THE PUBS OF HASTINGS & ST LEONARDS

1800–2000

BY THE SAME AUTHOR

Register of Licensees for Hastings & St Leonards 1500–2000

The Swan, Hastings 1523–1943

The Pubs of Rye, East Sussex 1750–1950

THIRD EDITION

THE PUBS OF
HASTINGS AND ST LEONARDS

1800–2000

◇————————◇

DAVID RUSSELL

Published by Lynda Russell

Copies of this book are available from the publisher.
Email: hastings.pubs@gmail.com
Tel: 01424 200227
www.hastingspubhistory.com

Printed and bound by Imprint Digital.net, Exeter
ISBN 978-0-9562917-7-6

Contents

Acknowledgements to:

The excellent staff of Hastings Reference Library and the East Sussex Record Office at The Keep, Falmer, East Sussex;

Members of the Pub History Society;

John Hodges for his photograph of the Old Golden Cross, now Flairz, on the front cover;

Jean Hope for her watercolour of the London Trader on the back cover;

Roger Povey for sharing his pub research;

Betty Austin, the late Charles Banks, Vic Chalcraft, Alan Crouch, Jim Davidson, Julian Deeprose, Pat Dunn, Sonja Eveleigh, Michael Errey, the late Ron Fellows, Gerry Foster, Alan Garaty, Marie Garaty, John Hodges, Trefor Holloway, the late Minnie Howlett, Tony Howlett, Terry Huggins, Philip Littlejohn, Steve M, Dot Mitchell, Michael Monk, Cyril Pelluet, Roger Povey, Tommy Read, Michael Rose and Peter Skinner for their pub memories and family histories.

Picture Credits

Noel Bucknole: page 114

Patrick Chaplin: page 272

Late Ron Fellows: page 14

Alan and Marie Garaty: pages 214,215

James Gray: pages 38,112,221,314

John Hodges: pages 13,17,23,29,32,33,37,47,49,59,63,67,75,79,
83,87,91,100,101,107,115,123,125,129,133,139,145,151,157,162,
167,171,175,179,187,190,195,201,219,227,233,241,247,253,261,
263,269,285,290,295,296,300,303,309

Tony Howlett and the late Minnie Howlett: pages 291,292

Terry Huggins: page 212

Hastings Museum: page 294

Hastings Reference Library: pages 73,259

Brian Laws: page 68

Philip Littlejohn: page 82

Roger Povey: page 207

Tommy Read: page 174,267

Lynda Russell: pages 16,22,25,28,36,42,43,48,52,58,62,66,71,74,
86,90,95,104,111,124,128,132,143,144,148,150,156,160,163,170,
178,182,183,191,200,203,204,205,206,216,217,218,222,223,226,
230,231,232,236,237,246,256,261,262,265,267,268,273,274,283,
294,298,299,301,304,305,308,315

Arthur Taylor: page 211

J. Watts: page 120

Introduction

It has been estimated that there were only 15 public houses in Hastings in 1824. Obviously there were other drinking places, including unlicensed premises on America Ground* and elsewhere, and a few beer houses.

Six years later the 1830 Beer Act saw the start of dozens of beer houses opening in the town, a trend which continued for the next 40 years. In due course many of these became fully licensed public houses.

From 1828 the population grew rapidly with the building of St Leonards and the expansion of Hastings into the Priory Valley. Later, with the development of America Ground and the town centre from the 1850s, more public houses opened. By the 1870s the town was expanding outwards and new licences were granted in all districts of the town.

The high point of this expansion was 1860, when Hastings and St Leonards had a total of 128 pubs and beer houses, an average of one pub for every 112 people indicating a high pub-population ratio.

The Licensing Act of 1904 was the sting in the tail. This Act gave local magistrates the power to close down public houses on the grounds that they were redundant and no longer needed.

From 1905 the licensing magistrates applied the new law with indecent haste, encouraged by the chief constable and the local temperance lobby. The St Leonards branch of the British Women's Temperance Association cheered at its annual general meeting in 1905 as the closure of the first five pubs under this Act was announced.

During the First World War the Lloyd George government reduced the strength of beer by 50% and doubled the price of a pint. Opening hours were reduced by two-thirds and 'treating' was banned. These draconian measures affected all of the Hastings and St Leonards pubs, in particular the Roebuck, Horse and Groom and the Royal.

*An area of marshland created by a receding sea in the 18th century and inhabited by squatters until 1837.

Ten years after the war, in 1928, Hastings had one pub for every 330 people, which compared to Eastbourne (1:574) or Blackpool (1:711), indicated that the town still had a large number of public houses for its population. In 1945 the chief constable reported that 89 pubs had been 'extinguished' since 1905, although 53 new licences were granted in the same period. This brought the pub-population ratio down to about 1:450.

In 1939, in contrast to the First World War, pubs were seen as an essential element in the war effort. In Hastings they accommodated large numbers of US and Canadian Military in, for example, the Moda, York and Clarence. Many pubs were bombed including the Norman and the Warriors Gate, and most notoriously the Swan and the Bedford, which were completely destroyed. In these conditions 33 Hastings and St Leonards pubs closed 'for the duration' especially after the Battle of Britain.

After the war, the policy of the Hastings magistrates was to transfer licences 'in suspension'. Licences of war damaged premises and others which had closed, were transferred to new pubs mainly in the outlying districts of the town. Among these, the Swan licence was transferred to the Wishing Tree, the Fortune of War licence to the New Broom in Malvern Way, the Denmark licence to the Comet in Harley Shute Road and the defunct St Leonards pier licence to the Pump House in George Street.

Since this book was first published in 2009 it has been much in demand. This edition is enhanced by the inclusion of new photographs by Lynda Russell, and by further research.

Four more pub histories have been added. These are the Coach and Horses, Priory Tavern, Privateer and the first Tivoli Tavern. The history of several other pubs has been updated. The appendix on 'Lost Pubs' has been removed but a list of all 341 Hastings and St Leonards pubs is now available in a separate publication the *Register of Licensees for Hastings & St Leonards 1500–2000*. This third edition of *The Pubs of Hastings & St Leonards* is favoured with a sister volume: *The Swan, Hastings 1523–1943*.

David Russell, St Leonards-on-Sea, March 2014
www.hastingspubhistory.com

Admiral Benbow
London Road, St Leonards

Yorkshire Grey before 1995

The Admiral Benbow first opened its doors in 1833. It was the third public house to be built in the new town of St Leonards-on-Sea, being erected at that time by James Burton. It was first known as the Saxon Shades, a plebeian taproom at the rear of the Saxon Hotel. The hotel is now the Lotus Chinese restaurant on the corner of London Road.

The Saxon Shades existed for half a century serving the drivers and coachmen of the six-horse coaches that stopped there and the ostlers and stablemen who serviced them. The name 'shades' was a term used in the south-east for a tap room located behind a hotel, indicating that prostitutes used the premises.

In 1884 the Saxon Shades changed its name to the Yorkshire Grey[1] and in 1898 the landlord was summonsed for allowing gambling on the premises, a story which hit the national headlines.

The landlord, Lewis Hobbs, organised a Derby sweepstake on the run up to Derby day every year. This was run on the calculation that selling 1,000 tickets at 2s 6d [12½p], would generate a total of £125. Ten per cent was deducted for expenses and printing, leaving £112.10s [£112.50] for prizes. Tickets were sold openly over the bar. However, the police employed a man called Mawle, who formerly worked in the pub, to observe ticket sales and to note whether or not the gambling law was being broken. On Mawle's evidence the police raided the pub and the landlord was charged.

A jury convicted him at Lewes Assizes but he appealed. The case went to the Queen's Bench where, finally, five judges decided that the Yorkshire Grey sweepstake was a lottery that the landlord managed 'for the purpose of adding to the popularity of his house'. He received no profit and took no tickets. The prizewinners were decided, not on the outcome of the horse race itself, but on the drawing of the tickets. The conviction was quashed and Lewis Hobbs was exonerated. This case helped clarify what was and was not gambling in pubs all over the country.[2]

The Saxon Hotel finally closed in 1905 leaving the Yorkshire Grey to continue as an independent public house.

Saxon Hotel c1900

SAXON HOTEL'S PASSING
ELDRIDGE. THE "SAXON KING."

To the Editor of the Observer

SIR, — Now that the Saxon Hotel has been closed, the question has been more than once put to me, "When and by whom was the building erected?"

The answer is this: — Nos. 1 to 12, Adelaide-place (now Grand-parade), were built by Messrs. Towner, Jenner, and other persons, from the plans and designs of the late Walter Inskipp, in 1831, and the adjoining house was erected for the late William Mantel Eldridge by the builder Smith. It was, I believe, completed in 1832.

"Give your verdict," said an eminent Vice-Chancellor, "but assign no reason." This was just what the Magistrates did when they refused Mr. Mantel Eldridge a licence for the Saxon Hotel: for whatever might have been their reasons for the refusal, they assigned none. Albeit, in their case, the Vice-Chancellor's advice was acted upon to their detriment. The "King" – as those who delighted in pseudonyms were wont to style Mr. Eldridge – was not to be denied his suit by any less regal body: and he therefore summoned the Magistrates to Lewes to show cause for their refusal. Their plans were deemed insufficient, and Eldridge, the "Saxon King," came off the conqueror.

In a very short time the Saxon Hotel became a licensed house, and during 72 years of its existence has been successively managed by Mr. Eldridge, Mr. Hutchings and other persons. But, like the old Swan Hotel, of which the same Mr. Eldridge at one time became proprietor, it has ended its career as an hotel, and will be replaced by something more modern, and let us hope, more generally successful.

It is probable that in Eldridge's case the then Magistrates judged the licensed houses to be more than sufficient for the needs of the public, and thus the former declined to accede to Eldridge's request. There were at that time the Harold Hotel, the Conqueror Hotel, the St. Leonards Hotel, each with its so-called tap, the Horse and Groom and the Warrior's Gate Inns, all within a stone's-throw distance.

But the defeat of the Magistrates at the Lewes Court made them very chary as to future refusals: hence, within a comparatively short period licences were readily granted for the Anchor, the Coach and Horses, the Fountain, the Black Horse, the Sussex Tap, the Old England Tavern, the Norman Hotel, the

White Hart, the British Queen, and the St. Leonards Arms, the last-named in connection with the St. Leonards Brewery, of which Mr. Eldridge was proprietor.

Yours truly,

T.B. BRETT.

1905 (Edited) [3]

Around 80 years later the large upstairs room had become a popular 'pub rock' venue known as Blades. It was one of a few live music venues in Hastings at the time and was organised by Phil Little, drummer with local group The Pullbacks.[4] Award-winning pianist and jazz singer Liane Carroll played here with the Trevor Francis Quartet, as did the Roger Carey Band and many others.

Trefor Holloway recalls: "The pub I remember with affection is the Yorkshire Grey. It's closed now but in the 80s I worked sometimes in pub security. I worked as a bouncer on the door there. The Yorkshire 'Gay' as it was dubbed was the most lively, popular and successful pub in the town."[5]

The music stopped in 1995 when the pub closed temporarily after the landlady ran off with the takings and the jukebox. Soon after, it was renamed the Admiral Benbow, commemorating the seaman John Benbow (1650–1702), who died fighting the French in the Caribbean. The pub finally closed in 2008 and is now used as a studio.

Anchor Inn and Coach & Horses
East Ascent and Mews Road

Anchor passage

The Anchor Inn, one of the lost pubs of St Leonards, was located in a passage or twitten* behind East Ascent. The passage, Anchor Passage, led into St Leonards Mews – later Royal Victoria Mews and later still Victoria Dwellings – where coach houses, stables and coachmen's cottages were located. This beer house opened in about 1833, to cater for this small residential and working community.

It had an anchor above the door, a 'fouled anchor' with a rope curled round it. James Burton incorporated the sign of the anchor into the Burton family arms in 1902 and, at a later date, it became the coat of arms of St Leonards itself. Other versions of the St Leonards' anchor can be seen on the Clock House, St Leonards Gardens, above the arch of North Lodge and on an old cast iron boundary marker.

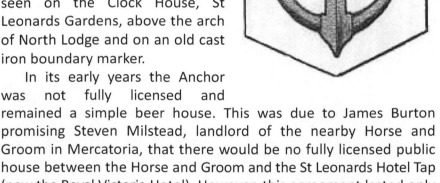

In its early years the Anchor was not fully licensed and remained a simple beer house. This was due to James Burton promising Steven Milstead, landlord of the nearby Horse and Groom in Mercatoria, that there would be no fully licensed public house between the Horse and Groom and the St Leonards Hotel Tap (now the Royal Victoria Hotel). However, this agreement lasted only a few years.[1]

In the 1830s the bulk of the population was illiterate and newspapers were highly taxed to prevent poorer people having access to them. The Anchor, the Horse and Groom, the Tivoli Tavern and other local public houses had news rooms, where they employed 'Sunday readers' to recite the newspapers to the assembled customers. Amateur politicians of the day would gather to listen, discuss and criticise issues of local and national government.

* Sussex term for a narrow passage or alleyway.

A local schoolteacher was Sunday reader at the Anchor Inn for many years, a practice that stayed until the tax on newspapers was removed in 1855. Also a Mechanics' Institute, where newspapers could be read, was established in St Leonards in the 1850s. These were exciting years and, although it might not seem much to us now, one of the major issues up for discussion was the 1832 Reform Act, which gave the vote to men who owned or leased land worth £10 or more. This was the start of popular suffrage and the right to vote, which was celebrated by thousands of people in Hastings with bonfires on the beach and overflowing pubs. For many years after 1832 the Anchor celebrated the anniversary of the Reform Act on 'the glorious first of June'.

One landlord in the 1850s was under the impression that he could serve his friends when he wished. On more than one occasion drinkers, cautioned by the police after hours, claimed they were only there as friends of the landlord. During one case the clerk of the court asked a customer: "How do you address your friends in the Anchor?" "Good morning. I want a pint of Porter." [laughter]

In 1869, landlord Thomas Vido was fined for allowing gambling on the premises. Ostlers who worked in the stables in Mews Road looking after the horses for the coaches of the nearby Victoria Hotel, were among the customers who played cards for money. This sometimes got out of hand and led to cheating and argument.

In its final years the Anchor was tied to the Blyth Brewery (later Ind Coope) for draught beer, but was a free house for bottles and spirits. Tom Wells was landlord for 25 years but, it was said, he died penniless, totally impoverished and destitute.[2] The Anchor started to lose trade around 1900 and the police complained it was difficult to supervise the pub through the twitten. From 1900 it had at least five different landlords before being forced to close by the licensing magistrates in 1905, using their new powers under the Act of 1904.

Other Hastings' pubs in twittens included the Duke of Cornwall in Post Office Passage, the Prince of Wales in Waterloo Passage and almost certainly the Robin Hood in North Passage, North Street. The Anchor was one of the first pubs in Hastings to be declared redundant along with four other lost pubs, the Hastings Castle, the Eagle Tavern, the Warrior's Arms and the Free Trader.

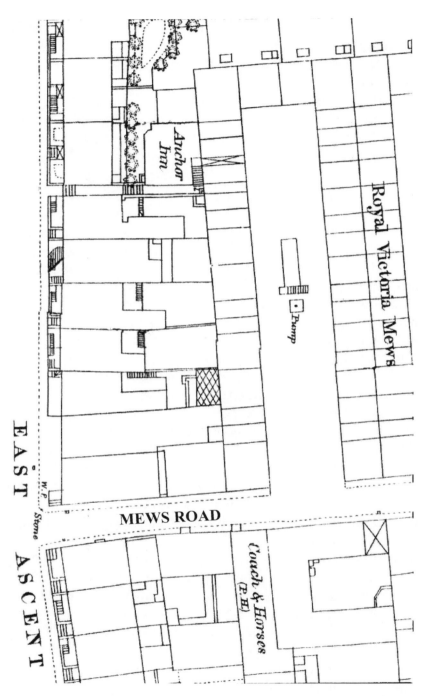

Ordnance survey map showing Anchor Inn and Coach & Horses 1873

The Coach and Horses first opened its doors in 1846 bringing competition to the Anchor Inn. A large number of shopkeepers and tradesmen of St Leonards attended its inauguration dinner in a large attached room.[3] The first landlord, William Birch, was described 'as a man of considerable energy and genial disposition' who, among other things, kept the keys of the St Leonards Fire Engine House and owned several pleasure boats on the beach.

The Coach and Horses was the starting point of the St Leonards Bonfire Boys procession on the 5th November 1891 and probably in other years. At the end of the evening customers were often driven home in a donkey or mule chaise rather than walk.

Marjorie Martin, born in 1907, lived in Victoria Dwellings opposite (demolished in the 1960s) and remembered her parents and other residents buying jugs of beer from the Coach and Horses in the inter-war years. Michael Rose, born in 1932, also lived in Victoria Dwellings. He said: "My dad usually drank in the Kicking Donkey but on Sunday lunchtimes he used the Coach and Horses. When lunch was ready my mother would send me across the road to fetch him. As you went into the pub there was a door on the right hand side leading into the public bar, which was the size of a small living room about 12 foot x 14 foot [3.66m x 4.27m]. Further along the passageway there was a small snug bar and then stairs up into the landlord's accommodation.

"The shovepenny board was located just inside the door of the public bar. I used to sit on the step with a glass of lemonade and watch my father playing shovepenny with his mates.

"After the war it provided bed and breakfast. In about 1946–7 I remember some American tourists staying there for a few days. They arrived on a 'Red Indian' motorbike decked out in leather tassels, which was an attraction to the local children."[4]

In 1950 the landlord, 72-year old Robert Thompson, attended the licensing session which wanted to close his pub. The police had visited the pub seven times and found the average number of customers was 2.1. The landlord said he had evacuated early in the war when he only had five customers aged between 78 and 95. He returned in 1942 and could open only one day a week. Air raids affected the evening trade.

There were garages, workshops, builders and bakers nearby, which all provided customers, and there were visitors in summer. The house was built into sandstone and it was claimed that beer kept in the cellar was always 65 degrees. People used to come up from the beach for beer and sandwiches but he had 'lost his catering licence'.

Bad trade was due to a shortage of money and the price of beer. The brewers said he was a victim of circumstances with ill health, tax, low-income groups and evacuation during the Battle of Britain. The Coach and Horses was his home, business and livelihood. There was not much else in the poor districts of Hastings and St Leonards. Was the town to have only 'swell pubs'? Sadly it was declared redundant and closed in 1950, just over a century old.[5]

Coach and Horses 2014

Anchor Inn
George Street, Old Town

Another Anchor Inn dating back to at least 1680, once stood outside the Old Town wall, near the fish market. The current Anchor Inn, George Street, dates back to 1798, when the licensee was Anne Thwaites.[1] This was an era when the population was largely illiterate and when pubs were recognised by visual symbols and signs, instead of written names. Hence the small anchor embedded in the wall above the door. The sign of the Anchor was a popular one for pubs near the sea.

For over two centuries the Anchor has had a wide variety of customers. In the early 1800s, military personnel were billeted in the Anchor and in the surrounding streets, in anticipation of an invasion by Napoleon. At this time vessels from around the world arrived off Hastings, ferried passengers ashore and replenished their ship's stores from Thomas Daniels, landlord from 1805 to 1840.

> Arrived off Hastings on Monday, the ship William Nichol, Capt. John McAlpin, from Sydney to London, 106 days, and landed at Daniel's Anchor Inn J Bettington Esq and Mr Hillditch.

1838 [2]

> On Saturday, the ship Hindus, Capt. McFarlan, commander, from China to Amsterdam, out 6 months, arrived off this port, being short of provisions and water. She was immediately supplied by Mr Daniels, of the Anchor Inn, and a pilot taken on board to proceed to the Downs. Crew all well.

1839 [3]

Thomas Daniels also owned the building opposite (now the Pump House) which he used as a store, and the pump which supplied water to George Street residents.

Tom Daniels lives here, a most worthy old chum,
Who sells the best brandy, gin, hollands and rum—
He caters for tradesmen and sailors alot,
And serves up for farmers, good dinners all hot;
With nimblest of feet and the strongest of nerves
It's said that his patrons be very well served
From widow Anne Thwaites he the Anchor obtained,
In 1805 he the licence first gained.

From 1753 to 1833 the Assembly Room next door was itself a pub called the Rose and Crown. In 1833 the Rose and Crown was replaced by a new market which later became the Assembly Room. Today it is known as the Black Market. Over the next century the Assembly Room was used by a variety of groups and individuals. These included political parties during elections, a large branch of the Odd Fellows friendly society, temperance campaign groups, suffragettes, fishermen (5am licence), auctioneers, the organised unemployed and later, the annual darts tournaments organised by the *Hastings & St Leonards Observer*. It was also the location of the Victoria Cinema from 1909 to 1910.[4]

An important event which took place here was organised by local Chartists in 1852, when Chartist Henry Vincent gave a lecture on political and constitutional history.

Former Assembly Room

Henry Vincent. Chartist

Chartism was an important stage in British labour history between 1838–1848. They campaigned for political reform and took the name from the People's Charter of 1838. Chartism began among skilled artisans, such as shoemakers, printers and tailors, as a petition movement, trying to mobilise a 'moral force' for reform. But it also attracted men who advocated strikes, general strikes and 'physical force'.

The only other Hastings pub known to accommodate the Chartists was the Star, High Street (see page 241).[5]

From 1840 to the late 1860s the landlord was Charles West, who kept a respected and well-run public house, and leased the Assembly room next door. In the 1850s the centre of Hastings moved from the Old Town to the Priory Valley and Charles West went with the flow and moved into Robertson Street in 1868, where he took over the premises now known as The Electric Stag, but then known as West's Cellars. One of his last acts before leaving was to raise money for new bells for St Clement's Church. The Anchor was then sold for £2,500 and the Pump House opposite for the 'knock down price' of £500.

With the departure of Charles West, the Anchor slid downhill into a murky period of its history. Local prostitutes were allowed to ply their trade, thieves and pickpockets were among the customers and the pub was always in the news for drunkenness, gambling, riotous and immoral behaviour. Not surprisingly it was often threatened with closure, but has somehow managed to survive.

In a typical incident in 1871, a prostitute called Harriet Clapson was charged with assaulting a woman from London. The London woman came into the 'little room' of the pub and Clapson remarked that she would "show these ... from London who come down here and do the bounce on us". She delivered a violent blow with her fist to the woman's head, for which she was fined 10s [50p] plus 9s.6d costs.[6]

In the 1870s, the Victoria Lodge of the Oddfellows Friendly Society with 680 members and capital of £3,000 (today's value £138,000), moved out of the Anchor, where it had met since its formation in 1831, and into the Central in the town centre. The Victoria Lodge claimed to be 'the largest lodge of Oddfellows in England'.

In 1876 one of the most serious riots in the history of the town broke out at the Anchor. A drunk refused to leave when asked, and assaulted the landlord. He was arrested and a riotous crowd assembled. Stones were thrown at the police in response to the man's incitement of the crowd to rescue him. "This is a good chance to hustle the police", he shouted and a large, violent crowd did just that. More stones were thrown, one seriously denting the constable's helmet. In response, the constable had to call for assistance and it finally took four constables to overpower the man and take him away. A violent mob followed them to the station house and remained outside for some time until they were cleared. In Hastings Borough Court the man was found guilty of assaulting the landlord, refusing to quit the pub and incitement to riot. He was sent to Lewes prison for a period of hard labour.[7] The police station was one of the few civic buildings to remain in the Old Town where it was needed in the late Victorian period.

In 1882 another riot broke out. This time at a large temperance meeting in the Assembly Room, campaigning for pubs to be closed on Sundays. Temperance supporters were admitted early and took all the front seats, forcing their opponents to the back. This meant they had to shout to be heard. Eventually fighting broke out and a mass wave of people stormed the platform. 'The uproar ended in a riot the like of which had never been seen in Hastings in living memory. Women fainted and chairs were thrown.' Ironically, the key temperance speakers on the platform had to escape through a connecting door into the Anchor and then out onto George Street![8]

In the late 1930s the Assembly Room was a venue for the finals and semi-finals of the Hastings *Observer* Annual Darts Tournaments, which included several Old Town teams.

In 1876 the Anchor Assembly Room was used by the judge and jury from the sessions held in the Town Hall in the High Street. Reports from that time quote 'a disadvantage was the echo of persons walking across the room. This was found to be a great inconvenience'.

This could explain why the ghost of a judge in a dark suit and black hat haunts the back bar, making sure that today's customers are behaving! Thus the Anchor covets the title of 'most haunted pub' in Hastings and the Old Town Ghost walks start from here in the summer.

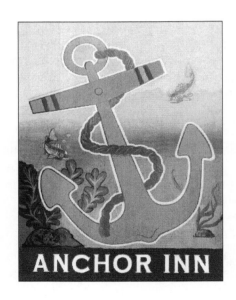

Angel and Plough
West Hill

These two pubs on the West Hill both opened as beer houses in 1835.[1] The Angel, first known as the Brisco Arms, took its name from the Brisco family who resided in Bohemia House. Musgrave Brisco was the Conservative member of parliament for Hastings in 1844. The name changed to the Angel in 1837, when Henry Morley, formerly a tailor, became the landlord. He was also a journalist and a Liberal, and probably changed the pub name for political reasons.

At that time the Angel stood in the Long Field, now called St Mary's Terrace, while the Plough stood in the Mill Field, so named because there was a cluster of four windmills on the West Hill, with another further away on the site of a former school in Priory Road. One windmill was situated in the garden of the Plough, and the last survived until 1874.

In the 1840s, the landlord of the Plough worked as a wheelwright, running the beer house as a secondary occupation.[2] The Plough got a full licence in 1854 but in 1856 the landlady, Martha Rhoden, became bankrupt and was unable to pay the General District Rate of 18s [90p]. She had to move out and apply for a 'distress warrant'.

Both inns must have had the custom of the millers, carters and other workers in the corn trade, as well as those who worked in the local slaughterhouses in the area. As the West Hill was developed in the last 30 years of the 19th century and the first houses were completed, itinerant building workers and travelling tradesmen were customers of both pubs. Some used the Angel as a lodging house.[3]

The Angel stands over St Clement's Caves, which cover a large area under the West Hill. It is thought that the Angel used the caves as a pub cellar for several years, although the management of St Clement's Caves cannot confirm this.

The American artist, James McNeil Whistler (1834–1903), probably used both pubs when visiting his mother at nearby Talbot House, St Mary's Terrace. Over a period of six years he painted her portrait, which now hangs in the Louvre in Paris. Nearby, Whistler's Steps lead down into the Priory Valley and the town centre.

In 1871, Angel landlord, John Crouch, was summonsed and fined 'for having his house open during the hours of divine service on Good Friday'.[4] Some years later another landlord, Harry Johnson, spent a lot of time as a soapbox orator, debating with socialists in the cut and thrust of local Edwardian politics.

In his younger days, Johnson had been an Independent Labour Party speaker, but changed his politics in later life. In a debate with the Hastings firebrand Alf Cobb, Johnson became irritated by a remark about the iniquities of brewers and publicans. He was also upset by jibes about 'publicans, beer and angels'. "What about strawberries?" his supporters replied. (Cobb was a barrow boy later summonsed for obstructing the roadway, whilst selling strawberries outside the Old England.)

During the First World War, the Angel was closed from May 1916, when the landlord was called up into the military. He didn't return and the pub stayed closed until December 1920. This led the licensing magistrates to conclude that the pub was redundant and in 1921 it was referred to the compensation authority for closure, along with the Little Brown Jug, a beer house 'forty-five paces away' in St Mary's Terrace.

In 1921 several surprise visits were made by the police to pubs in the area to establish their custom. In nine visits they found a total of '121 customers in the Angel, 264 in the Granville, 136 in the Whitefriars, 128 in the Plough, but only 47 in the Little Brown Jug'. However, the more middle class Red House was ignored by the police and left alone.[5] The Angel and the Plough were both opposed by the temperance lobby, in this case the Sunday School Union and the British Women's Temperance Association, but finally the magistrates decided to close the Little Brown Jug and not the Angel, as there was not enough money to compensate both.

The Angel came to attention in 1977, when 18-year-old Mark Greenaway of the Angel darts team got within one second of the world record for 'round the board doubles at arm's length'. The landlord of the Warrior's Gate in St Leonards, held the world record of 9.2 seconds.[6]

Years before the smoking ban in public buildings, the Angel supported National No Smoking Day campaigns. As early as 1988, along with the local Health Promotion Unit, the landlord designated the ground floor of the pub as a 'No Smoking' area. He said the smoke free area was being promoted to encourage people to give up smoking and to reduce the incidence of passive smoking.

Although the campaign didn't have total national support, one and a half million people attempted to give up smoking, but it is not known how many succeeded. The Angel was the only pub in Hastings known to participate in the national 'No Smoking' campaign at that time. The Angel finally closed in the economic recession of 2008.

The Plough is a building of Dutch design which maybe connected with the windmill that once stood in its garden. Its sign depicts the plough constellation.

An early photograph of the Plough

Barrattinis's Sports Bar
Marina, St Leonards

Burtons Bar 2008–2009

James Burton built the Marina in 1829, as part of the new town of St Leonards-on-Sea. For 146 years, 42 Marina was the home of Addison's, the town's oldest established bakers and confectioners.[1] Addison's advertised itself as 'a connoisseur of exotic food', supplying the upper class market of Victorian St Leonards and in later years the large American export market, until the last member of the family, K. E. Addison, retired.

**Mr Cherry's
Free House**

St Leonards

*Don't Miss
Mr Cherry's Disco*

Saturday Lunchtimes,
Monday and
Wednesday evenings

Enquiries concerning
Wedding Receptions, Functions,
Dinner Dances and Meetings
Tel Mr or Mrs MacGlade —
HASTINGS 422705

Mr Cherry's
42/43 MARINA, ST LEONARDS-ON-SEA

1976

In 1975 the property was sold and became Mr Cherry's Wine Bar, which was opened by TV star, David Lloyd Meredith, of *Softly, Softly* fame.[2] It got off to a good start, supported by the Hastings branch of the Campaign for Real Ale, which had been formed in the Prince Albert, Brook Street. CAMRA used Mr Cherry's for branch meetings[3] and the pub quickly became established for its real ale and as one of the town's best known 'pub rock' venues. In 1976 it celebrated its first birthday with optimism and was listed in the CAMRA *Good Beer Guide*.

In 1983 a micro-brewery was installed in the basement, the home of Addison's original bakery, and started brewing Conqueror Bitter.[4] Because of its strength (it had a gravity of 10.66) it was sold only in half pints. This was the first micro-brewery in Hastings in modern times, three years before the FILO brewery opened in

1986, although the FILO brewery is still operating. Subsequently, Mr Cherry's was listed in the *Good Beer Guide* from 1983 to 1986.

In 1983 the Hastings' Jack in the Green festival was revived on May Day, after an absence of three quarters of a century. The route of the procession in the first few years visited St Leonards Gardens, behind Mr Cherry's, (where the original 19th century Jack in the Green celebrations took place) and refreshment was taken in Mr Cherry's by revellers dressed as trees, before they marched back to the Stade.

In 1988 the magistrates refused to renew Mr Cherry's music licence due to complaints about noise. A few weeks after this decision, the pub suddenly closed and reopened as the James Burton, with the promise of strict noise control, for the benefit of the middle aged and elderly residents in the area.[5]

After a steady start and a new music licence, the James Burton spiralled into a tumultuous existence, with a continuous conflict between the licensees, the Marine Court Residents Association, the licensing magistrates and Hastings Borough Council. It acquired the nickname of 'the hash joint' and there were continuous complaints of a 'hooligan element, injuries to off-duty police, noise, loud music, a riff-raff occupying the front pavement, drugs, motor bikes and general mayhem in the evenings'. It seems however, that these complaints were only half accurate and certainly exaggerated.

From 1975 until 1990 many popular bands and musicians from Hastings and elsewhere played here. Roger Carey's Upstarts, Buick 6 and Pass the Cat, three popular Hastings groups, performed here, as did the Liane Carroll Big Band and the 18-piece Sounds of Swing. Among the musicians from outside the town were Howlin Wilf and the Vee-Jays, known for their album 'Blue Men Sing the Whites'.

Once more the renewal of the music licence was refused and six months after the closure of Mr Cherry's the James Burton was served with a Noise Abatement Notice, but the music continued. Eventually the two joint licensees were each fined £2,000 plus £2,500 costs, although they had spent £8,000 insulating the proposed Burtoneon Club in the basement. In 1990, after a heady two years, the pub suddenly closed for a second time.[6]

The closure was of concern to the Hastings pub rock community and, with fewer venues available to them, they started to organise, and the Hastings Live Music Forum was set up in 1993. It was chaired by Phil Little, drummer with the Pullbacks, and began to lobby for more venues. In 1994 another pub music venue, the Carlisle, which had been threatened with closure, was reprieved. A second pub music venue, Pissarro's, opened at the same time, while ironically Phil Little moved to Canada.

The local press reported the James Burton as 'Gone For a Burton' and with the licensees bankrupt, the business went into receivership. In 1994 it was put up for sale, but it was not until 2003 that it reopened as Kollege Kantina, which ran for four years and was popular with students of the college in Archery Road. Kollege Kantina closed in 2007 and reopened in 2008 as Burton's Bar. In 2009 it had another name change to Barrattinis's Sports Bar but closed in 2011.

Kollege Kantina 2007

Bo Peep
Grosvenor Crescent, St Leonards

c1901–1914

New England Bank/Bo-peep c1746–1846

The Bo Peep is linked with the coming of the railways to Hastings, with smugglers and a well-known nursery rhyme. Over its lifetime it has had four name changes and been rebuilt at least twice. It was apparently shown on a map of 1746,[1] and by 1777 it was leased to William Clarke.

Two years later, in 1779, the lease was held by Thomas Hovenden the well known Hastings publican and brewer, for '1½ acres of waste ground with a cottage called New England Bank or Bo-peep'.[2] Hovenden had been brewing in Rye and Hastings for at least 30 years, most recently at the Star, High Street.

It seems the 'cottage' was rebuilt in about 1780 when it included 'a kitchen, 2 parlours, 4 bed chambers, 1 garret and stables'. The landlord was then Thomas Everard.

The *Sussex Weekly Advertiser* reported in 1788 that the Excise Officer at Bo Peep, 'assisted by members of the 11th regiment of Light Dragoons, seized 48 casks of brandy and geneva loaded on 4 horses' from local smugglers.[3] Because of the intense smuggling activity the pub was sold again in 1794 and again by auction in 1803.

> TO BE SOLD BY AUCTION,
> By W. CARLY,
>
> At the house of James Phillips, the sign of the Cutter, in Hastings, on Saturday the 26th day of February, 1803, between the hours of Five and Six in the Evening,
>
> ALL that Leasehold PUBLIC HOUSE, known by the name of BOPEEP, or NEW ENGLAND BANK, situate and being in the parish of St Leonard's, near Hastings; together with the stable, buildings, waste ground and premises thereto belonging, in the occupation of Robert Dunk.
>
> The above Premises are capable of great improvement, pleasantly and desirably situated near the sea, about two miles from Hastings, on the road to Bexhill.
>
> For further particulars apply to John Carey, Attorney at Hastings

1803 [4]

The Hastings Guide, published in 1797 by James Barry, described the Bo Peep as 'a public house by the roadside, where company may have an excellent dish of tea and good cream al fresco'.[5] The pub is mentioned again in 1815 as 'a wretched public house by the roadside', although this didn't deter the poet John Keats and the beautiful Isabella Jones from staying there when he visited the south coast in 1817. Keats portrayed Isabella Jones, 'the lady from Hastings', in his poem Endymion,[6] a poetic romance published in 1818 depicting a nymph rising naked from the Fishponds, a local beauty spot. The poem is famous for its first line: *A thing of beauty is a joy forever.*

When the railway arrived along the coast from Brighton in 1846, the original pub was demolished to make way for West Marina station.

> *Where sailors, soldiers, smugglers all*
> *Hob nobbed in days of yore;*
> *That wayside inn whose site just now*
> *The railway covers o'er.*[7]

By all accounts riotous times were had in the old pub. A musician who played there in the 1840s observed that the 'dancing created abnormal vibration. The visible contraction of the old walls was such as to threaten a general collapse!'[8]

The landlord was compensated by the South Eastern Railway Company and in 1847 he built a new pub, just east of the new station. The new pub was at first called the Railway Terminus Inn and supplied beer to passengers waiting for the coach into Hastings. The name reverted back to Bo Peep when the tunnel was dug through the cliffs behind, and the railway line continued into St Leonards. In 1972 when the site of the New England Bank was excavated and developed, old wine bottles, a silver fork and a mineral bottle dated 1808 were found.

In the mid-Victorian era the Bo Peep was a popular venue. Apart from political meetings, balls, quadrilles and parties were held here on a regular basis. It was a meeting place for the St Leonards Vestry, who discussed parish matters and elected the local rate collector.

In 1843 two overseers
Not one of whom in flesh now appears
A rate prescribed at that New England Bank
Which bounded St Leonards western flank.
That wayside Inn, near where grazing sheep,
Made way for railway station at Bo Peep.

As a 'railway pub', coroner's inquests into accidents on the line took place here. A moment of tragedy came in 1877, with the death of a guard on a train travelling through Bo Peep tunnel. He must have been looking out of the window when a train passing in the opposite direction struck him dead. Nobody saw anything as the tunnel was full of steam.[9] There was a second accident a few years later, when a body and severed head were found on the line by a signalman, who took them to the stables at the rear of the pub. Both accidents were severe shocks to the local community.

The photograph on page 37 was taken before the First World War when Charles Webber was landlord. Firemen pose on the ladder for the photographer after a fire in the attic. The Webber family ran the Bo Peep from 1901 until 1933.

Postcard of Bo Peep c1912

Academics and others have tried to explain the connection between Bo Peep and smuggling. In fact the Bo Peep nursery rhyme is a metaphor. Its exact origin is uncertain, but locals claim it as an old St Leonards tale and there is no doubt that the pub was used by smugglers, as shown on one side of the pub sign. The other side shows a shepherdess. The Bo Peep double sign was unveiled in 1977.

The metaphor of Bo Peep refers to the customs men (looking and peeping), the sheep refers to the smugglers (who they cannot find) and their tails to the contraband (barrels of rum and brandy).

The double-sided pub sign

Brass Monkey
Havelock Road

2010

1899

The Brass Monkey first opened as the Provincial Hotel in 1865. In its early days it was the meeting place of local postmen from the nearby town post office. In one year, at least, it was the base for 'Beating the Bounds' of the parish. In 1868 the parish overseers, the vestry clerk and parishioners 'searched out the Parish landmarks for three hours on Ascension Day. They were accompanied by a group of boys who were rewarded with nuts and oranges. Afterwards they adjourned to the Provincial for tea provided by Mr Longhurst.'

In the 1880s when Hastings was known as a 'health resort' the Provincial catered for invalids and was the town's main hire centre for bath chairs. The Provincial yard had stalls for 21 bath chairs and the bar was popular with bath chair men.

By the 1960s it was only one of two Hastings' pubs with a chess team and by 1970 it had closed, but then reopened in 1977 as the Golden Hind. In 2010 Julian Deeprose, landlord at that time, recalled his time there.

"I was licensee of the Golden Hind", he began, "from 1977 to 1979 and of the Carlisle from 1987 to 1990. The history of the Golden Hind, as I remember it, was that it used to be the Provincial Hotel for many years, and finally closed its doors in the late 60s. The building became derelict and was bought for next to nothing by Jimmy Demetris, who owned many Old Town properties many of them restaurants, including the Mayfair at the end of Pelham Crescent, where the family lived. He used to give some pretty seedy characters a place to live, in return for them working for him renovating properties. The Provincial was one of these and they only ever finished the ground floor and part of the first floor. He then gave the pub to his sons to run, the older son, Steve, being responsible for the opening of the Golden Hind and for inventing the persona of the pub. The younger son Akis was the 'accountant'.

"It would have opened around 1976 or 1977 and was a disco bar in the back and a lounge bar in the front. Steve Demetris had, and still has, another career as a musician and he quickly tired of being the face of the Golden Hind and left it to various bar staff to run.

"Disaster ensued", continued Julian. "I had always fancied being a publican and had been working part-time in the pub. I told him of my ambition and he literally handed me over the keys. I was 19 years old at the time. We had a bit of a task assuring the magistrates

Steve Demetris , landlord of the Golden Hind (second right) with rock band 'Stallion' in 1977

that a 19-year-old could run a very busy and successful pub in the town centre, but I mollified them by holding a joint licence with Steve for the first year. I think I am the youngest licensee in Hastings to this day.

"It really was tremendously successful and as the real ale renaissance was just starting, and I had a huge interest in this, I quickly turned the front bar into a haven for beer enthusiasts, which proved very successful. As did the pub games I introduced into the back bar for the early part of the week. We ended up with winning darts, shovepenny and soccer teams as well as the disco, packing both bars at the weekends, with excellent local DJs like Tony Davies and Johnny Francis. Great times.

"Eventually Steve received an offer he couldn't refuse from a consortium of chaps who used to work at a factory on Ponswood Estate. They already ran the Crown House social club and wanted to expand. Steve, by this time, was never seen. I only used to see Akis once every so often when he came to collect the cash. The frontman/woman were Howard and Diane Haskell and in the background were Phil Bebb and John Wilkinson. Steve ensured that they kept me on. I worked for them for a couple of years before leaving to join Martlet Brewery as their free trade rep. They ran the pub successfully for another couple of years before leasing the building to John and Barbara Gadd (I am unsure of the surname), who used to run the East Hastings Angling Club. I am guessing they took the pub in around 1983.

"Since then the pub has been totally ripped out inside. The Golden Hind was very much using the old Provincial interior, including some wonderful wooden panelling in the back bar; unfortunately long since gone.

"The local Citizens Band Radio (the Bluebeard Breakers) used to meet in the Golden Hind and did indeed operate from the pub. A 'breaker' is American CB slang for somebody breaking the silence— as simple as that. In typical CB fashion they nicknamed the Golden Hind: 'The Bluebeard', as Steve Demetris had a very dark beard. The name stuck and after he sold the pub to Howard Haskell et al I arranged for the production of a Royal Wedding ale known as Bluebeard in 1981. I signed some labels as did Howard, and there was also a run of unsigned but numbered bottles.

"The beer was brewed by Martlet of Eastbourne and the Golden Hind had its own draught version on sale at all times—one of the first if not *the* first house beer!

"As far as I am aware Bluebeard Bitter was the first beer brewed especially for a pub in the real ale renais- sance—it was actually a mix of Martlet Regency Bitter and Brighton Special Bitter, which was extra dry hopped and had a character all of its own. It was not a standard beer sold under another name."

The label shown here was designed by a group of Golden Hind customers and real ale enthusiasts for Martlet. Apart from designing the labels, this group also bottled the beer.

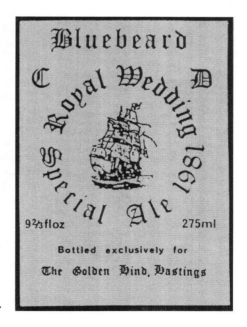

"Although Martlet brewed the beer specially", added Julian, "they did not bottle it as they did not have a bottling plant. It was bottled manually in the pub while enjoying a pint or three at the same time."[1] The same group was also responsible for labelling and bottling beer at two other Hastings' pubs: the Duke of Wellington and the Wheatsheaf, which were then tied to Charrington and Shepheard Neame respectively.

John Hodges was one of the customers involved in this. "We made pencil sketches in the bar", he explained, "which were then developed on the computer and printed off. After we had sterilised the bottles we filled them with beer and capped them. These bottles became collector's items. I had one of the largest collections of bottles and labels. However, we never drank the bottled beer; it became undrinkable after three months!"[2]

Many of these bottles are traded on the internet. "Beware many of them are fakes", warned Julian.

The Golden Hind later became Rockwells and then the Brass Monkey.

Brass Monkey in 2010

Bulverhythe
Bexhill Road

c1990

This pub was located in the old Cinque Port 'lymbe' of Bulverhythe, one of the 'lost villages' of Sussex.

The old English name hythe simply means 'people's landing place'. Although Pevensey is the officially recognised landing place for William the Conqueror, the precise spot where he landed is still a debating point among a minority of historians, some of whom claim that Bulverhythe, as the port of old Hastings, is a strong contender.

The pub sign had nothing to do with William the Conqueror or the Cinque Ports, but portrayed a ship wrecked off the Bulverhythe coast in a severe gale in 1749. The ship in question was a Dutch East Indiaman called the 'Amsterdam' and the pub sign was a copy of a painting of it, commissioned by the *Holland Herald*, an English language Dutch newspaper and painted by Jean Moore of St Leonards in 1975.

The Amsterdam, on her maiden voyage from North Holland to Indonesia, encountered a severe storm in the North Sea and lost her rudder. She attempted to anchor but drifted ashore at Bulverhythe where she sank into the beach mud.

At night at low tide, the crew clambered down the sides of the ship and were taken to safety by the locals. Smugglers quickly raided the ship and removed a large number of silver coins from the hold. After the rest of the bullion was officially removed, the town crier tried to locate and recover the missing silver, but without much success.

The wreck sank further into the soft beach mud and the remains of three decks are still buried, with much of her cargo and supplies, including onion-shaped bottles of Monbazillac, a French wine, intact. In 1969 an attempt was made to salvage the remains of the cargo and during the dig, some of the wine, vases and a cannon ball were looted.

The Bulverhythe is listed in the *Sussex Directory* for 1855[1] and was almost certainly a beer house from the 1840s, serving the railway navvies building the line into Hastings, and stage coach travellers on the Bexhill Road. A beer house which may have become the Bulverhythe was located on the Salts behind, in 1845.

COUNTY BENCH, TOWN HALL, APRIL 19.—Before F NORTH, Esq., Major JEFFRIES, and R. WETHERELL, Esq.

FRANCIS FARCEY appeared to answer an information of the Excise, for selling beer without a license.

It appeared the defendant had been keeping a Tom and Jerry shop in a booth erected on Salts, near Bulverhithe, in the parish of Bexhill, for the accommodation of the labourers at work on the Brighton Railway. He had been cautioned by the excise officer not to sell without a license; but the officer stated a license would now be granted to him.

Farcey admitted he sold beer without an excise license, but he had a license (certificate) from the gentlemen of the parish which he thought was sufficient.—Fined in the mitigated penalty of £5 and 21s. costs.

1845[2]

At the time beer houses were known by a range of nicknames. The popular and colloquial term 'tom and jerry shop' was derived from Corinthian Tom and Jerry Hawthorn, whose adventures made a best seller of the 1821 novel *Life in London* by Pierce Egan.

In 1900, along with some other local pubs and shops, the Bulverhythe became a victim of a 19th century confidence trick known as the 'bright farthing'. The barmaid had to constantly watch out for customers who paid for their beer with a sovereign [£1], which meant that there would usually be a half sovereign in the change. A half sovereign was similar in size to a (polished) farthing, [quarter of a penny] which could, by sleight of hand, be substituted for the half sovereign and the change queried. This happened several times before the culprit was finally caught.[3]

Because of its location about three miles from the centre of Hastings, the Bulverhythe was also targeted by 'bona fide travellers', a new category of customer, created by the licensing laws of 1855 and 1872. These Acts introduced restrictions on pub opening hours, but gave travellers the right to be served in pubs outside of the usual hours. In 1910 two men from Hastings knocked on the door at 11.15 on a Sunday morning, asking to be served as travellers. At that time opening hours were from noon on a Sunday, but this did not apply to customers who had travelled at least three miles from where they had spent the previous night. They were observed by a policeman and charged.

In court they claimed they had travelled three miles. There was some dispute as to the distance from Hastings to Bulverhythe. The case was adjourned whilst the magistrates did some measuring. They decided that the distance from Hastings was 200 yards [183m] short of the required three miles, but when the men were re-summonsed, the case was dismissed. Thus, before the First World War, the Bulverhythe quickly developed a reputation as, a pub where Hastingers could claim to be 'bona fide travellers' and get a drink outside normal pub hours.[4]

In the 1980s the Bulverhythe was a popular off-duty rendezvous for members of the Hastings police force, many of whom resided in the police flats in Harley Shute Road. The Bulverhythe closed in 2010 and is now a supermarket.

2013

Carlisle
Carlisle Parade

Carlisle in the 1930s , with roof garden and public shelter (right)

The Carlisle, formerly the Pelham Arms, was built by Richard Chandler in about 1820 on the site of an old tannery. It was located next door to a boat hull on America Ground, known as Noah's Ark. The Pelham Arms remained in the Chandler family until 1864 and was a meeting place for early rowing clubs and licensed watermen. Live music was played here in the 1840s[1] and by the 1880s it was known as a Liberal house.

In 1892 the Pelham Arms became the Carlisle Hotel.[2] The landlord, T.C. Brown, was a county cricketer and straw hat manufacturer. On the road to bankruptcy, he ignored all the signs and continued to take money out of the till, played cricket for Sussex 'a few times' and gambled a little on the side. By 1894 he had become bankrupt.[3]

Selling toffee apples outside the original Carlisle, 1890s

In 1899 the pub was taken over by E.E. Chase, whose time here was to be even shorter than Brown's and he too became bankrupt within 18 months. A reckless, extravagant character, Chase founded the Carlisle Cup, which was presented annually to local footballers.[4] When the Cinque Ports Volunteers went to the Boer War in 1900, he sent them boxes of expensive cigars.

One morning in 1908 a military impostor walked in pretending to be deaf and dumb. He produced a begging letter addressed to himself as a band sergeant from an army captain and was given a shilling [5p]. He got away with it until someone suddenly asked him if he would like a drink. "A small Bass", he replied, and got three months for deception!

During the First World War, when the town was taken over by the military, a soldier from the South Wales Borderers sold his boots to a fruit hawker in the bar for 4s 4d [21½p], two oranges and a pot of beer. He was punished by his regiment and the hawker was fined. The licensee was then Harry Bishop, who at various times ran the Rising Sun, the King's Head, Ore, the Provincial and the Lord Nelson. He was called up into the army in 1917 and his wife took over.

During the inter-war years, the pub grew in success. Sometime between 1926 and 1933 it was rebuilt with a roof terrace,[5] and dance floor for large-scale social occasions. As the 'Carlisle Saloon' it became a major venue for some of the town's annual billiards, snooker and darts tournaments. In 1938 it staged the first ladies'

1930s postcard

snooker match to be played in public in Hastings, between N. Lawrence and T. Kirkpatrick.[6]

The Carlisle closed in the Second World War until May 1945, when it was one of only two local pubs with a music licence.[7] The Debonair's Dance Band played here in the evenings and by the 1950s Carlisle Parade, then known as Teddy Boys' Walk, was the scene of clashes between 'Teds' and soldiers from Lydd Army Camp.

One popular Ted known as the Lemon Drop Kid used to sing Buddy Holly numbers and the pub hosted a Teddy Girl disc jockey called Bebopa Lula.

Good evening! . . .
and the place to enjoy it
CARLISLE HOTEL
SEA FRONT
CARLISLE PARADE • HASTINGS

★ THE DEBONAIRES ★
play in the UPPER SALOON BAR EVERY EVENING from 7.45 p.m.
ADMISSION FREE ★ POPULAR BAR PRICES

1951

By the 1960s the lounge had become the Ocean Bar, hosting the Commanders Show Band. From then on it attracted different youth cultures including Rockers, Greasers and Hell's Angels.

From 1983 to 1986 the licence was held by Tony Shipley who also ran the Lord Nelson. When Tony Shipley took over the Carlisle a number of bikers, customers of the Lord Nelson, followed him to the Carlisle,[8] which from then on gradually became a haunt of bikers from all over the country.

Between 1987 and 1990 the Carlisle was licensed to Julian Deeprose and Mike Ford. "Mike Ford and I took over the Carlisle in 1987", said Julian, "after it had been run into the ground by an ex-Hong Kong policeman and closed for six months. He was banning people for wearing leather jackets and denims. He was known to the locals as 'Stiff' but for the life of me I cannot remember his real name."

Their worst moment was in 1989 when the leader of a Birmingham motor cycle gang, the 'Cycle Tramps', was shot dead outside the pub by a member of the rival London Road Rats. This was unexpected. "Among the motorcycle chapters", according to Julian, "Hastings was considered to be neutral territory, so there was never any inter-club trouble. The murder violated that agreement and we feared reprisals, but fortunately they never happened, at least not in the Carlisle."[9]

1992

In 1992 Hastings Borough Council, who are the freeholders, threatened to close the pub down. A campaign was launched in its support and 12,000 people signed a petition. At one point 'thought waves' were sent out by the high priest and priestess of British white witches, Kevin and Ingrid Carlyon, in an attempt to cleanse the mind of the town council and persuade it to leave the Carlisle alone.[10] It was proposed to burn an old motor bike with an effigy of the council leader, below the high tide mark on the beach. At a crowded council meeting, Gus Cummins, a local artist, said that "the Carlisle was unique to the town and had a colourful and diverse clientele". Finally, in 1994, the council decided the pub would stay open.

Every May Day thousands of bikers ride into town on the 'Hastings Run' and the Carlisle is at the hub of the day's activity. On May day 2010, for example, an estimated 20,000 bikers turned up.

There is some irony in the fact, that the pub is named after the crown agent who evicted the original inhabitants of America Ground in 1835, when today's customers are the true inheritors of the spirit of those times.

Carlisle 2014

Cinque Ports Arms

All Saints Street, Old Town

c1960s

The Cinque Ports Arms is one of the oldest pubs in Hastings. It was formerly known as the Chequers, which apparently existed on this site in 1642, although the building has not been open continuously as a pub since that time.[1] It has been claimed that the current building replaced the original one several years ago. What is known is that the present building was partly rebuilt in the mock tudor style after a fire in 1925, and that the cottage next door was also 'tudorised' after the Second World War.

The fortunes of the Cinque Ports Arms have ebbed and flowed across the centuries following the changing social fabric of the Old Town itself. In the 17th century it was described as a 'tenement block' with a dubious status, attached to an equally dubious brewery. The first mention of it as the Cinque Ports Arms was in 1827, when William Wood purchased the pub for £260. It is recorded that smugglers used the pub as a rendezvous and for storing contraband.[2]

In 1850 this fairly large pub, with a bar, tap room and three parlours, was auctioned off.

FREEHOLD INN FOR SALE.

To be Sold by Auction, on Friday, April 19, 1850, at Six o'clock in the Evening, at the Cinque Ports' Arms Inn, Hastings, by

MR. WOMERSLEY,

A FREEHOLD MESSUAGE and INN, or Public House, situate in All Saints-street, in the parish of All Saints, Hastings, and called the CINQUE PORTS' ARMS INN.

The house comprises a bar, three parlours, tap room, four bed rooms, kitchen, cellarage, and offices ; together with a detached laundry, and bed room over. Also, a GARDEN, 93 feet 6 inches in length, and about 22 feet in breadth, in part of which stands a building used as a skittle alley ; and an outhouse.

The above is in the occupation of Mr. ELIAS COUSSENS, as yearly tenant.

For further particulars and conditions of sale apply to Messrs. SHORTER and PHILLIPS, Solicitors, or to the Auctioneer, Hastings.

1850

In the mid-19th century the pub included a 'Common Lodging House' in a temporary building at the back. This was run by Ann Holt who paid the landlord 12s [60p] a week for it. Four beds were let to eight men at 2s [10p] a week each. The premises was badly drained and the cesspool was always over-flowing.

A common practice for those without money was to offer goods for drink. In the 1870s a tramp tried to exchange a slop (a loose outer garment or smock) for beer. He asked the landlord to let him have 'three pots on it', but was refused and went outside and sold it for 1s [5p] in the street.[3] During these years of poverty, the pub couldn't shake off its rough image. An attempt was made to auction it off again at the start of the last century, but there were few bids; it didn't even make the reserve price and was withdrawn. Soon after, the chief constable tried to close the pub down, on the basis that it was just a common lodging house with a bar attached. The landlord quickly made some alterations to prevent communication between the lodging house and the pub, by separating the two. The Cinque Ports Arms was reprieved, but only just.

By 1905 it was still feeling the pinch of poverty. The pub was now only open part time and the landlord was forced to work as a hawker during the daytime. In 1919 there was a further attempt to close it down, this time because the chief constable considered the pub to be 'ill conducted' and, he said, because it was still attracting an undesirable custom. But again it was reprieved.

In recent decades the middle classes have moved back into the area and land values have dramatically increased. Ironically because of this, the Cinque Ports Arms was again threatened with closure in 1989. This time not because of poverty, but because the brewery, with an eye on the building as a valuable and desirable residence, considered turning it into a normal house. However, some think the brewery may have been opposed to the fact that the pub was generally seen as a gay pub. Fortunately it remained open.[4]

The Old Town, now one of the more affluent areas of Hastings, has found new fortunes and the Cinque Ports Arms has benefited from an improved local economy and from tourism. It is probably the only Hastings pub where the landlord calls time on a brass bell and, true to its age, a dark medieval atmosphere pervades its single bar.

The Cinque Ports of Hastings, Hythe, Romney, Dover and Sandwich have had their own coat of arms for many hundreds of years. Early common seals suggest that the design of three lions 'passant guardant' (full face), with one paw raised, conjoined to three ships' hulls, came into use between 1194 and 1305. The arms are derived from the golden lions used on the arms of England, except that the lions are joined with ships' hulls, to denote the provision of ships and men by the Cinque Ports to the Crown, before England had a navy.

The arms of the town of Hastings, on the other hand, differ in that they have only two lions conjoined to ships' hulls. The third lion is complete, which denotes Hastings as the chief Cinque Port.

Clarence
Middle Street

Before 1995

The Clarence, Middle Street, was built and licensed in 1868 as a small, town centre hotel.[1] Since then it has served a wide variety of customers, including army volunteers, building workers, trade unionists, benefit societies, football supporters and many others.

The 1st Cinque Ports Rifle Volunteer Corps, formed in 1860 and supported by public subscription, had its drill hall two doors away. Military personnel of all ranks were customers of the Clarence, who in the 1880s used the pub to host naval artillery suppers.[2] A beer house called the Volunteer, now gone, was located two doors away in Middle Street.

Before the mass production of cigarettes at the end of the 19th century, clay pipes were commonly smoked in pubs and it was the custom for the landlord to supply them free. The Clarence kept a jar of clay pipes on the bar. When a customer had finished his smoke he replaced the pipe in the jar for the next customer. Squeamish customers would break off an inch of stem to get a clean smoke. It was also the custom for the landlord to leave clay pipes in a cast iron rack

THE CLARENCE HOTEL
AND
WHOLESALE AND RETAIL
WINE AND SPIRIT ESTABLISHMENT
(next the Town Clerk's Office),
2 minutes from the Railway Station or the Beach,
MIDDLE STREET, HASTINGS.

Private Apartments for families.
DINNERS PROVIDED ON THE SHORTEST NOTICE
Chops and Steaks.

Visitors staying at this Hotel will find the comforts of home—special attention being paid to their requirements by the Proprietor, whose Hotel experience is well known. Visitors staying at the Hotel are also furnished with a Pier Ticket free of charge.
WINES & SPIRITS direct from bond. A single bottle at wholesale prices.
T. WILLCOX,
From VICTORIA STATION,
Proprietor.

Thomas Willcox 1874–1876

over the fire at night, to sterilise them for the following day's patrons.

The 19th century town centre was always busy with hawkers and on one occasion in 1872, a peddler walked in selling clay pipes. He had 70 for sale, for which he wanted 9d [4p]. "Here's a little lot that will suit you Sir", he said to the landlord. When challenged by a constable he admitted he didn't have a hawker's licence, "only one or two marriage certificates at home"[laughter].[3]

The period from the 1890s to the First World War was the heyday of the Clarence. These were very busy years. The Hastings Cabmen's Benefit Society held monthly meetings here. Their 'distress fund' was organised for the relief of members fallen on hard times. On one occasion a donation was made to a member whose trap had been smashed in the town centre. The cabmen also spent many evenings in 'harmony' (singing).[4]

The Clarence was also the meeting place of the Amalgamated Society of House Decorators and Painters, who ran an impressive campaign on wages and on the levelling up of the painter's rate to 7d [3p] an hour.[5] This determined the income of one drinker, Robert Tressell, who became the pub's most famous customer.

The Hastings branch of the Postmen's Federation, originally formed at the Clifton, St Leonards in 1895, also met here. The Hastings branch of the Amalgamated Society of Tailors, defunct in the 1890s, reformed here in 1906.[6] It was perhaps inevitable that the Hastings and St Leonards Trades Council was founded here in 1894. Following this, the Hastings Labour Party, then known as the Labour Representation Committee, was formed by the Trades Council and the National Democratic League at the turn of the last century. It was here that debates about municipal housing, direct labour, public baths, fair wages, local hospital provision and other issues were debated, before being passed on to Hastings Borough Council and other authorities. It was from this pub that the Trades Council lobbied the candidates in national and local elections and then decided whom to support, on the basis of their replies.

By the time of the 1906 general election, the local trades union vote was significant enough for local candidates to canvas the votes of Trades Council members. This resulted in the Trades Council supporting the Liberal. Nevertheless, although 29 Labour MPs were elected nationally and led by Keir Hardie, Hastings returned yet another Tory MP. In fact Hastings and Rye were the only two Conservative gains in the country.

In the same year the Hastings Labour Representation Committee split into two, when the trades unionists refused to break their links with the Liberals and Conservatives.[7] The Hastings and St Leonards Trades Council was still meeting here in 1951.

The Clarence has also been patronised by many other organisations over the years. These include Hastings Rowing Club, the Cinque Ports Foresters (a large branch with hundreds of members), the Victoria Lodge of the Oddfellows and the Hastings branch of the Equitable Society. The latter met here from 1901 and in 1910 the landlord formed the Clarence Benefit Society, which had 176 members and a total fund of £1,276, a considerable balance for those days. Between them, the members of all the above organisations provided the Clarence with a wide customer base.

During the Second World War the Clarence was patronised by Canadian troops billeted in the town. The late Charles Banks, then Police Inspector Banks, recalled that "Hastings' police were frequently called to the Clarence to deal with assaults, brawls and wilful damage. The ringleaders were frequently Canadian soldiers, members of the Princess Louise Dragoon Guards."[8] During the war parts of Middle Street were bombed, but the Clarence was spared.

Clive Vale Hotel
Old London Road, Ore

c1914

From the 1870s there were several applications for new licences for premises on the Clive Vale Estate in the north-east district of Hastings. One was for a proposed 12 bedroom hotel, 'to be erected at the junction of Alfred Road and the Old London Road', on a plot

Landlord William Luck and wife 1886–1894

of land set aside for a new public house by the British Land Company. The application, opposed by the Hare and Hounds, was refused at least five times but was finally granted in 1886 to William Luck, previously landlord of the Millers Arms.[1]

The British Land Company dated back to the 1850s. Its policy was to acquire building land that could be divided into plots. Ownership of a house on one of these plots qualified men to vote, through the 'forty-shilling freehold'.[2]

The pub had a variety of customers in its early years. In the 1890s the Clive Vale Bicycle Club met here, as did a branch of the Equitable Friendly Society and the Ore and Clive Vale Rifle, Bowls and Quoits Club. In 1909 this club celebrated a 'quoits handicap on the American system, on their enlarged and improved ground' beside the pub in Alfred Road.[3] This club was still going strong in 1920.[4] The Clive Vale was one of the few pubs where quoits was played in Hastings, although the Edinburgh Castle on the West Hill had a quoits club, as did the Norman in St Leonards. There may have

Ore & Clive Vale Harriers & Bowls Club 1909–1920

been other pub teams. Hastings Borough Council provided facilities for the game in Alexandra Park in 1911 and the current Alexandra and Clive Vale Bowls Club stems from that time. The game was played outside by throwing metal rings down a pitch at target pins embedded in the ground.

By 1915 the pub was showing middle class credentials by hosting suppers for the All Souls Church Choir and for the local cricket club. But in the 1920s its social base began to change and by the depression of the 1930s it was a popular pub with 'webbers', men who drove rabbits into long webbed nets, placed at right angles along two sides of a field. A successful night's webbing could produce up to 150 rabbits, which were then sold in the community and in the pub.

In an interview with Hastings Local History Group, Tom Blackman (1915–1981), an old customer, recalled: "I can remember them all that used to come here. And one pub in particular called the Clive Vale, it's still there, but altered now, and if you went in that pub on Sunday dinner time, it's no exaggeration, in them days there were a row of seats all the way round, and they used to sit there,

69

and you didn't dare put your foot under the seat, because there'd be about 20 dogs lying under there. And there'd be rabbits and everything else in that pub. And them dogs the breeding wasn't worth four pence as the saying is but them dogs was worth their weight in gold … they'd watch one hole for you and if the rabbit came out they'd grab it, and if the ferret come out they'd squeak and tell you the ferret was out."

He continued, "They weren't actual poachers because poaching is when you take game. It was quite an honourable profession in them days … you never looked down on a rabbit catcher. If you got caught the charge was: 'trespassing in search of conies'. It was just a way of life: they lived rabbits, talked rabbits and hunted rabbits. Things were so hard that a few rabbits meant everything … And they say the good old days!"[5]

In 1987 the pub changed its name to Brunel's and in an advert, a piece of pure marketing hype, the Clive Vale gave itself some false history:

Originally named the Railway, this pub was designed by Isambard Kingdom Brunel in 1886 as a small hotel outside the proposed site of Ore railway station. In the event the railway engineers couldn't blast through the rock and Ore Station was resited where it is today. It was renamed the Clive Vale Hotel.[6]

The fallacy of this statement is self evident. Firstly, engineers wouldn't build a railway uphill when they could follow the Ore Valley and secondly, the local rock is Hastings sandstone. Furthermore, the pub was never known as the Railway and Brunel had nothing to do with the Clive Vale Hotel, Ore railway station or the South Eastern Railway.

The idea comes from a mistaken belief in the Ore community, that the Clive Vale Hotel was a folly erected in anticipation of Ore railway station being built nearby. The fact that Francis Thompson, an architect who worked for Brunel, lived in Alfred Road in the early 1900s, most probably influenced this idea.

The name Brunel's lasted only 12 months before it was renamed again as the New Clive Vale, in 1988.[7] After an active century the Clive Vale closed soon after.

Clown
Russell Street

2009

The Clown claims the title of 'Hastings' cosiest pub', and it is certainly one of the smallest. It is first mentioned in the Hastings Licensees Register for 1872 after the licensing act of that year but was almost certainly in existence before that time. The landlord was then Albert McConky who also had a small shop counter on the premises.

In 1905, immediately after the 1904 Licensing Act came into force, the Clown was nominated by the chief constable, along with 24 other Hastings pubs, for closure on the grounds that it was 'no longer required' and should be made redundant. He claimed that 'the premises were such that no magistrate would grant a new licence'.[1]

However, the locals who drank there attended the licensing sessions and put up a rigorous defence. One of them described it as 'a round the corner sort of place with respectable customers'. The Clown was reprieved, but the magistrates closed down five other pubs that year and the threat never really went away.

Eight years later, in 1913, Edwin Turner, an old army man 'invalided out after six years in the colours', bought the business, still a simple beer house, from Smith's Lamberhurst Brewery. It must have been a successful business, for nine years later he bought the freehold for £755, which in 2006, using the historic retail price index, was equivalent to £28,000. This made him, at that time, a rare person in Hastings, the owner of a free house.

The licence was opposed again by the chief constable in 1928, but the pub was reprieved a second time, as it was not possible to compensate a free house with money from the brewery. On examination it was found that trade was not large, but as a free house the Clown sold the 'better beers', where the profit margin was proportionally greater and perhaps three times that of ordinary mild ale. The Clown was basically a single bar divided into two and the jug and bottle (a beer takeaway) was the smallest in Hastings, measuring only 7 feet 7 inches by 4 feet 8 inches [2.3m by 1.4m].[2]

In 1930 the licence was opposed for a third time and the pub's regulars went back to court to protest yet again. "It's a restful little place", they said. "It's a shame to take it away from us." The Licensed Victuallers Association pointed out that the landlord had a

Late 1950s

good record. He had previously been landlord of the Black Horse, Halton and had 'never had an upset in 15 years'. Again it stayed open.[3]

The Clown seems to have remained open during the years of the Second World War, when it entered a team in the *Observer* Darts Tournament. The Clown was (and is) a working class pub and most of its competition came from the Castle Shades, the Gaiety and the York Hotel (all now closed), the Central Hotel (now Moda, which caters for a younger customer) and the Bedford, which was bombed in 1940.

The Clown's trade has always increased in the summer months. In the 1890s it was popular with 'excursionists' who travelled to Hastings by train. By the 1930s they had become 'day trippers', travelling to Hastings by charabanc from London. They often loaded up with crates of beer for the return journey. Cricket fans who came for the matches across the road on the Central Cricket Ground were also good customers.

After Edwin Turner's time as owner the Clown became tied to George, Beer and Rigden and then to Fremlin's of Maidstone. In 1949 it was granted a licence for the consumption of wine on and off the premises, ending its 77 years plus as a beer house. This was followed by a full licence in 1954.[4]

The name 'Clown' stems from the 1870s. During that decade cricket teams, made up of actors from the London theatres, dressed as clowns, and some genuine cricketers toured several venues in the south-east including Hastings, Lewes and elsewhere. Accompanied by a band these carnival occasions were frowned upon by some of the more serious cricketing fraternity and for that reason didn't continue. However, the Clown was used by members of the visiting team and gained its name from them.

One regular in the 1990s was Roger Povey, who remembers there was much talk of a ghost at that time.[5] More recently another customer, Hastings resident Betty Austin, said: "The Clown always feels busy even with just a dozen or so people it feels full".

Cricketers
South Terrace

The Cricketers was first licensed in 1864.[1] Its most famous customer was Robert Tressell, author of *The Ragged Trousered Philanthropists*, a novel set in Hastings, incorporating the 'Labour Theory of Value'. Tressell drank here in the early years of the 20th century and this was the pub where he observed the drinkers who became the prototypes for the characters of the Semi-drunk and the Besotted Wretch.[2] The description of the Cricketers which follows is paraphrased from Tressell's book.

The pub was arranged in five bars. There was a saloon bar, a jug and bottle for taking away beer and two private bars, with room only for two or three people looking for 'four pennyworth of spirits'. These private bars were 'much appreciated by ladies, who liked to indulge in a drop of gin on the quiet'. Finally there was the much larger public bar, with sawdust and spittoons.

The polyphon, an early jukebox

In the public bar a 'large automatic instrument', a polyphon(e) (an antique music player with a cylinder, a forerunner of the jukebox) stood close to the counter. Nearby was a ring board, about 15 inches [38cm] square, where players threw rubber rings onto numbered hooks, and a shovepenny board, played with old French pennies kept behind the bar. Above it a neatly printed framed notice said:

> *Gentlemen using this house are*
> *respectfully asked to refrain*
> *from using obscene language.*

'The landlord was a well fed and prosperous looking individual, in a fancy waistcoat, gold watch chain and a diamond ring. The landlady was a large woman with a highly coloured countenance ... a large bust encased in a black dress and several gold rings on her fat, white hands.'

One of the regulars, 'a shabbily dressed, bleary-eyed, degraded, beer-sodden, trembling wretch', spent the greater part of every day and all of his money in this bar. He was a miserable looking wreck of a man about 30, but was a very good customer.

The other main regular was a shabby, semi-drunken man in a bowler hat with a 'very thin, pale face and a large high bridged nose, bearing a striking resemblance to the first Duke of Wellington'.

"Wotcher", said the landlord affably, greeting the customers, "Ow goes it?" "All reet me ole dear", was the usual reply. "Well wot's it to be." "Ere's the skin orf yer nose", was the usual toast. The landlord would put a penny in the polyphon(e) and it would start to play. The Semi-drunk would rise to his feet unsteadily and begin shuffling and singing:

> *"They may build their ships, my lads,*
> *And try to play the game,*
> *But they can't build the boys of the Bulldog breed,*
> *Wot made ole Hingland's—"*

"Ere! Stop that, will yer?" cried the Old Dear, fiercely. "I told you once before that I don't allow that sort of thing in my 'ouse!" "I didn't mean no 'arm", he said unsteadily, appealing to the company. "I don't want no chin from you!" said the Old Dear with a ferocious scowl. "If you want to make that row you can go somewheres else, and the sooner you goes the better. You've been 'ere long enough." Tressell observed the pub games, the Besotted Wretch throwing the rubber rings at the ring board. The customers laughed when he missed and applauded 'when he threw a good ring'.

On one occasion he watched the two regulars play each other. "You can't play for nuts", said the Besotted Wretch. "Can't I? I can play you, anyway." "Right you are! I'll play you for a round!" cried the Semi-drunk. "Come on then. What's it to be? Fifty up?" "Anything you like! Fifty or a 'undred or a bloody million!"

'Holding the six rings in his left hand, the man stood in the middle of the floor at a distance of about three yards. Taking one of the rings between the forefinger and thumb of his right hand and closing his left eye, he carefully "sighted" the centre hook, then he slowly extended his arm to its full length then, bending his elbow, he brought his hand back again until it nearly touched his chin, and slowly extended his arm again. He repeated these movements several times, whilst the others watched with bated breath. Getting it right at last he suddenly shot the ring at the board, but instead of hooking on No 13, it went over the partition into the private bar' to the huge delight of the watching customers.[3]

Ninety years later, there was a series of problems with flooding. In 1992 the Cricketers was flooded five times and after the Environmental Health Department had condemned its cellar, the pub closed down for a time. In 1995, the cricket ground opposite was redeveloped into Priory Meadow Shopping Centre and construction work brought complaints of cloudy beer. Sediment in the barrels was disturbed by the vibration caused by pile driving and turned the beer cloudy, making it unsaleable.

In 1996 it became the Priory and then the Jazz and Blues House. It is now a gambling venue called the Hastings Terrace Club.

Crown Inn
All Saints Street, Old Town

Ye Olde Crown Inn, prior to 1921

The original Crown Inn was located on the south corner of Courthouse Street and High Street and dated from the 16th century. It was re-built with other buildings after a fire in the Tudor period, which all but destroyed the High Street. There has been a pub on the recent site since 1794 when the Crown was a coaching inn licensed to William Smith, and then to his widow Sarah Smith from 1815 to 1832.

In the early 19th century, the Crown and the nearby Swan were described as 'the principal rendezvous of gentility'. As early as 1817 Hastings was so crowded in the summer months that the Crown had its loft fitted up as sleeping quarters for the servants and engaged up to 30 other beds off the premises.[1]

Coaches set off for London, Brighton and Dover from here. An advert in 1816 said: 'The Crown Inn coach sets off every morning at 8am and arrives in London at 6pm. It is driven by the most experienced coachman.'

Powell's *Hastings Guide* for 1831 said Mrs Smith 'deserves particular commendation and support, as being the first (with a family of seven children) to add to the accommodation of visitors by every species of comfort, neatness, and domestic attention'.

Mrs Smith's time as landlady ended in 1832 and marked the beginning of a period of decline for the Crown Inn. In 1839, for example, two members of the Hastings police force, an inspector and a constable, were charged with 'neglecting their duty wantonly' and 'degrading the character of the Hastings police', by drinking ale and rum in the Crown from 'noon till 7pm in the company of two prostitutes'. In the evening when they retired to an upstairs room 'the Inspector was so intoxicated', a witness stated, that 'he went upstairs on his hands and knees'.[2]

Another example was reported on an evening in the 1850s. A 'preventive man' [customs officer] had his purse stolen while having a quiet drink in the bar. The purse was eventually retrieved from a woman's bosom, empty, after she tried to swap it for a glass of gin. On another occasion a constable heard 'indecent, noisy language' coming from the Crown and found five men and seven 'girls on the town', in a side parlour. One of them asked him to have a brandy, and a butcher, who was having supper in a little back parlour, admitted there were some 'improper characters' in the bar.[3]

Around the same time, an Irishman known as Old Jack was buried at All Saints Church. A wake was held in the Crown and it was reported that 'everyone was thoroughly inebriated and set the neighbourhood in an uproar with their strange freaks'. In 1856 a German, who lodged at the Crown, was also buried at All Saints', after cutting his throat. A German band played the *Death March*.

Like most Old Town pubs, the Crown also ran a common lodging house located in a yard in Crown Lane, where on one occasion a man had his dinner (a sheep's head) stolen by a drinker in the Crown Tap.

The Crown lodging house was included in a survey of the sanitary conditions of Hastings in 1850. In the Crown yard the survey found 13 beds in a converted stable loft without running water, drainage or a 'privy'. The accommodation was organized by John and Mary Huggett who charged two shillings [10p] per person per week. Mrs Huggett paid the landlord half the income she received, did the cooking and washing and supplied coal and candles. There was no toilet, water supply, drainage or electricity. Lodgers used buckets which when full were dumped in the street.[4]

Forty years later things had improved. A large Buffaloes Lodge was established in the 1890s. Their meetings raised primo members to 'degrees of knighthood', where they drank each other's health dressed in Buffalo regalia.[5]

In 1898 the All Saints' Conservative Association held social evenings here and in 1900, when the Boer War broke out, a large gathering of local dignitaries gathered to give patriotic, nationalist and jingoistic support to the local volunteers who had been dispatched to South Africa.[6]

In the early 1900s this once large inn, now known as Ye Olde Crown House, was reduced in size. The landlord from 1902–1907 was Alexander James Littlejohn. After his time at the Crown he went to sea with the White Star Line as a steward, and in 1912 he joined the ill-fated Titanic on its maiden voyage. His grandson Phillip Littlejohn explained: "My grandfather was a first-class steward on the Titanic but survived the ordeal after being ordered to row lifeboat 13. It was in this boat that the youngest passenger aboard, nine weeks old Millvina Dean, was rescued. She became the longest surviving passenger and died in 2009 aged 97."

Alexander Littlejohn later described his experience in lifeboat 13. "We could see the Titanic sinking by the head", he remembered. "Her forward ports were under water and we could see the lights gradually go out on E deck .... All her other lights were burning brilliantly and she looked a blaze of light from stem to stern. We watched her like this for some time then suddenly she gave a plunge forward and all the lights went out. Her stern went right up in the air; there were two or three explosions and ... immediately after there were terrible cries for help. They were awful and heartrending."

Landlord A.J. Littlejohn before and after the Titanic disaster

In 1921 a fire destroyed the pub and it was rebuilt.[7] In 1985 it was completely refurbished and became Harvey's first Hastings' pub.

In 1998 the landlord was Alex Napier ex-drummer with rock band Uriah Heep. When Phillip Littlejohn visited the Crown whilst researching his book, a biography of his grandfather, he was astonished to find that Alex Napier called time on a reproduction 'Titanic' brass bell kept behind the bar. This was pure coincidence, as the connection between his grandfather and the Crown was unknown outside the family.[8]

Cutter

East Parade

The Cutter Hotel pre -1927

The Cutter was built in 1769 and rebuilt 37 years later, as a ship-lap timber building in the centre of the Hastings fishing industry.[1] James Bell was landlord from 1807 to 1823, when the pub had a sign which read 'Ship representing a Cutter' and 'James Bell, dealer in Ale. Bottled 4d'. During the Napoleonic Wars he was a valet to Lord Nelson.

In 1813, the Cutter became the first meeting place of the Derwent Lodge of the Freemasons. Alfred Chatfield, formerly a footman and then a barber, became landlord around 1840, and in 1860 the poet and Pre-Raphaelite painter, Dante Gabriel Rossetti, stayed here before marrying Elizabeth Siddal in St Clements Church. The sight of the sun sinking in the west over the Hastings coast left an impression on him. His stay is recorded on a blue plaque.

The Poet and Painter
DANTE GABRIEL
ROSSETTI
(1828 - 1882)

Stayed here during 1860
Prior to his wedding
On 23rd May, 1860
at nearby
St Clement's Church

O.H.P.S.

A popular drink at the time was 'three pennyworth of rum and eggs', an early type of 'eggnog' served to upper middle class customers in the smoking room.[2]

During the last 40 years of the 19th century, the Cutter followed the general decline of the Old Town and another class of customer began to turn up. In 1868 an engine driver fell asleep on a bench opposite the pub. Around 10pm, a woman called Elizabeth Evans woke him up asking: "Will you stand me a drink?" This was a common approach used by prostitutes at the time. They went into the Cutter and called for a 'quartern of whisky', in a small room at the side of the bar. Later, he realised the woman had stolen four sovereigns [£4] from his pocket. A policeman later found her in the Royal Standard and she was arrested.[3]

In 1872, a costermonger [barrow boy] was summonsed, for trying to obtain sixpence [2½p] by false pretences. He walked into the pub and asked for three ha'pennies [1p] worth of gin, for which he paid with a shilling [5p]. He said: "Will you give me six coppers [2½p] for a sixpence piece?" The barmaid laid six coppers on the counter, but before she could pick up the coin, he asked for 'a shilling for a sixpenny piece and six coppers'. She gave him a shilling and he put a sixpenny piece on the counter, with the coppers. He attempted the same trick at the Hastings Arms, but was caught out. The police finally picked him up in the Alma, another Old Town pub long since disappeared.[4]

In 1876 two vegetable hawkers left their carts outside the pub, while they went inside to 'wet a deal'. When they came out one cart was gone, only later to be found in Eastbourne with 4 hundredweight [203kg] of potatoes missing. Other customers included fly drivers, grocers, fish buyers, butchers, marine store dealers and waiters, of whom the landlord sometimes complained of their 'picky' (i.e. bad) language.

In the 1890s the Hastings and St Leonards Bicycle Club held their annual smoking concerts here [see page 285] and prizes were awarded for an annual '100 mile' ride to Worthing and back followed by a programme of songs and entertainment by a 'glee party'.[5]

The Cutter was rebuilt in 1927 and refurbished in 1957, when the house on the west side was added. When it reopened, the landlord, in the company of local fishermen and the lifeboat crew in oilskins, was presented with a painting of a cutter and the Hastings lifeboat was presented with a cheque by the brewery.

Adjacent to the Cutter was a centuries old navigation system for boats coming ashore, known as the 'Hastings' Upper and Lower Lights'. When boats at sea had the two lights in line they could turn inland into a safe channel between two ridges of rock. In the 19th century the upper light was located at the top of Light Steps, George Street and the lower light was to the east of the Cutter.

In the 1990s, the leaseholds of the Cutter and four other Hastings' pubs were held by Ray Lee, who by 1995, owed a massive £20,000 to the brewery for beer supplied to the Cutter, the Norman, the Marina Fountain, the Royal George (later the Priory) and the Dolphin. Under pressure of debt, he suddenly left Hastings and absconded with his wife to South Africa.[6]

Cutter 2009

Dripping Spring
Tower Road, Bohemia

Dripping Spring c1950

The triangle of land between Bohemia Road, Cornfield Terrace and Tower Road contains some of the earliest housing in Bohemia including, at one time, at least four pubs on Bohemia Road. In 1866 Richard Moy, landlord of one of them, the Prince of Wales, complained about the competition from 'two more beer houses in Bohemia'. One of these was the forerunner of the Dripping Spring, a grocer's shop and beer house run by Thomas Stubbenfield, at 35 Tower Road. Number 34, now the saloon bar, was a bootmakers.[1]

Stubbenfield's shop continued until 1899, but the beer house became separated from it in 1892 to become the Dripping Spring. Mrs Phoebe Tapp held the licence that year but proved herself to be 'ill-fitted' for the life of a publican. In her first year she was fined for permitting drunkenness and her licence was revoked.[2] The next landlord was Sydney Smith, who remained until 1896.

VALUABLE FREEHOLD PROPERTY,

WHICH

MESSRS WOODHAMS, SON & PARKS

Have received instructions to SELL BY AUCTION, at the CASTLE HOTEL, HASTINGS, on MONDAY, DEC. 5th, 1904, at Seven o'clock in the Evening.

LOT 1.--A capital Freehold Property, being No. 28, SEDLESCOMBE ROAD NORTH let at 6s. 6d. per week, the tenant paying the rates.

LOT 2 – A Pair of Freehold Semi-detached Cottages, Nos. 46 and 48, CORNFIELD TERRACE, BOHEMIA, each let at 5s. per week, the tenants paying the rates.

LOT 3 —The Freehold Detached Cottage, No. 49, CORNFIELD TERRACE, BOHEMIA, let at 6s. 6d. per week, the tenant paying the rates.

LOT 4.—The valuable Freehold Licensed Beerhouse, known as " THE DRIPPING SPRING," No. 35, TOWER ROAD, BOHEMIA, with good return frontage to Tower-road and Cornfield-terrace, and containing three bedrooms, sitting-room, two private bars, two public bars, bar parlour, and private entrance, kitchen, and good cellar in basement. It is let to Messrs. Ballard and Co. on lease (about 7½ years unexpired), at £50 per annum

Auction 1904

Before the First World War, the Dripping Spring ran a slate club, which in 1909 paid out £1 7s 2d [£1.36] to each of 76 members. The club came to an end when its members were recruited into the military.

In 1915 the potman was called up into the 'territorials'. A short time later in 1916 the landlord, Fred Smith, was also called up. He appealed to the Hastings Military Tribunal and explained that he and his wife now ran the Dripping Spring alone. He did all the cellar work himself and explained that the lightest barrel was a quarter-hundredweight [12.7kg], the heaviest four and a quarter-hundredweight [218kg] and a two dozen crate of beer was a quarter-hundredweight. His appeal was refused and he was granted an exemption of one month only, before being sent to France.[3] After his departure his wife struggled on with help from the customers but Fred was lucky: he returned from France alive and well and remained landlord until 1921, when the 'Drip' was taken over by Charles Martin.

Charles Martin successfully applied for a wine licence in 1938 supported by a petition signed by 153 customers, although the Bohemia Arms, the Tower Hotel, the Prince of Wales and the chief constable opposed it.[4]

Unlike many pubs, the Drip stayed open during the Second World War and in 1940 the building was improved. In 1943 and 1944 the Drip entered two darts teams in the Annual *Observer* Darts tournament. It managed to escape the bombing, unlike the Tower Hotel, which had to remove a bomb from its cellar.

In 1950 the Dripping Spring was granted a full licence and its 84 years of life as a beer house came to an end. As the Licensing Act of 1910 stipulated that only pubs with two bars could have a full licence, the house next door was acquired and its ground floor turned into the saloon bar still in use today. Before this the entrance to the single bar was on the corner of Cornfield Terrace. In the same year it was included in the Whitbread miniature inn signs series.[5]

Cyril Pelluet remembers the pub from 1957. "Sometimes we went to the Dripping Spring", he says, "which we considered a better quality pub. The inside was smarter and husbands and wives went there together. Wives just didn't go to the Prince of Wales or the Bohemia Arms. The Dripping Spring was a bit higher up the social scale. Not very far up but just a bit".[6]

In 1992 the Dripping Spring became a free house and was known as the New George and Dragon, until 1995.[7] It started selling real ale in 1994 and in 1995 was listed in the *Good Beer Guide*. In 2000, the pub was voted CAMRA Sussex Pub of the Year and also runner-up as National Pub of the Year, to become the second best CAMRA pub in the country. The pub was listed in the *Good Beer Guide* for 10 years from 1997 to 2007 and again in 2009.

The pub is located on a part of Tower Road once known as Spring Terrace. The area is said to have several springs, one of which is thought to flow in a culvert beneath the pub cellar. Why or where it drips is a mystery. The present sign dates from 2008. The previous sign, last seen in the back garden, portrays a 'dandy' with a cane and a glass of wine, standing by a spring in an unknown location.

present pub sign

previous pub sign

Duke of Cornwall
5 Post Office Passage

Duke of Cornwall 1960s

These premises were built in 1768, rebuilt in 1816 and partly rebuilt again in 1899, due to the house sinking during drainage work. The pub was located in a poor district of Old Town, which had many pubs and beer houses. At one count there were 18 within 300 yards. Landlord William James Wenham applied for a full licence in 1850 and again in 1853 when he told the magistrates he 'had occupied the house for 13 years'. Post Office Passage was badly lit and it was difficult to see from one end to the other. The beer house was described by the police as 'uncomfortable and uninviting', and if there were no customers the landlord would turn the gaslights off in the passage to save fuel.

In 1865 new neighbours arrived in Post Office Passage in the form of the Rescue Society, a temperance organisation. Their mission was to 'rescue people from the evils of alcohol' which, as can be imagined, did not make for an amicable relationship.

William Wenham was the owner by 1872, so it seems he had done well as a publican with a second occupation making fish baskets.

> **THE CHARGE OF FELONY AGAINST A PUBLICAN.**— On Tuesday, WM: JOHN WENHAM, who keeps the Duke of Cornwall Inn, was again examined on the charge of stealing a number of fish baskets, the property of James Ball. Mr. W. Savery prosecuted, Mr. F. A. Langham defended. The baskets to the number of 100 dozens were left in a loft over the Crown stables, and about two months ago, 14 or 16 dozens, worth £1 or £1 5s. were missed. Last week, a shoemaker, named Loper, deposed to taking a number of baskets by a circuitous route to prisoner's house, but denied taking them from the Crown loft. It also appeared prisoner had sold and given away a number of baskets, Loper said he got the baskets from Mr. Wenham son's loft, the entrance to which was in the Crown yard, and not from prosecutor's, in the Crown Lane. John Harker, basket maker, proved that he made the baskets produced for Mr. Baldock (prosecutor's late partner), and said they were not commonly made for fish buyers now. George Page deposed to carrying baskets for Messrs. Baldock and Ball, to the loft in Crown Lane, many being similar to those produced. James White was called and proved having made baskets for Mr. Wenham, senior, for three or four years, but had never made any like those produced. Matthew Sargent, a baker and fish buyer in John Street, had had conversation with prisoner about the charge, and he admitted having taken two dozen and six, and that was all; what others had done he said he knew nothing about but if he was to split he should bring two or three more into trouble. In answer to Mr. Langham, witness said prisoner did not tell him that he found them in his father's loft.

1862 [1]

Charlotte and Walter Wenham were the tenants in 1881 thus the Duke of Cornwall was in the hands of the Wenham family for at least 40 years. A large Wenham family of nine is listed in the 1881 census and they are mentioned again on the website 'Romany-Gypsy Connections'.

WASHERWOMEN'S DINNER

BONNETS AND SHAWLS ROUND THE FESTIVE BOARD

BEEF PUDDING

Quite a unique social function took place in the Old Town recently, when washerwomen in the district gathered together for dinner at the Duke of Cornwall Inn.

The dinner was confined to women who take in washing for a living and do their washing at the public wash-houses. About 40 were present, all attired in bonnet and shawl, and the evening was a thoroughly jolly affair. For months past the women had paid into a central fund to provide the dinner, which it is hoped will become an annual affair.

The long parlour of the Duke of Cornwall was decorated for the occasion and the tables with their snow white cloths and gleaming cutlery made a bright scene.

Councillor J.H. Tingle, who is a representative of All Saints Ward, presided, and the dinner was served and eaten with rapidity The menu was:-

Beef pudding.

Joints of beef and mutton.

Vegetables in season.

Appropriate refreshments.

It should be pointed out that the last item included mellow old Duke of Cornwall ale, as well as lemonade and ginger beer. Mine host, Mr. Ben Page, supervised and attended to the needs of the company.

After dinner the Royal toast was duly honoured, and thirty washerwomen raised their voices in accord to sing a verse of the National Anthem. Then followed an impromptu programme, which was as varied as it was enjoyable. Old time songs were prime favourites and the refrains were taken up with rare gusto. The washerwomen came forward one after the other to give their turn and there was no "stage fright." They sung, lustily, songs which were popular forty years ago.

Altogether it was a very jolly affair and the washerwomen enjoyed themselves to the full.

1924 [2]

The Duke had a wide customer base and, it seems, some large rooms. In the mid-19th century the Cinque Ports Band practised here for 25 years and in 1903 the local magistrates noted that the Bagatelle Room was very popular with costermongers.

During the Second World War the Duke of Cornwall closed from 1940 until 1946. The magistrate's record states that the pub: 'Closed for trading from 10pm on the 30th September 1940; the reason being that the licensee's nerves were very bad and the conditions prevailing did not warrant a continuance of trade'.[3] After reopening in 1946 the Duke of Cornwall acquired the nick-name 'The Silver Dollar'. This was because the bar allegedly resembled a wild west saloon![2]

By 1966 this pub was feeling the pinch and stopped functioning in December of that year. The police, the magistrates and the brewers all agreed its redundancy and the pub closed in 1967. In 1976 Watney's applied for permission to use the site for storage. However, it was within a conservation area and the application was refused. It was later replaced by a block of flats.

Stanley Hayward and wife, licensees 1964–1966

Electric Stag
Robertson Street

The Electric Stag was almost certainly an entrance to the former music hall, at one time situated above Yates next door. In 1861 Charles Dickens appeared at the music hall and gave readings.

MUSIC HALL, HASTINGS.—FOR ONE NIGHT ONLY

MR. CHARLES DICKENS

WILL READ at the MUSIC HALL, Hastings, on WEDNESDAY EVENING, November the 6th, at Eight o'clock, his

CHRISTMAS CAROL & THE TRIAL FROM PICKWICK

The time occupied by this Reading will be within two hours.

Stalls, (numbered and reserved) 4s. ; Second Seats, 2s. Back Seats, 1s. Tickets to be had at Mr. Lockey's Pianoforte Saloon, Robertson Street, Hastings, where a Plan of the Stalls may be seen

1861 [1]

READING BY MR. CHARLES DICKENS.—The world-wide fame which Mr. Charles Dickens has obtained had the effect of securing for him a most flattering reception, at the Music Hall in this town, on the evening on Wednesday last, when the reading of his " Christmas Carol," and " The Trial from Pickwick," took place. For a long time both before and after the hour announced for the commencement of the reading, carriages continued to arrive at the entrance to the hall, and many persons, who had not secured tickets, were unable to obtain admission ; indeed, it is thought, that such a numerous and brilliant audience has not been witnessed in the hall since the opening concert. The reading of " The Christmas Carol" occupied the greater part of the evening, and, as one might suppose, seemed to produce the greater impression upon the audience. It served also to show not only Mr. Charles Dickens's unrivalled talent and ability as a writer of fiction, but also the efficiency he has acquired as a reader. His change of voice and countenance produced a good effect enabling him to bring the varied characters before the audience with a degree of accuracy which a personal representation of each individual could scarcely have excelled. The reading produced frequent manifestations of feeling, and the loud and repeated applause of the audience afforded a proof of their approbation.

1861 [2]

96

It was reported that he drew a crowd of maximum capacity, with a large number unable to get in. Two lines of waiting horse drawn carriages stretched up Cambridge Road for half a mile.

The building has been licensed for many years, although not from when it was first opened in 1858. The first licence was granted in 1868 after the cellar had been enlarged into a wine vault. The first landlord was Charles West, formerly of the Anchor, George Street, 'for the store adjacent to the Music Hall'.[3] It was first known as

---

THOMAS ORGER,

WEST'S CELLARS,

53, ROBERTSON ST., HASTINGS.

𝔚ine & 𝔖pirit 𝔐erchant,

BREWERS' AGENT AND BOTTLER.

☞ CELEBRATED HOUSE FOR OLD WHISKIES, VINTAGE PORTS & CHAMPAGNES.

A Large and Well-Assorted Stock of
— OLD PORTS, SHERRIES, HOCKS, MOSELLES, CLARETS, — CHAMPAGNES, BURGUNDIES, &c.

YOUNGER'S No. 1 SCOTCH ALE

On Draught and in Bottle.

LENEY'S CELEBRATED ALE,

In 4½, 9 and 18 Gall. Casks, with Patent Taps.

Per 1/- Gall.

BASS & ALLSOPP'S ALE & GUINNESS & Co.'s EXTRA STOUT in Cask and Bottle.

1890

West's Cellars and the licence was granted on condition that the bar 'would be used as a refreshment room, rather than an ordinary inn and not on Sundays'. The licence was opposed by the Havelock Hotel, which no doubt feared the competition.

In 1872 it became known as the Cambridge Arms and in 1877 as the Cambridge Arms Wine Vaults. The name changed again in the 1880s to West's Stores and Billiards Saloon and again in 1902 to Bodega Wine Merchants. At that time the premises had private accommodation upstairs for a caretaker.

In 1893 an entrance was opened up in Havelock Road, leading down to the original wine vaults, which had been fitted up as a second bar and billiard room.[4] The licensee at the time was Frederick O'Hara Hoar, who had been an architect in London and a gold miner in Colorado, where he made a lot of money developing a 'machine for washing gold ore'. He then spent a few years in South Africa buying up gold claims, before ending up as the licensee of the Bodega.

O'Hara Hoar and his business partner Mrs Clifford borrowed £1,000 from the brewers and among other things installed a Battle Shoot as a commercial enterprise. They overspent and became bankrupt with debts of £3,385.[5]

The Battle Shoot was almost certainly a shooting activity using small air rifles, popular at that time in pubs in the Midlands—an ideal activity for the Bodega cellar. The target was probably a bell target, 'a metal clock shaped device, with a small aperture in the centre, surrounded by rings. The scoring surface was coated with non-drying paint. A bull through the centre scored five points and rang a bell. Shots slightly off target scored 4, 3, 2 or 1, depending on whichever ring they hit. Once shooters had finished their six shots, their score was totted up and the surfaces were quickly recovered with more paint.'

In later years a local shopkeeper recalled that in the final years of the 19th century this saloon was the 'best known rendezvous in Robertson Street. Here would gather in the forenoon the leading business and professional men and some town councillors, over a morning glass of wine or ale'. An advert from that time describes the premises as a 'celebrated house for old whiskies, vintage ports and champagnes'.

For at least 60 years from 1902, the Bodega maintained a reputation for quality, and other establishments in Hastings measured themselves against its high standards. Bodega wines were considered quality products and regarded as the best that Hastings had to offer. The Bodega may have been a branch of the Bodega national chain.

This reputation continued throughout the Second World War. If you got caught in the town centre when the bombers came, what better than to take a glass in the Bodega. During one air raid in 1944, a middle class woman and her 16-year-old daughter took shelter in the Bodega, where they were observed by a policeman drinking port and lime. The mother was cautioned for allowing her underage daughter to take alcohol but explained that it could have been her last drink and her daughter's only drink. She was let off with a warning.[6]

Twenty years later the Bodega still maintained its 'cultivated atmosphere'. Peter Skinner, a customer in the early 1960s, remembers the house from that time. "We went there quite a lot", he says. "It was a very civilised place. Local solicitors drank there, sherry and things like that".[7]

It then became Forte's Wine and Spirit Merchants and in 1968 the York Bars, when the second entrance in Havelock Road was reopened. The cellar, underneath the York Bar, was extended in 1970 to become the Crypt and the name changed again to the York and Crypt Bars.[8] In 1990 it became the Street .

In 1991 the Street became a music venue. Roger Carey organised successful jazz nights for three years until 1994, with star musicians such as John Etheridge, Mornington Lockett and Claire Hamill. "Everybody expressed great enthusiasm for the club", he recalls and "many have been introduced to jazz for the first time".

The Street closed in 2011 but re-opened in 2013 as the Electric Stag.

Bodega

First In Last Out and Prince of Wales beer house,
High Street and Waterloo Passage

Waterloo Passage on the right

From 1849 to 1869 a poor beer house was located in Waterloo Passage—a twitten alongside the First In Last Out (FILO). A letter from a Reverend Alfred Barrett to the Mayor of Hastings in 1849 complained of a 'disorderly house in St Clements'.

'There is a beer house called the Prince of Wales in Waterloo Passage leading off the High Street. It is kept by Tilden Tolhurst. He has music and dancing without a licence every Monday evening from 10pm till 12am, drunkenness, conduct quarrelsome and disorderly, obscene language, gambling among children, open prostitution in and above the house. It is a fearful nuisance to the neighbourhood. After the music ceases many of the party retire into private rooms and gamble until 2 or 3 o'clock, then to avoid the police the persons are let out in sets of three and four ....'[1]

Excise v. Robert Swain, adjourned from Thursday last. A summons for selling spirits without a license.

Edwin Thomas Salt, excise-officer of Battle, deposed that on the 16th of May last he went into the defendant's house, the Prince of Wales, Waterloo passage, with his wife and family, and purchased of Mrs. Swain a quartern of brandy (for which he paid a shilling) out of a bottle which she took from a cupboard. Witness also had a glass of gin, for which he paid 2d. Other persons were in the room drinking brandy, which was also served from bottles from the same cupboard.

The defendant said it was a private room, and the persons were his relations from London.

The witness believed the room was entered for the sale of beer.

Mary Ann, wife of the first witness, corroborated his testimony.

Frances Vidler, a married woman, stated that on the day in question she saw the witnesses come into the Prince of Wales, and bring a pot of ale from the bar into a room in which witness and some of Mr. Swain's friends were sitting. Salt asked Mrs. Swain for some brandy, and she said she had none. He then asked for gin, and the same answer was given. The persons, however, in the room gave him a glass of gin from a pot on the table, which witness had fetched just before from the Crown for Mrs. Swain, to treat her husband's relations with. When the person went out he threw a 6d. on the table. 'She had been in the habit of coming for gin for Swaine. Fined £50 but as it was a first offence reduced to £12.10s.

1853 [2]

42 Bourne Walk, formerly the site of Prince of Wales beer house,
Waterloo Passage

However, the Prince of Wales managed to stay open for another 16 years until 1869 when its licence was revoked because the premises were 'insufficiently rated'. Landlord William Oakley said: "This is a hard case especially after I kept it 15 years. The rating was high enough until the Rating Committee put it down!"[3]

In the same year the building, which now houses the FILO, was a corn dealers, run by Charles Pearson. In 1876 he started selling beer and by 1880 the premises had been transformed into a beer house.[2] George Crampton took over in 1889 and gave the First In Last Out its distinctive name. He remained landlord until 1901 before moving to the newly licensed Railway Stores, Hughenden Road, near Ore Station.[4] He left the FILO owing money to a local beer wholesaler, which suggests that he didn't brew beer himself.

Before the First World War, the FILO ran two very successful slate clubs, one for men and one for women. The fact that it had a female club suggests it had female customers, which was advanced for that time. We know that many pubs were negative about female custom and, in the majority of cases, women were not served. The slate clubs met regularly to organise sick, unemployment and death benefits and for social occasions and dinners. In 1909, for example, the men's slate had 30 members and paid out £40 1s 9d [£40.08] in sick pay.[5]

Twenty years later, the chief constable claimed that there were too many pubs in the Old Town and attempted to close down the FILO. The landlord in 1929, Samuel Mepham, was accused of being drunk in charge of the bar and it seemed a foregone conclusion that the pub would close.

However, the case was unusual. The landlord had served in France in the First World War and claimed to suffer from 'neurasthenia', a condition brought about by trench gas in the Somme. He had also suffered a kick in the head by an army horse and these two things, he claimed, were the cause of his depression, strange appearance and unusual behaviour. Although he had medical witnesses, the court obviously disbelieved his story and fined him two guineas [£2.10]. This was in July 1929 and by August he had lost his licence, which was temporarily transferred to a manager of Ballard's Brewery, Lewes.[6] The police then stopped opposing the licence 'having no further evidence to offer against renewal' and the life of the FILO continued.[7] This brought the total number of landlords between 1908 and 1929 to eight.

FILO brewery, 2009

The FILO slate club was still very active and by then had 58 members, including several men over 50 years of age. A second argument put forward to the magistrates was that if the pub closed, these members would not be able to join any other slate club because of their age and would lose their benefits. FILO regulars Arthur Wood, Albert Colbran, George Jackson and George Gallop, among others, appeared as witnesses for both the pub and the slate club. Arthur Wood described the

FILO as 'a nice little house which doesn't pretend to be a Gin Palace'. The FILO was reprieved with a new landlord.

In 1933 the FILO applied for a wine licence. The landlord told the magistrates that he was interested in promoting 'the wines of the British Empire', which was bringing 'wine within reach of the middle and working classes' for the first time. However, a wine licence was refused[8] and the FILO had to wait another 20 years before it could legally sell wine. After 78 years as a beer house, the pub was granted a full licence in 1954.[9] It has been a free house since 1976, having previously been tied to Charrington's.

In 1982, the FILO acquired a milk pump and was the first (and only) Hastings pub to sell pints of draught milk.[10] Four years later the St Clement's micro-brewery was established on the premises, using four milk pasteurising tanks, by landlord David Harding. This was three years after a micro-brewery was established at Mr Cherry's on the Marina, although the brewery at the FILO is still operating.

In 2001 the brewery was updated and modernised and currently produces Crofters Best Bitter, Cardinal (Sussex Porter), Ginger Tom and Filo Gold (Premium Ale) and also occasional beers for special events such as bonfire night. The FILO has appeared in the *Good Beer Guide* over several years and it has been home to the Hastings branch of the Society for the Preservation of Beers in the Wood.

The pub name possibly stems from the fact that it was, at one time, the last pub before Halton. The pub sign shows a Hastings stage coach. A previous double sign showed a cat being put out at night on one side and being let back in the following morning on the other.

The FILO End of Summer Festival

on Fri 13th, Sat 14th & Sun 15th Oct

FEATURING

Friday 13th
Steve Winchester and Andy Neate

Saturday 14th
Bo'ville
Roger Hubbard

Sunday 15th
Liane Carroll

plus other guest performers

Appearing on all 3 Days

WADWORTH'S
Malt & Hops

MANSFIELD'S
Old Bailey

ARCHER'S
Best Bitter

ASH VINE'S
Challenger

BUNCES
Best Bitter

HOGS BACK'S
T.E.A.

HOOK NORTON'S
Old Hookey

HOP BACK'S
Summer Lightning

SUMMERSKILLS
Indiana Bones

FILO'S
Crofters & Cardinal

THEAKSTON'S
Old Peculier

Guest Appearance DRAUGHT "BUDVA"

First In Last Out
14/15 High Street
Old Town, Hastings
(01424) 425079

1995

Flairz
Havelock Road

Old Golden Cross

This pub was first licensed in 1857 as the Old Golden Cross. It was then a much smaller building than the present one.[1] In 1867 the landlord applied for a licence for another premises at 53 Havelock Road, to be called the New Golden Cross, which was granted.[2] The Old Golden Cross was extended in 1890, when the house next door was purchased.[3] The two premises were completely rebuilt in 1899 and taken over by A.J. Jones, formerly a draper at Whiteley's. At the turn of the last century this new pub was, with one or two exceptions, considered the best that Hastings had to offer; a fine artistic building in the Renaissance style. The following description paraphrases a report from that time.[4]

Its chief feature, apart from the cupola with the resplendent cross on top, was a series of handsome columns which outlined the windows. The rooms on the first floor comprised a billiard room, a lodge room and a reception room. The billiard room was well lit and magnificently decorated with a heavy embossed wallpaper having a large and beautiful chrysanthemum design. The room was fitted all round with rich leather and dark wood lounge seats. The final touch was a high and graceful fireplace, which occupied one end of the room and completed the harmony with the rest of the furniture.

The billiard room ceiling was panelled in plaster relief that extended down onto a frieze of considerable depth, whose pattern was partly based on the chrysanthemum wallpaper. All the upholstery and furnishing was the work of Maple's of Tottenham Court Road. It was a room where the locals came not only to play billiards but also to admire and experience some luxury.

Next to the billiard room was the lodge room, fitted for the use of secret societies, dazzling with the symbolism of the Druids, the Freemasons and the Buffaloes. At its far end, in front of a projecting carved window, was a curtain dais where the druid's throne was located. Decorated pedestals, appropriate to the druidical ceremonies, were prominent. The lodge room was furnished with long mahogany tables and handsomely decorated chairs.

From the first floor a grand staircase came down to the ground floor. At the foot it separated, one side to the main entrance, the other to the saloon bar. The ground floor was divided by handsome dark wooden partitions into four sections. The public bar, the plainest of the four, was a model of comfort with substantial wooden benches of a perforated design.

Similar to the description of the Cricketers given by Robert Tressell, there were also two private bars. The saloon bar was a luxurious lounge of sofas and easy chairs upholstered in Moroccan leather. It contained some handsome tapestry work designed around historical subjects and framed in heavy plush velvet, which lent the room a dignity and comfortable appearance.

The report from which this description is taken described the barmaids as 'a bevy of damsels as dexterous and charming as ever was the celebrated Hebe, who waited on the assembled gods of Olympus, who, however delicious was the nectar they drank, certainly never took their refreshment in a maple fitted bar like that in the Old Golden Cross'.

The report mentions finally the electric lighting, pointing out the lamp brackets as a most striking feature, especially in the downstairs bars. The whole installation was carried out by the Southern Electrical Engineering Company on its free wiring system, 'and was a splendid example of the latest in art glass globes and art brackets'. Including the great sign that was originally out front, there were about two hundred lamps in the house, requiring no small amount of current when all were turned on at once. Spacious cellars and vaults completed the scheme of this palatial public house.

 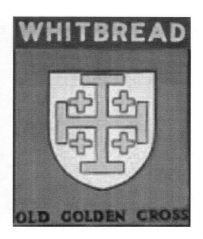

In the years before the First World War the Lodge room, on the first floor, became licensed for 'cinematographic performances'. From 1911 it was one of Hastings' first cinemas showing occasional early films.

The Old Golden Cross closed during the Second World War and suffered severe blast damage from a bomb explosion on nearby buildings. In 1950 its sign was included in Whitbread's miniature inn signs series.[5] In the same year the brewers vandalised the building by ripping out all of the interior for use in a pub conversion in London. In 2003 it was renamed Hero's Venue Bar and redesigned as a teenage music venue. With the arrival of the University Centre opposite, it will no doubt stay that way. In 2008 it was renamed as Laila and in 2011 the name changed again, to Flairz.

Hero's Venue Bar

Foresters Arms
Shepherd Street

2009

The building of St Leonards in the 1830s required a large workforce, many of whom were itinerant travelling tradesmen who had found accommodation on America Ground, Hastings. America Ground was an area of unowned land on the Hastings shoreline inhabited by a large community who had raised the Stars and Stripes as a symbol of their independence.

The 'Americans' were evicted in 1835 and a large number of them moved to St Leonards, taking their homes with them. One 'American', Daniel Thomas, was landlord of an old gin house named the Black Horse, on the site of what is now Holy Trinity Church in Hastings' town centre.

The Black Horse was dismantled and re-erected in Shepherd Street, St Leonards, by James (Jemmy) Hyland.[1] Many other buildings from America Ground stand in the surrounding streets.

For most of the 19th century, the Black Horse was both a beer house and a small, crowded lodging house where, if you weren't careful, you would find your belongings in a nearby second-hand shop. Lodgers slept two to a bed. One evening a policeman checking on closing time found the ground floor empty but insisted on going upstairs, where he found six men drinking beer from earthenware pots in a room with three beds.

In the 1850s some customers spent all day here drinking and playing 'Four Corners'.[2] This was a game played by throwing a large wooden bowl or 'cheese' weighing 6 to 8 lbs [2.7 to 3.6 kg], at four

A game of Four Corners in 1856
Note the man sitting down is smoking a 'Churchwarden',
a 2 feet long clay pipe, popular at the time.

large pins placed at the corners of a square frame, from a distance of about 10 feet [3m]. Because of the space required, it was usually played in a Four Corners shed or alley, which must have been in a rear outbuilding. Customers at this time included the railway navvies, building the line through to Hastings.[3]

In 1864 the Black Horse hit the headlines when there was an 'Attempt at Murder and Arson'. Thomas Bowsteed of Gensing Road was charged with shooting William Tew with a pistol and of trying to set fire to a workshop behind the pub that Tew rented from the landlord. The case was referred to Lewes Assizes and Bowsteed was imprisoned for several years.[4]

In the 1870s the landlord, George Earle, 'an elderly man with a wooden leg', was cautioned for allowing late night drinking. In his defence he said that one man found on the premises by the police was a cellarman who came in every night to tap the barrels, because 'I only have one beer engine'. He couldn't do it himself because he 'couldn't stoop and if the tap busted, beer flew all over the bar'. Another man, George Copley, a lodger, said he 'had some beer drawn but it was so full of froth he wouldn't pay for it'. The case was dismissed with a warning that 'it is unusual to tap beer this time of night'. The court was attended by several of George's customers including an artistic decorator, a grainer and a shoesmith.[5]

Before the arrival of the railway St Leonards had its ice, coal, timber, building materials and other goods delivered by boat onto the beach opposite the end of London Road. Some of these boats often arrived late on Saturday night or early Sunday morning, when pubs were supposed to be closed. A provision in the law allowed pubs to serve 'bona fide travellers' including boat crews, outside of normal hours, but this did not include the men who unloaded the boats. When the boats were in, police often checked with a knock on the door. "Who've you got in the kitchen, lodgers?" "No", replied the landlord, "men working on the collier just come ashore", and got into trouble for it.

Between 1886 and 1888 the Black Horse was rebuilt and renamed the Foresters Arms.[6] In 1905 the chief constable tried to get the Foresters closed down and the magistrates questioned Breeds Brewery on the need to keep it open. In the rear yard, a cottage was let at 4s 6d [22½p] a week and three workshops at 6d [2½p] a week each. These were reached by a twitten called Black

Horse Passage, formerly Valentine's Passage, which had its own entrance.

At this time the landlord worked as an upholsterer during the day. The previous landlord had been an army pensioner and local bandmaster. The pub takings averaged £11 a week and the rent was £18 a year. They sold 204 barrels of beer a year and a lot of bread, cheese and pickles. One hundred loyal customers signed a memorial in support and the pub stayed open.[7]

A quarter of a century later, during the depression, a more upmarket landlord took over. He had been a steward at the Constitutional Club in Crowborough and licensee of the Sussex Hotel in Tunbridge Wells. In 1933 he applied for a wine licence, claiming that there was an all-year-round demand for wine in Shepherd Street.[8] This was refused and it was not until 1952 that the Foresters was granted a full licence.[9]

The last landlord was Eddy Churchill, who arrived in 1959. When he moved to a restaurant in Hastings in 1969, the Foresters closed its doors for the last time.[10] It was one of three Whitbread houses in St Leonards, including the Warrior's Gate and the British Queen. Originally, however, it was tied to St Leonard's Brewery which was situated next door in Shepherd Street. The building later became the Photogallery. This photograph by Noel Bucknole shows an exhibition of the Masai in 1980.

1980

Fortune of War
Priory Road

c1930s

During the Napoleonic Wars Halton, a district in the north-east of Hastings, was the site of a barracks for infantry, cavalry and artillery. The Fortune of War was built and opened in 1810 by Thomas Sinnock, to serve the troops.[1] About 30 years later, long after the troops had gone, this 'poorly constructed inn' had to be partly rebuilt and an old ice vault or 'tub hole' for depositing contraband spirits was discovered at the back of the pub. This indicated that the Fortune of War might have been an early rendezvous for local smugglers.[2]

After soldiers and smugglers came the railway navvies. The latter arrived in the 1850s to find work digging out the Ore tunnel and laying the track for the line to Ashford. The navvies were a law unto themselves and lived a hard and rough life. Many of them lived in tents and temporary huts alongside the line and were heavy drinkers. Landlords of the Fortune of War and other pubs were charged for serving 'out of hours' and for permitting drunkenness and disturbances on more than one occasion.[3]

An inquest in 1866:

SINGULAR DEATH FROM FRIGHT. —An inquest held at the Fortune of War Inn, Halton, on Saturday afternoon, on the body of Maria Robinson, an aged bathing woman, who is well known in Hastings, who died from fright at seeing a bull.

Mrs. Jane Monk—I was in Mount Pleasant-road on Thursday evening, and saw a stout woman whom I did not know, near the road to Broom's-grove. She said, "Oh dear, how troubled I am to walk. How bad my breath is." I saw a bull up the road, and I said to my child, "Dear me, there comes a bull, we had better get out of the way." The woman (who was afterwards shown to be the deceased) said, "My God, where shall we get to." I knew the fence of the shaw on the embankment was broken, and said, "We will get through the fence where it was broken." I ran with my boy, and saw the deceased run also. I could not see the woman when I looked back. After the bull had passed, I got into the road again, and I heard a woman scream. I listened and heard a voice say, "Oh, dear! Oh, help me!" As if from the midst of the trees. [At the spot in question there is a very steep embankment, about twelve feet deep, partially covered with trees]. I said, "The bull is past; it is all clear." The deceased continued to say, "Oh help me," and as my child was frightened I went to the cottages at the top of the road and got assistance. When I went back I found some one else was talking to the woman, and I went home.

Eleanor Tree deposed to having come up the Brooms Grove-road, and heard some one moaning. A woman's voice in the Mount Pleasant-road said "Where are you?" And deceased said "Down on the grass." Witness did not know if deceased had fallen down the bank.

Mrs. Blyde, a neighbour of the deceased (who had arrived within a hundred yards of her own cottage), went out when Mrs. Monk told her what was the matter. She found deceased lying on her side face on the grass and lifted her up. Deceased expired in witness's arms in a few minutes.

The evidence of deceased's daughter showed that Mrs.

> Robinson was a very nervous person, much frightened at the sight of animals of any kind. She was 66 years of age, very stout and fat.
>
> Charles Asherden, Esq., the surgeon who examined the deceased, proved that no bones were broken, and that there were no marks of violence. The appearance denoted that she had died from fright acting on a fatty, flabby heart. A thin muscular woman would not have died from the shock.
>
> The Coroner briefly summed up, pointing out that no one seemed to be at all to blame.
>
> Verdict—Death from natural causes, accelerated by fright.

1866 [4]

Halton has always been a poor district and in 1885 the pub was the location of another inquest into a sad case of suicide by drowning of a fish hawker, who lived around the corner and who had apparently been charged with cruelty to a horse. The evening before he died, the landlord of the Mount Pleasant Inn gave him a free pint. He was so poor he couldn't pay for it.

He simply left two sad letters. One was to a carman:

Dear Sir, Please pay my wife the sum of ten shillings for a half hundredweight of wheel grease delivered this day. If you want any harness oil there is 2 or 3 gallons. I have instructed my wife to sell it to you for 4s per gallon. If you pay it you will do my family justice. Adieu

And the second letter to his wife:

Madam, Please do the best you can as I have made up my mind to finish with this world at once. Take my little cart and keep it or sell it. Send to Mr Godden for 10s for the grease and if he wants any harness oil sell him the lot for 3s 6d a gallon. I am very sorry I can do no more. I have left my knife and glasses at the Duke of Cornwall, Winding Street, if you want them. They might be of use to you. J. Barton. [5]

Early picture of Fortune of War on far right.

At one point in the 1890s the Fortune of War was a 'Tory house' and several Conservative Smoking Concerts were held there around the turn of the century. It was here that the Conservatives organised the voting register of local working men. This part of Hastings, St Clement's Ward, was, in 1903, a marginal ward held by the Liberals, with a majority of only nine votes.[6]

The Liberals meanwhile held their meetings at the nearby Hope, a 'radical house', and often it seems both pubs held meetings on the same night. The Liberals offered 'radical beef pudding suppers', selections by the Cinque Ports Mandolin Band and discussions on Free Trade, an issue which the Conservatives saw as a cause of unemployment and the decline of British agriculture.[7]

In 1915 the landlord of the Hope was charged with allowing a woman to get drunk. When asked by the magistrate if she was sober he said: "She was more sober than usual for Halton". "What do you mean?" asked the magistrate, "are the people of Halton not generally sober?" The landlord replied: "They all like a drop at times".

The Fortune of War closed for a period in the First World War, under the restrictions of the Defence of the Realm Act, when the chief constable reported that the pub had given the Hastings police a lot of trouble and that it was frequented by large numbers of women. This was quite unusual, as most pubs at that time would not serve women on their own. However, many of its male customers had been called up into the army.

From 1929 to 1950 the landlord was John (Clifford) Errey. His son Michael (born 1932) said: "I was born and brought up in the Fortune of War. My father was landlord and I have very clear memories of the pub. The 'Fortune' was tied to the George Beer and Rigden Brewery of Faversham, Kent and in the early 1930s they used to deliver the beer in a steam driven Foden lorry and on delivery days I used to watch out for the puffs of steam as the lorry made its way up the hill. I was then able to warn my father that the beer was about to arrive.

"The Fortune of War was originally part of a military complex, and at the time when England was under threat of attack by Napoleon the pub was used as a sort of officer's mess. The 'other ranks' would have had to use another public house in a back street, probably the Dun Horse if it existed then.

"The Fortune of War was a big pub. It was the biggest pub in Halton anyway. It had five separate bars, a kitchen and a living room on the ground floor and a large cellar. One of the bigger bars was next to our living room. The bar and the living room were separated by a sliding door in sections so that we could extend the bar into our living room if it got crowded.

"When the bombers came during the war we used to take shelter in the cellar. During one heavy raid we all went down as usual. We had a piano in the bar and I remember when we came up it was missing. Although the pub itself wasn't hit reverberations from a nearby bomb blast had lifted the piano and hurled it from the bar into the living room.

"All through the war I used to look out of my bedroom window at night and I could see the bright red sky all lit up over burning London. We had a road sign attached to the pub which said 'London 61 Miles'. If I couldn't see the bright red London sky I felt quite deprived.

"When it was all over I remember the celebrations. One night there were so many people in the pub, it was so packed and with everybody dancing and singing my father thought that maybe the floor above the cellar might be in danger of collapse. He sent me into the cellar to stack beer crates up to the sagging ceiling of the cellar to support it and prevent the floor of the bar falling in. We were lucky it never gave way!

"Outside, the Fortune of War was unusual in that it stuck out into the roadway reducing the width of the road by at least a third at that point. I've since heard that this might have been a reason why it was eventually pulled down." [8]

In 1963 Fremlin's Brewery attempted to transfer the licence to another site on the Halton re-development scheme. The Fortune of War survived for another year before it was closed in 1964. By 1968 the magistrates had become impatient and wanted 'this terrible building out of the way'.[9] It was finally demolished in 1970 and the licence was transferred to the New Broom, on the Broomsgrove Estate. The New Broom later became the Malvern Tavern, now also closed.

"We want this terrible building out of the way"

Fountain
Queens Road

1923–1924

The Fountain was first fully licensed in 1853.[1] At that time it stood at the northern extremity of the town, which was gradually spreading out from the centre. A memorial signed by 54 'respectable residents' was presented to the licensing magistrates, in support of a full licence. The first landlord was Charles Edwards, who held the licence for 29 years before selling up to the Hanbury Brewery in 1882.

Early customers of the Fountain public bar included the employees of Hastings gasworks, then on the opposite side of Queen's Road. Employment in the gasworks was laborious, hot and dirty work, leading many men into heavy drinking. When pub opening hours were regulated by the 1872 Licensing Act, the Fountain applied for extended hours to correspond with the shifts of the gasworks, but was refused.

Apart from the gasworks, this area was still partly rural and the slaughterhouses and pigsties, also across the road, were considered a great nuisance. It was reported that: 'Cattle on the roads, pig keeping and offal boiling were an offence to the ladies and invalids on their way to St Andrew's Park' (now Alexandra Park) 'and slaughtering effected property values.' However, according to G.D. Coleman, 'cattle and sheep were still being driven along Queen's Road to the slaughterhouse in Waterworks Road' as late as 1929.[2]

Slaughterhouse employees were also Fountain customers, as were the numerous horse dealers who, on coming into town to trade, tethered their animals nearby whilst they drank and completed transactions in the bar.

The butchers of Hastings had some sort of informal organisation in the town during these years and the Fountain, because of its location near the slaughterhouses, was known for a time as a 'butchers' pub'. In the 1870s butchers not only drank here but also used the pub for more formal occasions. In 1879, for example, 30 butchers attended a wedding party of one of their members at the Fountain. The party turned into a riotous celebration and the licensee was fined 10s [50p], while a waiter, Gabriel Eaton, was also cautioned.[3]

In 1916 during the First World War, landlord Sidney Faulkner was called up to serve in France. At the Hastings Military Tribunal in July of that year, he pointed out that he was in sole control of the

Fountain and if it closed down, £500 investment would be lost. He was exempted by the military for two months before being sent off to fight.[4] At the end of the war the shop next door, in Stonefield Street, was incorporated into the pub to extend the saloon bar. The two separate bars still exist.

In 1937 the *Hastings Observer* 'put darts on the map in Hastings' when it organised the first Hastings Annual Darts Tournament. The Fountain team came to brief fame when it reached the semi-final, in which it was only narrowly beaten by the Hastings British Legion Club.

The match was held at the Cambridge (now the Union Bar) and 'the room was packed with eager supporters of both teams, who watched the flight of the darts with an intensity not bettered at a test match'. The British Legion team admitted that: 'There were only two teams we feared, the Fountain and the Cambridge'.[5] But little did they fear the immediate future. Three years later the town

1950s

was evacuated during the Battle of Britain and the Fountain closed down from 1940 until 1943.

In 1950 the Fountain sign was included in Whitbread's miniature inn sign series.[6] The present sign dates from when Shepherd Neame purchased the freehold in 1993.

Fox
North Street, St Leonards

1930s

Formerly known as the British Queen, the Fox has had a chequered history. It was listed in the *Sussex Directory* of 1855 as a beer house and most likely existed before then.[1] The first landlord was James Barnett, who had his own pewter mugs inscribed 'J.B. British Queen, St Leonards'. These were probably used only in the saloon bar. Beer in the other bars was served in enamelled earthenware pots in quarts [2 pints], pints and half pints. In 1858 he moved on to become landlord of the Tivoli Tavern in Silverhill and in later years the pewter tankards became collectors items.

George Linton applied for a full licence in 1862 but was refused, although his name appears in the licensees' register from 1865 to 1897 and the name of his widow Ann Linton from 1898 to 1909.[2] The pub was originally tied to the long gone St Leonards Brewery of

Shepherd Street and has passed through the hands of seven different brewers since.

As a tenant of the St Leonards Brewery it sold the original 'St Leonards Pale Ale', brewed by them over 150 years ago. In the 1880s the British Queen sold its own whisky in bottles of its own design, which on at least one occasion was found by an inspector to be very much under proof.

In the 1890s the British Queen had problems with bookmakers and their 'runners' collecting bets in the bar, and landlady Ann Linton was cautioned for allowing them access to the premises. The runners in question worked for George Talbot, who kept a furniture shop at 10 North Street and collected betting slips from hotels, pubs and cafes.

In the 1930s the British Queen was a popular darts venue, used by London General Omnibus employees residing at the Capel le Ferne convalescent home.[3] Ralph Peacock, formerly captain of the darts team, became landlord in 1938. In 1939 Whitbread completely refurbished the pub. The five bars and a private room were converted into three bars, large enough, it was claimed, for 100 customers. The doors were grained, leaded windows were fitted and the latest Coalite stoves were installed.

Along with the usual pub games, a new game of 'bull', played after the style of shovepenny, was installed.[4] Bull was played on an extended board with an extra bed, the tenth bed, containing the bull. "Shove-penny, as opposed to shove-ha'penny", explains Alan Crouch, "was the game found in Hastings and Eastbourne. The difference between the two was only in the coins used. Some players cheated by keeping a chestnut in their pocket. Rubbing the nut and then the penny affected its performance, as the oil in the nut made the penny stick. Shovepenny boards were treated with paraffin, water or beer and cleaned with newspaper or a beer mat. Players prepared the pennies by heating one up and putting it onto a block of wood, which made a mould. A cold penny was put into the mould and smoothed with emery cloth or a surface grinder. This enabled players to have pennies of different weights, giving each coin its own characteristics. However, before matches all pennies were weighed."[5]

In 1940 the British Queen darts team won the Annual *Observer* Darts Tournament, beating 54 other pub teams.[6] However, this record was marred in 1942 when the next landlord, Stanley Wood, was summonsed for 'harbouring' army clothing, Canadian cigarettes and tobacco, which he was selling from behind the bar. In court it was stated he had 'ten pairs of woollen drawers, vests, socks, boots and other clothing all marked War Department'. He also had in his possession 6,680 Canadian cigarettes and 7lbs [3kg] of tobacco. He claimed to have lent money to Canadian soldiers, who offered the goods as security. He was fined £50 and lost his licence.[7]

Thirty-five years later the British Queen welcomed customers from another Commonwealth country. Michael Monk, a regular at the time, remembers: "The Seychelles Islands gained independence from Britain in 1976. In 1977 or 1978, the Commonwealth Conference was being held in London. Among the delegates, the first president of the Seychelles, James Mancham, learned that he had been deposed by a coup d'état. Obviously he couldn't go back immediately and he and his delegation stayed in Hastings until it was safe to return. I don't know where they stayed but five or six ministers of the Seychelles Islands' government drank in the British Queen saloon bar for a couple of years and we spent many an evening in their company. It was quite friendly and relaxed and there was never any question of racism or anything like that. They must have eventually returned."[8]

From the 1960s to the 1980s the custom of the British Queen was boosted by employees of the Central Electricity Generating Board, then a nationalised company, employed on the construction of the two power stations at Dungeness. Many lodged in St Leonards and were bussed daily to the site. The first power station was connected to the National Grid in 1965.[9]

The Fox managed to stay open for over 160 years, although it did close down in 1990. After another refurbishment, when its three bars became two and the original pub sign of Queen Bodicea driving her chariot was taken down, it reopened in 1992 as the Fox. A new sign showing a fox was erected in 2009. The British Queen sign was included in Whitbread's miniature inn signs in 1950.[10] The Fox finally closed in 2010 and is now private housing.

Frank's Front Room

32 Station Road

1898–1913

Frank's Front Room, formerly the Priory, initially the Royal George, was a pub associated with Hastings railway station and its employees, and with the former Central Cricket Ground, now the Priory Meadow Shopping Centre.

The Royal George was originally an ordinary beer house serving the staff and passengers of the railway station, which opened in 1851. It was granted a full licence in 1864 and the first landlord was George William Thwaites. In his application he claimed his pub was different from the Old Golden Cross (now Flairz) on the adjacent corner, which opened in 1857. "We cater for the middle class excursionists", he said, implying a hint of snobbery.[1]

The pub seemed to have got off to a good start, selling 400 barrels of malt liquor in its first year. But the idea that it was a middle class house quickly evaporated when it developed a reputation as a 'house visited by tradesmen on tramp', particularly bricklayers, carpenters and plasterers, who travelled between towns looking for work. Whether they lodged in the pub is unknown.

Other customers were day visitors who arrived by train and who could legally be served as 'bona fide travellers' outside normal hours. The pubs were open to them on the production of a rail ticket. In the 1860s Hastings' magistrates complained that public houses, particularly near railway stations, were being kept open on Sundays because of excursionists.[2]

The Royal George was also a railwaymen's pub and by the early 1890s it had become the meeting place of the Hastings branch of the Amalgamated Society of Railway Servants. The members campaigned for a 'fair day's pay for a fair day's work' and for a reduction of the long hours worked on the railways at that time.[3]

In 1899 the pub applied for a 6am licence, to be extended to 5am in summer. This was in order to serve the employees of the station and of the goods yard opposite, some of whom worked all night and, as the landlord said, were entitled to an early morning pub as much as the workers in the fish market were. The application was refused.[4]

Before the First World War, the Royal George was granted another licence to put on 'cinematograph performances'. A first floor function room, with 70 seats, was used to show early films but this apparently ceased in December 1912.

During the First World War the government was particularly concerned about the amount of alcohol being consumed and in 1915 announced several measures it believed would reduce alcohol consumption. A 'No Treating Order' stipulated that people could not buy drinks for each other, especially soldiers. The following year the landlord of the Royal George was cautioned and a customer was fined a massive £5 for supplying a Canadian soldier with two quarts [four pints] of beer.[5]

For the next 50 years or so nothing much is heard about the Royal George but at some point it expanded into the house behind. In 1964 Watney's set up a pub football league in Hastings and customers of the Royal George, the Old England and the Belmont formed the first organising committee. This football tradition continued for many years and was later organised by Roger Povey. In the late 1980s the pub briefly changed its name to Grace's Wine Bar before becoming the Priory in August 2000.

However, its sign shows an early batsman in action, which has an interesting story. Roger Povey ran a Sunday league football team out of Grace's Wine Bar in the late 1990s. When a new landlord decided to change the pub's name to the Bat and Ball because of its location near the old cricket ground, Roger explained: "I obviously couldn't call the team after the new name as it wasn't, I thought, a suitable name for a football team. I had to register the team name and decided to call the team Sporting Priory. It was only then that the new landlord considered that perhaps he should call the pub the Priory for the sake of the team and after the old priory that once owned all the land in the area. I think this is the first time a pub has changed its name to the name of a football team."[6]

However, the new pub sign had already been painted and showed a cricketer in action over the name Bat and Ball. The name on the sign was changed to the Priory but the figure of the cricketer however, remained.

None of this should be confused with the nearby Cricketers (now the Hastings Terrace Club), another pub which experimented with the name Priory in 1996, although it seems to have been a passing phase.

The Priory closed in 2008, re-opened as Frank's Front Room in 2012 and closed again in 2013.

2008

2012

French's Bar and Priory Tavern
Robertson Street

French's Bar with former Wine Office on right

French's Bar stands in the middle of America Ground, Hastings. When Robertson Street was built in the 1850s French's Bar, then known as the Royal Standard, was one of its first licensed premises. It cost £1,500 to build which was a large amount for the time, and 87 local dignitaries, including many shopkeepers and the Hastings Member of Parliament, attended its opening dinner.

After a few months the Royal Standard applied for a full licence. The Victorian developers had stipulated that no taverns or public houses would be allowed without a special licence from the Crown Lessee. However, with the support of a London barrister, the licence was granted in 1851 and George Lindfield became its first landlord.[1]

The first licensed premises in Robertson Street, in 1850, was the Priory Hotel Tavern[2] housed in the same complex as the Royal Standard. The entrance to the Priory 'Shades Bar' was located at the rear of the building in Robertson Passage and a valuation of the bar contents in 1857 included bagatelle boards, framed pictures, stuffed birds in cages and spittoons. The Priory Tavern closed in 1859 and was later incorporated into the Royal Standard. Its last landlord, Thomas Turner, then moved to the new Havelock Hotel at the end of Robertson Street.

In 1856, when Robertson Street was still under construction, a series of vestry meetings were held here to discuss the possibility of building a church on the land opposite. Donations totalling £2,486 were received and the church was built with local sandstone. In 1857 the foundation stone of Holy Trinity was laid with a silver trowel, and the church opened the following year. A short time later the drinking fountain was erected.

One evening in 1865, the Royal Standard held a raffle for 'a horse and chaise' which, most surprisingly, at a sovereign [£1] a ticket, proved a great attraction among the town's flymen (drivers of horse-drawn cabs). A sovereign in 1865 would today be about £70.[3]

In 1866 the Royal Standard was acquired by the Kelsey brewery of Tunbridge Wells. A valuation tells us that the pub had 12 bedrooms, a bar, bar parlour, commercial room, smoking room and a billiard room. The bar contained a 16 foot 'mahogany panelled counter with a pewter top and a six pull beer engine'.

Holy Trinity church

The billiard room had 'a massive billiard table by Burroughs and Watts, Moroccan leather seats, rosewood card tables and earthenware spittoons. It also had a 15 foot zinc speaking tube to the bar enabling players to order their drinks without interrupting the billiards. A 'letter weighing machine' in the commercial room tells us that the pub also acted as the first post office in the new town centre.[4]

At this time the pub became an attraction for sessions of 'hustling the hat', a 19th century Hastings' pub custom where the players put a (marked) coin into a hat which was shaken and tipped out. All coins showing heads were withdrawn. The tails were put back into the hat and the process repeated. The final or 'true tail' had to pay for 'pots all round'. This custom was popular with commercial travellers, summer visitors and locals but often ended in dispute. At least one court case resulted from this activity. A further attraction was the barmaid Louise Macguire who was described 'as a young lady of somewhat prepossessing appearance'.

The Kelsey Brewery banned 'hustling the hat', but in the following year, 1867, it had to deal with attempts to pass off counterfeit money. A scam by two London men was discovered when a counterfeit shilling snapped in half. After their discovery and arrest it was found they had been spending a lot of 'bad' money in the shops and pubs of the town centre, most of it roughly cast from the same mould. They were both sent for trial in Lewes.[5]

In 1882 the Royal Standard became part of the Bodega chain selling the Bodega brands of imported bulk wines and lagers. The Bodega in turn became the Sussex Wine Stores in 1901, consisting of a large bar and 'wine office' and a small back bar—the original Priory shades bar—in Robertson Terrace. The Bodega then moved down the road into what is now the Electric Stag.

In 1927 it was taken over by Henekeys, another chain of upmarket bars owned by the Callingham family. The head of Henekeys, Clement Callingham, was married to Nora Turner who, after his death in 1945, became Lady Docker more popularly known by the soubriquet or humorous nickname of 'Lady Muck'. This association only added to the Henekeys aura.

Hastings' resident Betty Austin worked for Henekeys from 1945 until 1972. She remembers Henekeys as a good but strict employer with 12 staff and a doorman. Unlike barmaids in other pubs, Betty was not allowed to accept a drink or engage in conversation with customers. She was a cashier rather than a barmaid, and at first dealt with customers only indirectly via a waiter. However, when these work practises changed Betty took charge of a bar by herself.

Henekeys bars were known for their distinctive décor and ambience based on a 'churchy style' interior with wooden arches supporting the roof, seating in alcoves, leaded windows and a lot of oak and copper. "Each branch", said Betty, "had dark oak barrels with brass taps holding several gallons. Sherry, port, gin, brandy and whisky were all sold from the barrel. A Henekey's best seller was Alto Duro Port. Alto Duro was delivered in five gallon casks and the manager transferred the wine into the barrels behind the bar using a large copper funnel. We sold 12 different ports, 12 different sherries, mulled spiced wine and cider in blue mugs at 10 pence a mug. By this time the building was divided into a main bar, saloon bar, public bar, top bar and a ladies bar."[6]

In 1972 Henekeys was purchased by the owners of the Mermaid, Rye and the name was changed to French's Bar. French's continued with the Henekeys style selling draught ports and sherries from wooden casks located on the back of the bar. They included French's Old Alto Duro Port, French's Dry Fino Sherry, French's Old Selected White Port, French's Bristol Milk and Rye Custom House Montillado Sherry.

French's
(Formerly Henekeys)

'The Best
Meeting Place
in Hastings'
GOOD WINE AND LUNCH-
TIME FOOD
Robertson Street, Hastings

French's was purchased by the owners of the Mermaid in Rye in 1972

In 1995 there was a claim by the licensee that the pub was established in 1694 and preparations were made to celebrate its 300th birthday. However, this was done in error. The date '1694' which was then above the corner window, referred to the origin of the Henekeys organisation not to their Hastings branch. In 1695 America Ground was marshy no-man's land, later to be inhabited by squatters and Robertson Street did not then exist![7]

However, it does take its name from a notorious, 18th century smuggler called John French, who was very active until he was arrested in his bed by customs officers and removed to Hastings gaol. John French was one of the 'five hundred pound men' on account of there being a five hundred pound reward for information about him or his gang'.

A letter to the mayor of Hastings, John Collier, dated 31st October 1749, said:

"Last Saturday Mr Samuel Cruttenden, Geery, Bailey, Watson & Mr Coppard's man having Information of Smuggled Goods being in the house of Thomas Bayley, they went and Searched the Same, and Going up Stairs they saw a Man in bed, who they Imagined was Sick, but upon looking about the Chamber they found some baked Herrings in a plate, and Plenty of Other Victuals, which the officers thought was Odd dyet for a Sick person, they asked him what his name was, who reply'd Smith, Upon which Mr Bailey took up his handkerchief and which was tyed round his head and face, and knew him perfectly to be John French, a Notorious Outlawed Smuggler, Upon which he was Immediately Secured and Committed to Hasting Gaol, where he is to Continue till the Comrs further Order. —This French was one of the P'sons advertised in the Gazette, and stands charged with running Prohibited Goods with fire arms near the Sea Houses at Eastbourne, for which Offence Ashcroft has been Executed;- There was no soldiers or other Persons concerned in apprehending French, but the above five Persons."

A fortnight later a second letter reported that:

"French, the outlawed smuggler, was yesterday morning carried before Mr Nicoll who Committed him to Horsham Gaol; and Mr Sam Cruttenden, Mr Bailey, and four foot Soldiers are Gone to Escort him to that place." [8]

General Havelock
Robertson Street

The Havelock public house was originally a town centre hotel occupying the whole corner site between Robertson Street and Havelock Road.

This large building was first licensed in 1859 when Thomas Turner applied to the Excise to have his licence transferred to the Havelock from the nearby Priory Tavern. (See French's Bar.)[1]

In its first 20 years the Havelock did a brisk trade accommodating several different large groups. Trade Unionists met here, surrounding plots of building land were auctioned here and Priory Meadow itself was used for election hustings until 1869. Election campaigns and hustings were generally rowdy and violent and turned the town centre into a riotous area. An example was the

Havelock Hotel, & Commercial House,

HAVELOCK ROAD,

AND

ROBERTSON ST., HASTINGS.

CHARLES DAVEY,

(Of London),

Having purchased the above Establishment, begs to inform the Inhabitants of the surrounding neighbourhood, and the Public generally, that he has laid in an entire fresh Stock of Old and Choice Foreign WINES and SPIRITS of the Finest Brands, and hopes by strict personal attention to business to receive an adequate share of support.

C. D. having had many years' experience in the trade, guarantees that all articles vended at this Establishment will be perfectly genuine, and not to be surpassed in quality or Price by any House in the trade.

All Malt Liquors from the most eminent Brewers.

Clean Measures kept expressly for Jugs.

1871

by-election in 1869 following the death of Hastings' MP Frederick North. An election night procession 'passing the Havelock with whistles, pipes and lanterns frightened a horse' and the 'cabby' remonstrated with the crowd who started chanting: "he's a ... old Tory, turn him over". The flyman drove through the crowd 'and got clean away' to the Fountain in Queens Road!

In 1864 at a meeting in the Havelock it was proposed that the Priory Meadow should be procured as a cricket and recreation ground. There was great enthusiasm for this idea and an inaugural match was played between Hastings and Bexhill.

The following year the Havelock became the headquarters of the Hastings United Cricket Club and Priory Meadow became the town's official cricketing venue. Landlord Thomas Turner provided dressing rooms for the players, and management policy for the ground was decided at Havelock meetings.

One of the first international matches, if not the first, was played over three days in 1868 between an Australian Aboriginal team and a Hastings eleven. The match was unfinished because play ended early and the Aborigines gave a demonstration of boomerang throwing and whip cracking to the large crowd. The Aboriginal team was accommodated in the Havelock.[2]

By the 1870s the Havelock was doing a full trade, particularly in summer. On one occasion 180 children from the Licensed Victuallers' school in Kennington arrived by rail and marched to the beach 'to the merry strains of a well trained drum and fyfe band'. They went for a swim and a ramble and then marched back to the Havelock for dinner.

But not all the customers were as happy. In the same year a Coroner's Inquest was held in the Assembly Room into the suicide of a commercial traveller staying there. The police found the deceased hanging by the neck with a long handkerchief tied to the bedrail. The waiter, Alfred Briggs, thought 'he had seemed vacant, lost and in low spirits'.[3] The same room was also used for cases heard by the Sheriff's County Court 'and a jury of twelve Hastings tradesmen' who determined ownership of property in dispute.

In the early 1880s, just before the licence changed hands, a group of musicians playing outside was found to be blocking the road with a crowd nine feet [2.74m] deep. They told the constable that the landlord, who was about to transfer, had requested them to play a parting tune for him.

Perhaps he saw the 'writing on the wall', as from now on circumstances began to change and with the onset of the economic depression, the Havelock began to suffer. In 1883 the hotel company suffered from a reduction in profits, debts, a court summons and writs. Liquidation followed, the hotel closed and the Havelock became an ordinary public house much reduced in size following a pattern in the town's hotels.[4]

By the mid 1880s a tiled passageway ran through the building and although owned by the pub was used by the public as a thoroughfare. An interview in the book *Hastings at War*, mentions the Havelock passage in the Second World War: 'There was a god almighty explosion and we went into the passage of the Havelock pub, and we dived into that passage and threw ourselves onto the ground and lay there looking out. Along by Woolworths, a car was sent up into the air by the bomb and rolled over and over ... . While we lay there, there was another terrific explosion down by Plummer's and I'll never forget seeing a huge lump of yellow coloured masonry come over and land on the tram wires ... I saw the wires stretch down and then up and back it went. I never knew where it went to, but it was a huge lump of masonry. When it had quietened down ... this Canadian soldier came running over covered in blood and dirt. He picked up his motorbike which was lying on its side in the gutter, and dashed off towards Bexhill, about 80 miles an hour.'[5]

Cyril Pelluet recalls the Havelock in the late 1950s and another motorbike, under more pleasant conditions. "The Havelock's attraction, at the time", he recalls, "was the landlady's daughter. She was a star attraction, quite well built and she rode a 350cc motorbike. We all fancied her something rotten but none of us ever got anywhere."[6]

The passageway, now integrated into the pub, came to national attention in the 1990s when it was suddenly realised that its wall tiles were possibly Royal Doulton. The tiled walls in question include four separate pictures, each covering approximately half a wall, from floor to ceiling.

General Havelock

One shows General Havelock sitting astride a white horse in uniform. Another is titled 'The Battle of Hastings A.D. 1066'. A third shows the ruins of Hastings Castle and a fourth, a sea battle between three vessels. Of the three vessels, two are named. One is *Conqueror* which bears the port registration 'Hastings' and the other is a French ship *Le Cormoran Affamé* (The Hungry Cormorant). Local folklore states that the timber from the French vessel is the timber seen today forming the ceiling of the Havelock's ground floor bar.

It seems unlikely that the artist would have named the ships and depicted a battle in such a large picture with so much detail and presumably considerable cost, if the event was entirely fictional. The Royal Doulton Museum has suggested that the pictures date from between 1890 and 1917, although during alterations to the Royal Albion in 1911, the landlord said he would 'like pictures on the wall like the Havelock'. The pub was immediately listed Grade II.

Hastings Castle

In the 1980s the Havelock was renamed the Cask and Kettle and became a managed Phoenix pub. In 1984 it put on pensioners' mornings, with free newspapers and 20p off every pint. Other Phoenix pubs in the town complained to the brewery and got the same reduction. The new name lasted for a few years, but eventually reverted back to the Havelock in 1995. The Havelock closed in 2011 but after extensive refurbishment it reopened in 2012 as the General Havelock.

Hare and Hounds
Old London Road, Ore

The Hare and Hounds is known to have existed in 1777 but was probably much older. It has a special niche in local history because the town's first theatre, a small playhouse built in 1806, was attached to the pub, situated at that time just outside the town boundary. It was located here because theatre was thought to be a corrupting influence on the working classes and was not allowed in Hastings itself.

The Hare and Hounds was five minutes walk from Halton Barracks, built in 1804, where troops were stationed in readiness for the threatened invasion by Napoleon. The troops were good customers of the Hare and Hounds and on 1st July 1806 the first performance of a comedy called *The Soldier's Daughter* was shown here. But by 1809, when the garrison was reduced, the audiences dwindled and the theatre was forced, at times, to put on shows of performing dogs.[1]

Edmund Kean

Thomas Sidney Cooper

The Shakespearean actor Edmund Kean, on a visit to Hastings in the 1820s, offered to play Shylock in the *Merchant of Venice* for one night only. He was accompanied by Robert Elliston, a leading comedian of the day, and the evening was a resounding success.[2] The scenery painter, Thomas Sidney Cooper RA, worked in the theatre for a short period, and was hired to paint the scenery for a play called the *Battle of Hastings*.

'I was busy painting the tent of King Harold in pink and white stripes', he records in his autobiography, 'when an amateur actor sauntered up with the very insulting manner that was usual to him (for he was a very high-and-mighty young gentleman, and thought a great deal of himself), and said it was not a bit like the tent. I said, "Don't interfere with me and I won't interfere with you." But just as Mr Kean entered the theatre, he came again and called me an ass. Now as ill luck or good luck (I don't know which to say) would have it, I had in my hand what is called a pound brush full of pink paint with which I was laying on the pink stripes of the tent, and I suddenly turned and rammed it into his mouth. Upon this Mr Kean said to him: "Sir, I don't know who you are, but I heard what you said to this lad, and it is my opinion that you are no gentleman, and it served you quite right to have your mouth stopped with pink paint."

Cooper also recalled the whole company having lunch in the Hare and Hounds. 'In the course of an hour it was ready and we all sat down and enjoyed the repast. Spirits and wine were in abundance. The two great men were free with the bottle and several

Theatre, Hare and Hounds,
HASTING.

The Public are most respectfully informed, this Theatre will open for a short Season.

On Thursday, 17th Sept. 1818.

When the Majesties Servants of the Theatre Royal Windsor will Perform the Celebrated Comedy of THE

HONEYMOON

Duke Aranza Mr. SALTER
Rolando   Mr. GANN   Count Montalbin Mr. M. PENLEY
Balthazar   Mr. CRESWELL
Lopez   Mr. PENLEY   Campillo Mr. BENNETT
Pedro   Mr. W. PENLEY   Jaques Mr. JONAS
Lampedo   Mr. Burton
Juliana   Miss R. PENLEY   Volante Miss PENLEY
Zamora   Miss FISHER   Hostess Mrs. BEYNON
In Act 4th, a Rustic Dance incident to the Play by Mr. SALTER
Mr. BENNETT, Mr. YARNOLD, Mr. BRADSHAW
Miss R. PENLEY, Miss YOUNG and Miss E. PENLEY.

END OF THE PLAY
A COMIC SONG by Mr. BURTON.
And a Comic Pas Seal by Mr. Fellows.
To conclude with the last new Farce of

The Sleeping Draught.

*Written by Mr. Penley Jun. and Performed with unbounded applause
at the Theatre Royal, Drury Lane,*
Doctor Vincolo   Mr. PENLEY
Rinaldo   Mr. M. PENLEY   Popolino   Mr. GANN
Gabriotto   Mr. JONAS   Yaldo   Mr. BURTON
Bruno   Mr. BENNETT   First Fellow   Mr. W. PENLEY
Second Fellow   Mr. BRADSHAW
Signora Francesca   Miss FISHER and Nonna   Miss PENLEY

BOXES 3s,...*PIT* 2s,...*GALLERY* 1s.
Doors to be opened at 6 and to begin at 7
Tickets to be had of Mr. Austin, Printer, High Street at the Inn, & of Mr. Penley, at the Theatre
where places for the Boxes may be taken.
No Person may be admitted behind the Scenes.
Nights of Performance will be Mondays, Tuesdays, Thursdays and Saturdays.

Austin, Printer, Hasting.

147

This stone is on the site of the first theatre, Hastings. For it T.S.Cooper, R.A. painted scenery, and Kean and Elliston acted. This commemorative tablet was unveiled on June 2, 1914 by Sir Herbert Beerbohm Tree.

of the others followed suit. Elliston was lively with jokes, and did a good deal of flirting with the actresses. Then he danced, and, in his frolicsome hilarity, kicked over the table breaking the bottles and glasses. All the wine was spilt, everything else spoiled; and no one seemed to care much about it but myself, for I had only eaten and had drunk nothing, never having, up to that time, even tasted wine, while the rest of the company appeared to have taken quite enough.'[3]

The pub was considerably enlarged in 1810 with several bedrooms, stables for eight horses, one and a half acres of meadow and a fenced tea garden, but on Boxing Day 1867 a fire destroyed both the inn and the theatre. In 1868 the Phoenix Fire Office paid out '£400 for the destruction of the Hare and Hounds [and] the adjacent wooden building, which latter was quite destroyed'. A new public house was built on Old London Road, a little to the south-west of the old inn, which was in the area now known as Saxon Road. The theatre is remembered on an inscribed tablet on a nearby wall, unveiled by Sir Herbert Beerbohm-Tree, a famous Edwardian actor-manager, in 1914.

By the early 1900s the Hare and Hounds registered 410 members of the Equitable Friendly Society, which provided insurance against sickness, old age and death. The membership comprised 300 men, 20 women and 90 juveniles. Because the juvenile members were not allowed into the pub, the society had its own entrance to a large upstairs room, where they met and sat down to 'beef pudding and plum suppers'.[4] The branch may have moved to the Clive Vale Hotel a few years later.

During the First World War, the pub was revisited by the military, this time by Canadian soldiers, 7,000 of whom were billeted in the town. The landlord hinted at the headache of their custom in 1918 when he transferred to the Cricketers, which he said, 'was a much easier house to manage than the Hare and Hounds'.

The pub was also the home of a tontine club, a type of savings club with a fixed number of members who each received an annuity at Christmas. The tontine operated for several years and was run by secretary Isaac Pattenden. He collected members' weekly subs, kept an account and handed the total to the landlord. The money was then banked with the brewers, who took charge of it as an investment. The size of the annuity paid out increased as the number of members decreased through death. The remaining capital was 'scooped' by the last living member, who, in this case, died in the 1940s.

Hare and Hounds by Francis Grose during his tour of the south-east 1773–1779

Just before Christmas 1933, it was found that the landlord had absconded with £50 8s [£50.40] of the tontine funds. Tamplin's the brewers made good the deficit, remarking that at the time there were a lot of poor people in the district of Ore and they 'wanted to stand by them'. The landlord, James Pritchard, was committed for trial for fraud and given three months imprisonment.[5] The only other known tontine club in the town operated out of the Marina Inn in Caves Road.

For many years the Hare and Hounds ran popular darts and shovepenny teams. It fielded teams in the Hastings league and in the brewery league, but in the 1960s at least, the landlord and landlady organised their own championships and awards. Annual winners had their names inscribed onto silver trophies for darts and for shovepenny. In 1965 they added a third trophy, for cribbage.

This old pub closed in 2006. It had been an integral part of the Ore community for at least two and a half centuries. It is now residential accommodation.

Hare and Hounds 2009

Hastings Arms
George Street, Old Town

1950s

The Hastings Arms dates from at least 1794, when it was described as 'a commercial inn of good reputation',[1] serving the military personnel billeted in Hastings waiting for Napoleon.

In 1814, to celebrate the end of the war, the pub erected a sign described as 'an illuminated transparency, exhibited to represent the genius of Britain at whose feet lay in abject despair the fallen Corsican hero, with cherubs ascending to proclaim peace'.[2]

From 1827 to 1845, Richard Harman was landlord. He was at various times a tailor, an election agent, a wrecker and a promoter of the Hastings Rock Fair. He came to fame after a court case in which he sued the local Tory MP, Joseph Planta, to recover £24 6s 6d [£24.32] spent in the general election of 1837. In 1832 Planta had opposed the Reform Bill, which gave the vote to certain groups of men for the first time. Consequently he was not re-elected. He stood again in 1837 and engaged Harman, 'well versed in electioneering tactics' and a reform supporter, as his agent. Planta knew he had little chance without Harman's support but Harman agreed to act for him if he agreed not to oppose the Reform Act.

Planta agreed but many voters were suspicious. However, corruption was rife and many 'pinks'—or early liberals—were bribed. Planta gave several Hastings pubs 'carte blanche' to treat 'the pinks' with free beer and punch. The Horse and Groom, the Hastings Arms, the Sussex Tap, the King's Head and many others across town were involved in this corruption.

In court, evidence was produced to show that several public houses had received cash to treat customers who had the vote. More funds were distributed to tradesmen and artisan voters who were supporters of reform and their wives were treated to tea and sugar. Harman won the case and was granted £15.[3]

'Wrecking' was the practice of taking valuables from a shipwreck which had foundered on or near the shore. Usually an unregulated activity of opportunity found in coastal communities. Hastings most notable example was the wreck of the Amsterdam which foundered at Bulverhythe in 1749 and whose cargo was plundered by the locals. Another Dutch ship was wrecked in 1840:

SHIPWRECK.—On Sunday morning last, a vessel was discovered, bottom upwards, by the Coast Guard Station at Galley Hill, Bexhill, floating towards the shore, numbers of persons instantly proceeded to the spot. The sea at the time she came ashore was tremendous. The beach was shortly after covered with pieces of timber and small casks of wine. The vessel was laden with wine and brandy. She came ashore in front of the Parade at St. Leonards, close to the Conqueror Hotel. Mr. Harman, of the Hastings Arms Inn, instantly mustered all his men, and with his cables and anchors soon made the vessel fast. We are happy to say that most of the cargo was saved, and much to the credit of our intrepid fishermen they saved several casks of wine at the great hazard of their lives. On Monday a hole was cut into her side and the remaining part of her cargo was taken out, it consisted of pieces of brandy. The vessel was named "The two Friends of Dunkirk," was schooner rigged, and about 170 tons burthen. She appears to be nearly new, and it is supposed by our sailors that she capsised in the squall on Friday night, the 24th, off Beachey Head. We regret to say that we cannot hear any tidings of the crew; it is supposed they are all lost. Most of the casks were marked "Courtors and Von Reynschoote Cette."

1840 [4]

A court case of 1843 mentions several local institutions of the period—Hastings Bank, Hastings Town Gaol, the town crier and the Hastings Arms pot boy:

HASTINGS AND ST. LEONARDS.-

BOROUGH QUARTER SESSIONS, TOWN HALL, FRIDAY, OCTOBER 27.-

THOMAS STONESTREET was placed at the bar, charged with stealing a bank-note of the value of £5, on the 4th inst., the same being the property of John Tolhurst.

John Tolhurst deposed that he was an ostler residing in Hastings, and between seven and eight o'clock on the morning of the 4th instant, he was in at Wimble's eating-house, where he had a £5 note safe in his pocket. It was one of the Hastings Old Bank, and numbered 41297. He afterwards went into the shop of Mr. Thwaites, butcher, in All Saints-street, where he paid some silver. Between ten and eleven o'clock he went into the Hastings Arms Inn and had some drink at the bar, and paid for it with half-a-crown. Did not recollect who served him. He took the silver out of the same pocket as he had the note in. He could not feel distinctly with his hands, in consequence of a paralytic stroke. He first missed the note a little after three in the afternoon, and immediately made enquiries where he had changed money in the morning; but not finding it he went to the bank and stopped payment of it, and had it cried.

John Turner, a newsvender, deposed that on the 4th instant, about the middle of the day, the prisoner came to him for change for a £5 note, stating his mistress had sent him. He (witness) gave the prisoner in change £4 10s. in gold, and 10s. in silver. The note he then produced (which was identified by the prosecutor as the one he had lost) was the same he received from the prisoner. He afterwards heard a note cried, and on making enquiries on the following morning found it was the same as he had changed for the prisoner.

Sarah Harman, wife of Mr. Richard Harman, of the Hastings Arms Inn, deposed that the prisoner had lived in the service of her husband for about a year and a half as pot-boy, and as such it was his duty to sweep out the bar, which he did in the forenoon of the 4th instant. She did not, on that day, send the prisoner out for change, nor receive any money from him. She heard the note cried, and asked the prisoner if he swept it up among the sand in the bar, as the prosecutor thought he had lost it there, but the prisoner made her no answer. Witness had charged the prisoner, if he found any thing, to bring it either to herself, or Mr. Harman.

The prisoner said he had not been told so by Mrs. Harman, but had been told that whatever he found belonged to the sweeper.

Mrs. Harman replied that she had given such instructions to the prisoner, who had brought her several articles which had been left by the customers, such as snuff boxes, pocket handkerchiefs, &c. She was present when her husband searched the prisoner's box, in which he found a small box, which contained money, and which was handed over to Mr. Campbell, the police inspector.

John Campbell deposed that he apprehended the prisoner on the 5th inst., he received a small box from Mr. Harman, containing nearly £2; the box produced was the same.

Several witnesses then came forward, and gave the prisoner a good previous character, among whom was Mr. Harman, who stated that he believed the prisoner had always been an honest lad up to that time.

The Recorder briefly summed up, and the jury returned a verdict of guilty.

Sentenced to *ten days' solitary confinement* in Hastings gaol, and to be *once well whipped.*

1843 [5]

During this period, the rear of the pub was known as the Hastings Arms Shades, where it was socially acceptable for customers to snatch some sleep in the small back bar.[6] A fisherman, for example, could call in after a trip, take some beer and have a nap. In 1851, James Noakes, a higgler (hawker), is recorded sleeping with his head on his lap. Similar occurrences are recorded in the Queen Adelaide (three doors away) and also in the Cutter.[7]

One evening during the First World War, five Canadian soldiers in the same bar were drinking Canadian Red Seal Whisky. Although the landlord claimed they couldn't possibly be drunk on the amount he had sold them, they nevertheless appeared to be. In court they claimed they had been doped and that their drinks had been spiked with 'snow', otherwise cocaine, which must have been one of the first drug cases in the town. The chief constable claimed 'the whole Hastings police force were trained in the use of cocaine' and that the soldiers had perjured themselves. The landlord was fined £5 for permitting drunkenness.[8]

Secret hiding place

In 1961 old hiding places for contraband spirits were discovered underneath two windowsills in a bedroom on the first floor. One contained four flasks each three feet deep. The second sill contained another three flasks and all were connected to the bar by metal pipes. Each flask was capable of holding eight gallons [36 litres] and they were estimated to be 200 years old. The first recorded licensee was Mrs Sargent, a widow, in 1794. However, there is an account of smugglers adjourning to Pip Sargent's after running a cargo, which suggests the house may have been licensed before that date.[9] The pub itself claims to have opened in 1734.

In the 1980s the pub was featured in the *Flook* strip cartoon by Hastings resident and jazz clarinetist Wally Fawkes, along with other Hastings landmarks, such as the pier.[10] The pub sign shows the town coat of arms, which should not be confused with the arms of the Cinque Ports towns.

Bas relief of Hastings Arms

SHEPHERD NEAME

HASTINGS ARMS

Hole in the Wall and Kicking Donkey
Hill Street, Old Town

1960s

The Hole in the Wall and its sister pub the Kicking Donkey were located opposite each other in Hill Street. The 'Ole in the Wall started selling beer in 1858,[1] when it was a grocery shop with an on licence. The first landlord was John Heathfield, who transferred from the Kicking Donkey. The business gradually transformed into a simple beer house, a status it kept until 1952.

In 1926 magistrates considered closing both pubs on the grounds of redundancy,[2] which was a contradiction, as the police admitted there were more customers in the 'Ole in the Wall when they visited than in any other pub in the Old Town. The police described the pub as 'cramped and unsuitable'. They objected to the poor lighting of the bar, and to a small passage alongside which led to alleys and small cottages to the rear. The brewers purchased the cottage next door for enlargement of the premises, but in the same year the building suffered a severe fire. After renewal a more modern, larger pub appeared.

A popular landlord was William Smith who arrived in Hastings in 1912. From 1918 to 1931 he worked on the railways and then in 1931 he became licensee of the 'Ole in the Wall, which was described at the time as having a 'dark atmosphere'. It seems the enlargement had not improved the lighting. Nevertheless it was obviously a good business, selling 400 barrels a year and producing £300 annual profits. Smith died in 1937,[3] just before the pub found brief fame by reaching the final in the *Observer* Darts Tournament in 1938.

Many supporters accompanied the darts team to the Cambridge clubroom to watch the semi-final between the 'Ole in the Wall and the Victoria, Hollington and again the following week for the final with the Lord Nelson in the Market Hall, George Street. Admission to the final was by ticket only and by all accounts this was a major event with 'yells of jubilation and groans of disappointment from an excited crowd of 400 spectators'. The 'Ole in the Wall team was only just beaten, even though three of its players were under 20 and were not so experienced.

Fifty-four pubs entered the tournament with 110 teams and 1,000 players but both the finalists were from the Old Town, which suggested they 'had the best players' [cheers and boos]. The team had obviously much improved since 1935 when they entered the Watney's Darts Competition with 14 other pubs, but were knocked out early in the competition.[4]

Two regulars in 1944 were Bert Thomas and Charlie Thomset, who were both posted abroad with the Hastings Company of the Royal Sussex Regiment. Early that year Bert had the bad luck to lose his left foot to a German mine and was shipped home. "Job for you laddy", he said to Charlie on leaving, "find that foot, pickle it and fetch it home".

Some months later Charlie arrived home on leave and found Bert in the 'Ole in the Wall, in position at the head of the bar. "Where's my foot?" he said and Charlie had to tell him he didn't have it. "That's it, bloody typical. Give you a simple job and you let me down". "Sorry Bert", said Charlie, "but you can't get the vinegar, y'know".[5]

In 1952 the Hole in the Wall finally became fully licensed.[6] Ron and Rose French ran it from 1957 for its final 14 years, before moving to the Jenny Lind in 1971. Its sign showed a fist holding a bottle of beer through a hole in a brick wall.[7] The name is misleading as the pub was situated some distance from the old town wall. A second Hole in the Wall existed in Claremont in the 1860s.

The Kicking Donkey is listed as a beer house in the 1855 directory when the licensee was John Heathfield,[8] although the building is much older. It was inherited by Mary Glyde in the 1860s, described as a fly proprietress and beer house keeper who became bankrupt in 1866.

THE BANKRUPTCY ACT, 1861.

In the County Court of Sussex holden at Hastings·

IN the matter of MARY GLYDE, of No. 4, Hill-street, Hastings, in the County of Sussex, Fly Proprietress and Beerhouse-keeper, adjudged Bankrupt on the 26th day of July, 1866.

A Meeting of the Creditors of the said Bankrupt will be held before the Registrar at the County Court Office, Hastings, on the 18th day of December, 1866, at Eleven o'clock in the forenoon, for the purpose of declaring a dividend, and also whether any allowance shall be made to the bankrupt. Proofs of debts will be received, and Creditors who have not yet proved, and do not then prove, will be excluded the benefit of the dividend.

WILLIAM BLACKMAN YOUNG,
Registrar.

1866

In 1891 the Kicking Donkey was rebuilt with an additional storey. From 1894 it was known as the Seagull, a most suitable name for a Hastings pub, before reverting back to the Kicking Donkey in 1899. In 1903 the licensing magistrate described the Kicking Donkey as a general shop with a beer engine and a back parlour with rabbits, eggs and sausages for sale. In 1923 it changed its status from a simple beer house to a fully licensed public house. In 1926 it was declared redundant by the chief constable, but was reprieved.

In 1936 it was granted a licence for bar billiards, a game then coming into vogue, providing it was not played on Sundays, Christmas Day or Good Friday.[9] On these days the landlord was required to dismantle the billiard table and store it in a cupboard so as not to offend St Clement's Church at the end of the street. The Kicking Donkey was one of the first Hastings pubs to promote the game of bar billiards, which started in England in the 1930s and was developed from the traditional game of bagatelle. Sussex in particular was – and is – a hot bed of bar billiards activity.

In 1947 the Kicking Donkey became licensed to sell wine[10] but nine years later, in 1956, it was declared redundant a second time and was closed. Its history as a former pub made it a desirable residence and in 1995 it was sold for £97,000.

Both premises proudly display their history. Above the original doorway a bas-relief of a kicking donkey recalls this pub of the past, while the private house opposite has kept the name Hole in the Wall.

Hill Street, Kicking Donkey on the right and Hole in the Wall on the left
1894–1916

Landlord Thomas Rand 1917–1919

Horse & Groom
Mercatoria

2011

The Horse and Groom, St Leonards oldest pub, was built in 1829 by glazier Stephen Millsted, for the benefit of the workforce busy constructing the new town of St Leonards. It is on record that they were so thirsty that the pub opened before the windows were installed.[1]

Workers also came to the Horse and Groom on Saturday nights to be paid their wages and were called in from the street one by one. They came again on Sundays to quench another thirst, this time to listen to the newspapers being read aloud. Edward Thebay was 'Sunday reader' at the Horse and Groom for many years.[2]

The Horse and Groom was regarded as a 'Tory rendezvous' and in the parliamentary election of 1835, the Conservative candidate, Joseph Planta, had one of his committee rooms here. It was common practice to bribe the voters and the Horse and Groom gave out a butt of porter plus wine, spirits and ale every day of the campaign, in support of the corrupt Tory candidate (see the Hastings Arms).[3]

Among the staff who worked here were Mrs Raven the cook, and a potboy called George. A story was told that one day in 1834 George complained about Mrs Raven's beef puddings with suet in the crust. "I really can't eat it missus", he complained. "Well, if you promise not to tell that I make my puddings without suet, I will see what I can do". Afterwards George in blissful ignorance of the fact that the only difference from before was that the suet was chopped smaller said, he had 'never tasted a better pudding'.[4]

An early landlord, John Woods, was described as cheerful, with a simple integrity and a strict disposition, but ill-fitted to be a publican. For sport or for gain his customers, after taking a drink from their pots, would shout: "Look here Woods, do you call this a proper measure?" He refilled their pots, not realising he had been duped. After a year he gave up to become Hastings postmaster.[5]

On a Wednesday afternoon in May 1853 the body of a shoemaker was laid out for inspection at a Coroner's Inquest in the Horse and Groom parlour. The dead man, Stephen Smith, a regular of the Horse and Groom, lived and worked in a small room in Harold Mews behind the pub.

The previous evening he and his wife Sarah had been into Hastings drinking at the Queen Adelaide beer house but had become separated on the way home. This had led to an argument and to Sarah Smith fatally stabbing her husband with his shoemaker's knife. A neighbour called the police and a Doctor:

P.C. George Burgess, deposed—This morning about half-past one o'clock, as I was on duty near the Warriors' Gate, Mr. Gardiner came up to me and said, "I have got a case of wilful murder." I followed him to Smith's lodging, where I found deceased sitting in a chair with his head resting on a pillow. Sarah Smith and Mrs. Cope were in the room at the time. Mr. Gardiner, the surgeon, said deceased was quite dead. Sarah Smith, who was then sitting down, jumped up and said, "Oh, dear me! Why did I do it! I have done it, and no one else, and I must be hung for it." I then apprehended her....

Roger Cooper Gardiner, surgeon deposed—About half-past one this morning, I was called up from my bed. A message was brought that a Mrs. Smith had stabbed her husband. I got up, and went with Mrs. Cope. On entering deceased's room I saw him sitting in the position in which the jury have just seen him, his head resting on a pillow laid on the back of the chair. He was not quite dead; he lived about one minute after I got there, and breathed about two or three times. His clothes were open. The wound had been rubbed clean. Upon my entering the room Sarah Smith said. "I have killed my husband, I knew it would come to this." I asked her the cause of the quarrel. She said he was always jealous of her; that they had been out together at Hastings, but on returning home she had given him the slip, that she did not get home till after him and that when she did get home, he spoke to her about her not coming home before. She then threatened to stab him, when he unbuttoned his waistcoat and said "Then do it," and she stabbed him immediately. Witness continued, I asked her what she did it with? She said, "With a knife... .

The Inquest considered the case a foregone conclusion. The Coroner made a few brief remarks to the jury who, after a short consultation brought in a verdict of "WILFUL MURDER." Sarah Smith was then charged and sent to the Lewes prison where, a few weeks later, she was executed with two other women who had also committed murder.

1853 [6]

'Lost' pubs around Mercatoria include the Anchor, East Ascent (1830s–1905), the Coach and Horses, Mews Road (1846–1950), the British Hotel, now Clarence House, opposite the Horse and Groom (1833–1906), the White Hart, Norman Road (1856–1953), the New

Inn, Mercatoria (1830s–1869) and the Star in the West, Undercliffe (1852–1943).

In 1871 they were threatened by the London matchbox trick. A tramp who called in for a drink was accused of stealing a bottle of whisky. He took a light for his clay pipe from the gas lamp behind the bar and turned out the lamp. Whilst the barman searched for matches the tramp snatched a bottle of whisky. In court he claimed he had never heard of the matchbox trick, had never been to London and had walked straight from Edinburgh. He got three months.

During the First World War, many Canadian soldiers were customers. Mary Dann, who lived in Harold Mews, was charged with 'supplying intoxicants to soldiers, with intent to make them less efficient'. She had purchased a considerable amount of beer and spirits in the Horse and Groom and seven Canadians were found drunk in her house. She received a brutal three months imprisonment.

A few months later, landlord Ernest Tompkins was charged under the same Defence of the Realm Act, but this time three witnesses gave contradictory evidence and the case was dismissed. His lawyer remarked: "If this man is found guilty no pub in England is safe".[7]

In 1985 the Victorian windows were replaced and became the subject of a complaint by a local amenity society. Without planning permission, as the pub is listed, the landlord removed Stephen Milstead's original windows and replaced them with multi-panelled, imitation Regency ones.[8]

In 1999 the Horse and Groom had another brief moment of fame, when one of its customers hit the national headlines. Regulars were dumbfounded when they read in the national press that fellow drinker Alan Kelly, of Norman Road, had turned up in Serbia among a group of Kosovan freedom fighters being disarmed by NATO troops. Frustrated by the atrocities he had seen on television at home in St Leonards, he had volunteered for two months.

Landlord David Sansbury said: "He told us he was going to Kosovo and everybody in the pub chuckled and wondered how far he would get. Anyone who can help the Kosovars in any way is doing good, but you would hardly call him a prize-fighter and I have not heard that he has had any military experience. I defy you to dislike him. He is a bloke who likes a drink, real ale is his tipple."[9]

Jenny Lind
High Street, Old Town

The Jenny Lind was granted a full licence in 1851. It was built on the site of the Bell, a pub that dated back to at least 1613. It was a free house until 1898, when Watney's purchased the freehold.

Before the First World War, the chief constable threatened to close the pub down because 'it was not being conducted to his satisfaction'. However, not enough money could be found for the compensation payment and the pub was reprieved.

During the war landlord James Smith was convicted for serving out of hours. In 1918 he was convicted a second time, for serving a lance corporal at 4pm, an offence under the wartime regulations. When the constable who saw this entered the pub, Smith attempted to bribe him, and for this he was heavily fined and lost his licence. After an agreement was made between the brewers and the magistrates, the landlord was replaced.[1]

In 1932 the police opposed the Jenny Lind licence a third time, because of 'poor sanitation'. Watney's agreed to make improvements and acquired an adjacent house that allowed them to enlarge the pub to the size it is today, and the Jenny Lind was reprieved once again.

During these improvements some old woodwork belonging to St Clement's Church was discovered embedded in the walls. A spokesman for the church reported: "The various pieces of oak formed part of the ancient rood screen of the church, which was probably taken down during the Commonwealth. The larger pieces can still be seen in the roof of the south aisle, where they were used to repair the damage caused by the attack of a hostile fleet in 1652. The smaller pieces were for the most part destroyed, but some were preserved by being built into the wall of a house facing the north-east corner of the church. The main beam that spanned an aisle or the nave, the lintel of the central arch, three pieces of arcading and several uprights, were discovered; and the smaller pieces were handed over to the Parochial Church Council for preservation by the owners of the house."[2]

On the outbreak of the Second World War and with the evacuation of the town during the Battle of Britain, the Jenny Lind closed and in 1941 its licence was transferred to the brewers.[3] In 1943 it was badly bombed and after the war it was completely rebuilt. The old interior of the back bar was restored with old timbers and the pub re-opened in 1951, a century after it first opened in 1851.[4]

In 1957 the licence was granted to the British light-heavyweight boxing champion, Don Cockell, remembered for his famous fight with Rocky Marciano for the world title in 1955. However, he didn't stay long and in May 1959 he gave up the licence.[5]

In 1980 landlord Graham Browne had to argue to get his licence. He had previously been the licensee of Tumbledown Dicks in Farnborough, described as one of the toughest pubs in Britain and a favourite of military personnel returning from overseas duty. But by 1982 he was struggling. "There are too many pubs in this small area", he complained. "I would close down if I could get a satisfactory settlement. We have lost money this year."[6] But within

OPEN MIKE

AT
THE JENNY

First Session: Thursday 26th October at 8pm

Featuring
John Hendrickse

Sessions held every Thursday
(poets & performers 7.30pm)

Come and read, play or perform

*Bring your own or your favourite poems,
songs or act to our Open Mike Sessions at:*
The Jenny Lind, High Street, Hastings Old Town

For further details see local press or telephone 01424 420879

1994

10 years the local economy had improved and with it the Jenny Lind's fortunes.

In August 1990 the pub changed its name to the Penny Farthing, a name which lasted only a few months.[7] The pub was taken over by the Kingston Inn Co. in 1993.

Royalty apart, there are few women in pub names, but the Jenny Lind is an exception. Jenny Lind was a famous Victorian soprano known as the Swedish Nightingale and a hugely successful singer in Europe and America in the mid-19th century. The gold rush town of 'Jenny Lind', California, is named after her and she is commemorated on the 50 krona Swedish bank note.

In recent years there have been attempts to prove she was a resident of Hastings. A previous landlord claimed she spent her retirement in Ore. There has been another suggestion that she lived in Bohemia and sang in St Clement's Church. However there is no evidence for any of these claims. The nearest she got to Hastings was Brighton, where she appeared in concerts in 1856 for the huge payment of £1,000 a week.

The pub sign is the only sign in Hastings made of stained glass and matches a stained glass window on the staircase.

Jolly Fisherman

East Parade

The Jolly Fisherman was first licensed to James Mann in 1834 and was located in front of the Stade, three doors from the London Trader beer house. In the 1850s the pub had an active cricket team, known as the Jollies, whose matches were reported in the local press. A typical match was played in 1854 between 'fishermen and mechanics' on the West Hill. The Jollies won this particular match by 109 runs to 29 and 118 runs to 65. It was the custom for both teams to celebrate afterwards in the pub.

The following year, landlord Robert Swain was charged with 'disturbing the peace'. A police inspector claimed a fracas had developed when he asked him to close at 12.20am, ending in Swain's arrest. Swain was able to call several witnesses in his defence, who all said that the inspector was drunk and 'had some little ill feeling towards the Jolly Fisherman and its landlord'. Swain claimed he was outside the pub only 'to see if the brig was ashore'. The magistrate refused to accept that the inspector was drunk but agreed he 'had exceeded his duties and had acted harshly, hastily and intemperately'. When the case was dismissed, the court, 'which was crowded with fishermen, found the decision to their great satisfaction'.[1]

The previous year a woman was charged with being drunk and disturbing the peace at 3am. She claimed she and her friends had just left the Jolly Fisherman 'in consequence of a collier being ashore', which demonstrates that the Jolly Fisherman opened and closed on demand during the night to serve boat crews when they landed,[2] even though it was against the law to open before 4am but not illegal to open for the crews of colliers, London traders and brigs, who were classed as 'bona fide travellers'.

In 1883 a visitor to Hastings left a carpet bag in the third class waiting room at Hastings station. He returned to find it missing. The thief gave the bag to the landlady of the Jolly Fisherman for safe keeping! It contained a nightshirt, slippers, a scotch cap, a flannel shirt, cigar case, flask, kid gloves, neck cloth and hairbrush. A fisherman in the bar bought the slippers for 6d [2½p] and the hairbrush for 2d. The thief was finally caught in a nearby beer house, the Free Trader, near the fish market, trying to sell the remaining items. When he was arrested he was wearing the flannel shirt and the neck cloth. He was charged and imprisoned for one month.[3] Jack Hart, a fisherman from the 1980s, remembered:

"Before the 1914–1918 war all the pubs used to open at 5am. There used to be more fights before 8am than there is all week now. There were often fights with the Ramsgate men (off the smacks working in Rye bay) out in front of the Jolly Fisherman. This was the most popular pub with fishermen because it was right in front of the fish market."

Pub opening hours were further controlled from 1869, so when the fish market was built in 1870, the pubs around it were granted 5am licences. The Jolly Fisherman got its early morning licence in 1875 but subsequently lost it, probably because of the decline of the fishing industry from 1900. When pub opening hours were further restricted during the First World War, the Jolly Fisherman tried to get its early licence back, but was refused.[4]

In 1925 it again applied for an early licence from 6.30am to 8.30am, on the basis that 'several hundreds of people are out and about at the fish market during these hours' and if the pub wasn't open 'fishermen wouldn't get their glass of milk and whisky'. The landlord said there were 30 big boats, 45 small boats and in addition, fishermen from Rye on steam trawlers put into the harbour. But again the application was turned down.[5]

In 1942 the Jolly Fisherman, being on the front line, suffered from enemy bombs. Although it was not directly hit, it closed for the remainder of the war. "In 1945 we moved in when it reopened", recalls Tommy Read, son of the landlord. "Nearly all our custom was from the fishing community. I remember two in particular—Bodger Barton and Buller Griggs, sitting on the wooden benches discussing the fishing. The funny thing was they had different accents. One spoke in a typical Hastings accent, the other in the 'Folkestone harbour' accent!"

When the nearby Prince Albert public house closed in 1954 Hastings Winkle Club moved into the Jolly Fisherman. Landlord Brian Hone became Winkle Club Treasurer until 1959.

In 1959 the licensee of the London Trader, then a beer house a few doors away and still trading today, applied for the transfer of the Jolly Fisherman licence. The application was successful and the Jolly Fisherman closed down. In the application the landlord of the London Trader pointed out that half his customers were fishermen. In reply the magistrates' clerk remarked, "If the application is granted, they will all be jolly fishermen". The transfer was granted.[6]

Drawing by landlord, Henry Read, 1952

Lord Nelson
East Bourne Street

c2010

The Lord Nelson was built and first licensed in 1827. Formerly the Nelson Inn, it stands just within the line of the Hastings old town wall, on a site that was originally two blocks of stables adjoining an old brandy house, dating back to 1590.[1]

In 1874 John Neale, Hastings' last stage coach driver, died. He drove the Despatch a three-horse omnibus between the railway station at Bulverhythe Salts and Hastings. He was also the landlord of the Lord Nelson from 1853 to 1861.

In 1880 the Lord Nelson was in the news during the general election of that year, when the Liberal Party lost one of its two Hastings MPs in a swing to the Conservatives and decided to form local Liberal associations. A Fishermen's Liberal Association was formed at a meeting in the Lord Nelson on 17th April, 1880, when 100 fishermen heard a rallying speech by Thomas Brassey MP. The Liberals had been criticised for being out of touch with fishermen's issues, particularly on the question of the loss of rights to the beach.'

It is interesting that in 1882 the *Hastings and St Leonards News* believed that the fishing community was somehow cut off from the town and that 'the want of wider social sympathies impels fishermen to congregate in public houses', like the Lord Nelson.[2]

In 1904 the Nelson closed for several months and a notice in the window advertised the pub to let at £24 per year. No one was prepared to rent it apparently, which gave the police reason to claim it was redundant and should be closed. However, the year before it had been sold by the brewery and was now a free house. The new owner bought the house anticipating the restrictions of the new Licensing Act of 1904, which allowed pubs tied to breweries to be closed on the grounds of redundancy, even though they might have a good record.[3]

The police tried to close it again in 1911. This time they complained about the difficulty of supervising the back doors. But in court popular landlord Harry Haste was praised for the good conduct of the pub and, among other things, the 'well attended sing-songs'. "You'll make me blush, if you carry on talking like this", he said. Nevertheless the chief constable still claimed that the Nelson was redundant and should close. Finally, it was decided that the licensee of a free house could not be awarded compensation out of brewery funds and, as the house was not tied to a brewery, the case was dropped.[4]

For the next 27 years little is heard about the Lord Nelson until, in 1938, its darts team won the *Observer* Annual Darts Tournament. Fifty-four pubs entered the competition with 110 teams and over 1,000 players. The final between the Hole in the Wall and the Lord Nelson, both Old Town pubs, was held in the Market Hall, George Street and was attended by 400 paying spectators. The team captains thanked the players for their sportsmanship and both teams went to the Nelson to drink out of the winner's cup.[5]

In the 1960s new drinking companions joined the local fishermen. In 1967 a barman, who was also a folk singer, received a hefty prison sentence of 15 months for selling cannabis to German language students who used the bar during the summer. At this time it had a reputation as a 'trouble spot'.[6]

Peter Skinner was a Nelson customer at the time: "When we were young and very drunk", he recalls, "we used this pub which was very wild. If it was the same today they'd close it. There was a lot of folk singing, a lot of villainous characters and it was very exciting when you were drunk." And with an echo from 1882, Peter said, "a lot of fishermen drank there. They didn't really mix with other groups in the town—always a group unto themselves."[7]

Fifteen years later Terry Huggins was a Nelson regular. "I remember the Nelson when Tony Shipley and his wife Tracey had it. Tony was a great landlord with an incredible sense of humour. He was everything a landlord should be, never judgemental, always friendly and he knew exactly when to turn a blind eye and exactly when to intervene. At the same time he knew everything that went on in his pub and it was no place to misbehave. His customers were mainly hippies, bikers and old towners but everybody was made to feel welcome." Tony Shipley ran the Nelson from 1978 until 1994 and also the Carlisle from 1983 until 1986, as a favour to the brewers.

"My other pub", added Terry "at least until the mid-70s, was the Anchor. There was a certain nervousness and some hostility towards the 'Nellie-Anchor crowd' by some landlords in Havelock Street and the town centre. Many of them didn't want their pub to become another hangout for the 'Nellie-Anchor crowd' and wished to attract more 'trendy', better dressed and less controversial customers. The reason for this was because both the Anchor and the Nelson were used by drug dealers throughout the 1970s and early 80s. This only applied to soft drugs in the case of the Nellie. Hard drugs were not tolerated there. Also both pubs were used by Hells Angels as well as ordinary bikers and various other groups such as the local anarchists. There was rarely any trouble in the Nellie although as in most pubs, an occasional fight broke out. Drug dealing declined in pubs after about 1983." [8]

In 1988 the Nelson Tigers Social Club (formed in 1977 to play rugby) staged the first of many, annual open-air rock concerts on the Stade. Thousands of pounds were raised for the Hastings lifeboat and by 1994 it had become the town's 'premier annual gig'.[9]

By the 1990s the Nelson had been adopted by Old Town artists and in 1991 an art exhibition was held in the pub which, surprisingly, sold £1,500 worth of pictures, prompting the landlord to hold monthly exhibitions. The new Jerwood Gallery on the Stade opposite the Nelson, might easily influence and develop the art connection.

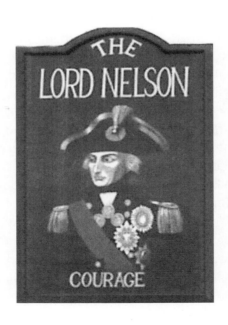

Marina Fountain

Caves Road, St Leonards

The Marina Fountain stands at the western boundary of Burton's St Leonards. Formerly the Fountain Inn, it was erected in about 1837 by Stanton Noakes, a blacksmith, on the banks of the River Asten, which then ran along the route of Grosvenor Crescent.[1] The river inspired Keats:

> So far her voice flowed on,
> like tumerous brook.
> That lingering along a pebbled coast
> Doth fear to meet the sea.

At that time, the area to the north was farmland and the pub served the needs of farmers and farm workers, many of whom resided in Caves Road.

The Fountain's trade was boosted in the 1840s when large numbers of railway navvies arrived to build the railway from West St Leonards to Hastings, and to dig out the tunnel in the cliffs behind. In January 1845 a dinner was held to celebrate the arrival of the railway and the opening of the new West St Leonards station. The 1851 census indicates the hard life of the landlord and landlady. Not only did they run the pub, they also had 10 children and 13 railway navvies as lodgers, with only one live-in servant.[2]

The cliffs behind the pub have often been a problem. In 1850 a horse belonging to a railway contractor fell over the cliff and was so badly injured it had to be put down. In 1860 twenty tons [20,321kg] of earth and rock fell onto a stable at the back of the pub, tragically killing John Barker, a homeless man who was living there.[3] Some other customers actually lived in the cliffs. In the 1850s William Smith and his family had a cave with all 'mod cons' including a stable, a kitchen and a chicken house. For insurance reasons, the cliffs are now bricked over down to the level of the pub garden.

After the railway navvies came the hop pickers. In October 1864 the *Hastings Chronicle* reported that 'large numbers of Irish hop pickers' had arrived in the countryside around Hastings and were lodging at the pub. At the end of the season, some of them stayed on to work on the new drainage system being built for St Leonards.[4]

At about this time the pub was tied to the Alfred Langford Brewery of Lewes. When the brewery became bankrupt in the

1860s the Fountain was sold and its fixtures and furniture were valued at £75, a very low figure. But a decade later its trade was boosted by London horse dealers and others attending the nearby Caves Road stables and auction house. In 1873, for example, a number of dealers paid high prices for local horses. The price paid for four horses was 333 guineas [£350] and the best 'a fine brown cob mare' fetched 140 guineas [£147]. Carriages were sold at the same time. The auction was reported as 'one of the most successful horse sales in the borough!

In the First World War landlord Walter Emery was charged with harbouring military goods. When the military police searched the pub they found two whole cheeses in a tub in a passage at the end of the bar, another 20lbs [9kg] of cheese on a shelf, 56lbs [25kg] of sugar, a large amount of cocoa, army blankets, three army sweaters and a Ross rifle, among other things. Walter Emery was jailed and the Fountain closed down,[5] until the licence was transferred. On the outbreak of the Second World War, licensee J.S. Clee was much more patriotic, acting as an unpaid air raid warden for the area.

By the 1950s the Fountain was feeling the competition from television and, along with other pubs, it lobbied the magistrates for an extra half-hour. "Customers with television stayed at home until 10pm, which didn't give them much time for a drink", claimed the landlord. The half-hour was refused.

Ten years later the successful Fountain Games and Social Club was refused an extension because it had not issued membership cards. In 1964 the club team became the Watney's shovepenny champions. In 1967 and 1968 they won both the shovepenny and darts shields, and in 1968 one customer, R. Ranson, was East Sussex, *News of the World* darts champion.[6]

In 1996 the Fountain was renamed the Marina Fountain when the Marina Inn at the other end of Caves Road closed. Today the Marina Fountain is a bikers' pub, catering especially for disabled bikers. The bar is a shrine to the Harley Davidson with a magnificent example mounted on the wall.

Biker Trefor Holloway recalls: "I've lived in Hastings for 40 years and used all the pubs here in my time. I've been a biker for many years and the pub that I use now is the Marina Fountain in St Leonards. The Marina Fountain has been a bikers' pub since about

2002 and it is used by the patch clubs, the guys with badges on the back of their leathers, because it's the only genuine bikers' pub in the town.

"In other pubs, drinkers you might think are bikers only dress that way", continued Trefor. "A lot of them don't even have bikes. We call them plastic, superficial. I'll give you an example. Some years ago I worked in an abattoir and a character known as Mad Dog Dan asked me for a pair of cow horns to attach to his crash helmet. He and his mates would go drinking, wearing cow horns on their helmets and beer mats sewn into their jeans. But the point is they don't ride bikes, they are just people who like to dress up. Why? Because this is Hastings and we're all a bit mad.

"Genuine bikers in the patch clubs, including the Chopper club and the Nomads among others, are regulars at the Fountain on music nights and at weekends when we drink beer. Other nights we go on ride-outs to places like Box Hill, Newhaven or Rye. The Six Bells at Chiddingly is a favourite ride-out. On these nights we only drink Coke. That's why it's expensive. They wouldn't make any money out of us otherwise.

"On May Day when Hastings is full of bikers who come in on the Hastings run, my girl friend and I and other bikers, drink in the London Trader and the Cutter."[7]

Merry Christmas
59 All Saints Street

All Saints Street in 2011

In Victorian times the Old Town of Hastings was a very poor area with a large number of pubs and beer houses. Several beer houses provided cheap accommodation for tramping tradesmen, fishermen from outside Hastings, hawkers, itinerants, and others, including a lot of women. They were designated as 'Common Lodging Houses', and some of them were licensed to sell beer.

As licensed premises, they had a bar attached and sometimes two. Between 1830 and 1869 anyone who paid rates could sell beer by purchasing a licence for two guineas from the Excise, bypassing the local magistrates.

In the main, these licensed premises did not have a 'pub name' and were simply known by the licensee's name. The Merry Christmas was one beer house with a name and was located in All Saints Street between 1848–1852, when the landlord was Edward Paris.

The Merry Christmas is listed in a document called 'Returns Under the Common Lodging Houses Act 1851'.[1] It had 12 beds to let, all lodgers sleeping two to a bed. In 1848 a tramping carpenter, called Thomas Wright, was charged with stealing a blanket from the Merry Christmas, and Eliza Paris, wife of the landlord, was a key witness. The prisoner was found guilty and sentenced to seven months in the Lewes House of Correction, which included 14 days in solitary.

This document was published in 1852 so we know that the Merry Christmas existed for at least four years. Its publication was a legal requirement under the 1848 Public Health Act. Hastings, along with other towns, was obliged to carry out a survey of the town's drainage and sewers because of concerns about a national outbreak of cholera in 1849. Drinking water in the Old Town was of very poor quality. Its main source, the Bourne stream, was filthy, which was a major reason why several premises sold beer and also why some were small brewers.

The survey of Hastings drainage and sewerage was carried out by E. Cresy, a government inspector, and published in 1850.[2] He described the Old Town as a festering slum where residents suffered the most decrepit conditions. Overflowing cess pools were discharged onto the beach and only a third of all housing had running water—but even this was contaminated by sewerage. However, you were lucky to be connected to the inadequate water supply and drainage system, when many hundreds, if not thousands, went without toilet facilities, drainage or running water.

The revolting conditions of the Merry Christmas were brought to Cresy's attention by the police who visited the premises in search of a stolen dog.

BOROUGH BENCH.—MAGISTRATES' CLERK'S OFFICE,
Nov. 19—Before the MAYOR and F.W. STAINES, Esq.

ELIZA PARIS, whose husband keeps the "Merry Christmas" lodging-house, in All Saints-street, and EDWARD WHITE, one of her lodgers, appeared in the hands of the borough police in the course of the afternoon, on a charge of assaulting police-constable Jeffery (E.S.C.) in the execution of his duty.

It appeared that Colonel Elliott, residing at Ore, had lately missed a puppy, and information having been received that the dog was at the "Merry Christmas," Jeffery went to the house in the course of this day (Monday), in company with a man-servant belonging to Colonel Elliott's establishment. The dog was found at Mrs. Paris's, and the servant endeavoured to carry it off, but Mrs. Paris refused to let it go, and caught hold of the animal. A struggle ensued, which threatened to issue fatally to the unfortunate animal, on perceiving which the servant desisted. The constable and the servant then went to procure a search warrant, which was speedily obtained, but the dog was not to be found on their return. Inspector Campbell accompanied them on this second visit; and while they were searching the premises, Jeffery was first assaulted by the male prisoner and then by Mrs. Paris, who were then taken into custody, and speedily made their appearance before the magistrates as stated above.

The bench fined the male prisoner 20s., in default of payment to go to prison for 14 days. They ordered Mrs. Paris to be remanded, and offered to set her at liberty if she would promise to appear before them at 10 o'clock the next morning, but her irritability was so excessive that she scouted any such obligation, and declared she would go to prison, whither she was accordingly conveyed.

TUESDAY, Nov. 20.—Before the MAYOR and F.W. STAINES, Esq.

ELIZA PARIS, remanded from the previous afternoon, was brought up and discharged—the missing dog which had led to such awkward consequences having been discovered, in consequence of information received from the irascible landlady. The animal was handed over to Colonel Elliott's servant, and Mrs. Paris proceeded homewards to await a visit from the Sanitary Committee, whose attention was to be drawn to the filthy state of the lodging-house, as discovered by the police in searching after the dog.

1849 [3]

Cresy mentions the Merry Christmas, the Cinque Ports Arms, the Crown Inn yard and several other licensed premises with attached lodging houses by name. At the Merry Christmas, Cresy reported: 'Edward Paris makes up 24 beds. Here the privy stands upon the highest level, from whence is a descent of 13 steps to the living room; the floor of the privy is on a level with the one pair window of the house in All Saints Street. The drainage proceeds from one platform [floor] to another, and eventually finds its way into the street.'

In 1849 there were at least 65 deaths from cholera in the Old Town alone, and many more went unregistered. Some other areas of the town were equally as bad. National and local government were forced to make the connection between the insanitary environment, bad public health and an average life span of only 31 years. This was bad news for Hastings. It was not what the town wanted visitors to know about or experience.

As for the Merry Christmas and the other common lodging houses, a major concern was drinking water. Those who were licensed to sell beer were in a much better position than those who weren't. Beer was obviously a healthier and safer drink and this is why there were numerous beer houses in the Old Town at that time.

The 1851 Census confirms the location of the Merry Christmas at 59 All Saints Street and lists a total of 16 people in residence on census night including:

Edward Paris, 39, licensee and bricklayer.

Robert Paris, 10, Son.

Claire Paris, 6, Daughter.

Thomas Paris, 4, Son.

(Eliza Paris, wife of the licensee and their son Edward Paris, the Younger, were not listed.)

The 12 other people listed were six couples all recorded as lodgers who had tramped from various parts of the country: Hampshire, Kent, Wales, Scotland and Loughton, Essex. The Merry Christmas is not listed in the 1861 Census by which time there seems to have been a change of use, but the copy is blurred.

It is not known if the present 59 All Saints Street is the same building dating from that time. All Saints Street has possibly been renumbered and in any case many properties have been 'tudorised' in the style of Mock Tudor and totally changed from their original design.

Moda
Queens Road

G.I. 1945–1962

This building dates from the 1850s, when it was part of Queen's Buildings. In 1866 it was known as the 'Wine and Beer Stores, formerly of George Street'.[1] It was granted a spirit licence in the same year and became the London Stores and Oyster Luncheon Bar. The term 'London stores' was 19th century slang and the term 'oyster' was slang for a part of the female anatomy, indicating that the premises were used by prostitutes.

In one of several cases involving prostitutes, following a visit by the police, the landlord was charged with 'unlawfully and knowingly permitting and suffering divers persons of a notorious bad character to assemble in his house against the tenor of his licence'. The police found what they described as a 'mare's nest' inside the pub, accompanied by 'a great noise, caused by female voices'. In his defence, the landlord said he was busy serving the employees of Manger's Menagerie, who were pulling down a marquee on the Central Cricket Ground behind the pub, and did not notice the women in the bar. He was fined £1 and asked the magistrate how he should deal with men from the cricket ground when they came into the pub to meet women. The magistrate's sexist response was a typical example of the double standards of Victorian morality; he simply said the charge did not apply to men at all.[2]

The bar became the Central Hotel in 1875[3] and narrowly escaped demolition in the late 1870s to make way for the new town hall built next door in 1881.

In the 1880s the Central Hotel was the headquarters of the Borough Bonfire Boys Society, one of at least four bonfire societies in 19th century Hastings. Large numbers of bonfire boys (up to 120) held their suppers and meetings at the Central but by 1887 they had moved to the Red Lion in Stone Street. Henry Link, late landlord of the Central, was treasurer of the society for eight years and was awarded a 'Handsomely Framed Illuminated Address' by them in 1887.[4] The society was still based at the Red Lion in 1890.

In the 1930s the Central had a large circular bar serving several cubicles, each of which had a velvet curtain which had to be pulled aside to enter. These bars were popular with people who wanted some privacy. Leneys, the brewery, removed these bars in the late 1930s. From 1942 to 1945 the Central was used by American troops when on leave passes. The late Charles Banks, then Police Inspector

Banks, remembered that: "On the whole they were well behaved, but there were quarrels at times with Canadian and British troops, mainly caused by the high rates of American pay".[5]

Tommy Read, son of the landlord, recalls that: "The beer was rationed and we often ran out. My father would put a notice on the door 'No Beer'. But the brewery expected us to keep open for tea and coffee. I was often sent to the Clock House off-licence in Queens Road for illicit supplies of Guinness. When the brewery found out they refused to allow my father to continue as landlord and in 1943 we had to move out!"[6]

In December 1945 the pub was renamed once more to become the G.I.[7] commemorating the war time patronage of the pub by American troops. Before the war, the American military had been told that they would be welcome in British pubs, if they remembered that the pub, generally, was a working man's place, where men come to meet their friends, not strangers. But after the war, Norman Longmate, in his book *The GIs* writes: 'The final proof that the pub, the most English of institutions had taken the American serviceman to its heart came, when the Central Hotel, Hastings was renamed the G.I.'[8]

At the renaming ceremony, Sergeant William Hastings of Texas, who had married a bride from Hastings, unfurled a new pub sign. He was presented with a silver tankard and many local, county, army and US dignitaries made speeches. The name G.I. put the pub into the *Guinness Book of Records*, as the shortest pub name in the

country and also into Whitbread's miniature inn signs series, published in the 1950s.[9]

But this was not to be the pub's final name. In 1962 it changed once more, to New Central. In 1979 it became the Town Crier, and then in the 1990s this elegant Victorian pub was gutted and 'remodelled'. In 1996 it was renamed again as Pitcher's Sports Bar and Diner. Ray Goode, Hastings's town crier (also one time national champion) was presented with the old pub sign, which was a portrait of himself. More recently it became Bar Moda, its seventh name change in over 150 years and is now simply Moda.

Town Crier 1979–1990s

Nag's Head
Gensing Road

2009

This pub adjoins an old boundary wall built to separate 'St Leonards Without' from 'St Leonards Within'. The Nag's Head opened as a beer house around 1835 but by 1850 it was tied to the local St Leonards Brewery in Shepherd Street. It was granted a full licence in 1853.[1]

In 1855 the pub and the cottage next door were sold and merged together,[2] and with more space it became a popular lodging house with eight bedrooms. Its lodgers included 'tramping tailors' 'who worked the same board', bath chair men who hired out wheelchairs on the seafront, building workers, sailors and itinerant hawkers.

MR. VOYSEY

Has received instructions from the Proprietor to Sell by Auction, at the SOUTH SAXON HOTEL, St. Leonards, on THURSDAY, September 13th, 1855, at Two for Three o'clock in the Afternoon, in one lot (unless an acceptable offer be made by Private Contract, of which due notice will be given),

A DESIRABLE FREE PUBLIC HOUSE, situate in Gensing Road, in the parish of St. Mary Magdalen, in the Borough of Hastings, and known as the NAG'S HEAD INN, together with the COTTAGE adjoining. The above premises are now let to Mr. THOMAS CHAMPION, as a yearly tenant, at the annual rent of £40.

The above contains, on the ground floor, a convenient and well-arranged bar and room adjoining, a parlour, tap-room, and kitchen; one-pair floor, a large club room, two bed rooms, and a water closet; on the two-pair floor, four bed rooms; and a roomy cellar under the bar and parlour. In the rear thereof is a commodious covered skittle alley.

The Cottage adjoining consists of a parlour, kitchen, wash-house, and two bed rooms; now let to Mr. CHARLES LEE, as a weekly tenant, at 4s. 6d. per week.

For further particulars, apply to Messrs. MARTIN, Solicitors, High street, Hastings; or to the Auctioneer, 4, Eversfield place, St. Leonards. Of the latter may be had cards to view, and the terms of Sale by Private Contract.

1855

STEALING CANARY BIRDS.—THOMAS SINNOCK, 33, and WILLIAM FRENCH, 40, mariners, for stealing, on the 3rd Sept., 10 canary birds from Henry Veller. Prosecutor, who is a foreigner, from Frankfurt in Germany, in September last, had 10 canaries in a cage at the Nags Head, Hastings, where he was lodging. Ten were missed, and it was ascertained that eight had been sold by prisoner French who had previously been convicted, *three years penal servitude*; Sinnock, whom two witnesses gave an excellent character —*three months hard labour*.

1862 [3]

In the 1880s the Nag's Head became the headquarters of the St Leonards' Bonfire Boys (founded in 1854), although in some years they used other St Leonards' pubs. Their annual dinners, held in the clubroom on the first floor, were well attended colourful occasions.

Every 5th of November the bonfire procession started here, headed by the St Leonards' Town Band and the society banner. A lot of people were involved. On a typical 5th of November parade they carried 400 torches and everyone wore a costume: hussars, lancers, admirals and colonels were followed by the 'guy', usually about 16 feet tall, on a coal wagon. Then more costumes: Turks, Irishmen, Chinese, Japanese and Indians followed by an illustrated banner depicting the arrest of Guy Fawkes. The procession marched around the principal streets of St Leonards before joining other processions in Hastings. Finally the guy was burnt on the beach, opposite the end of London Road.[4]

Twenty years later Robert Tressell and other building workers employed by Jarrett and Adams, who had a local workshop, drank here. These men were to become famous as the *Ragged Trousered Philanthropists* in the book of that name by Robert Tressell. In the summer their annual beanos were organised in and started from, the Nag's Head. In 1906, for example, they travelled by horse and trap to the John's Cross pub near Robertsbridge to play cricket.[5] Over the last century Tressell's book has sold over six million copies!

The controversial pub sign showing a woman's head in a muzzle is another example of a pub sign in the Whitbread collection of miniature inn signs issued in the 1950s. The reverse of the Nag's Head miniature states: 'The scold's bridle went out of fashion some time ago. According to men this was because of a shortage of good old-fashioned steel, but according to ladies, because its application was never really necessary. It is better to dwell in the wilderness than with a contentious and angry woman.' However, it is not generally realized that the sign was designed by a woman, Violet Rutter.[6]

In the 1950s and 1960s the Nag's Head was renowned for its darts team. On one memorable evening the team played a local archery club. The archers brought their own 'dartboard', an archery

House of Whitbread magazine 1955

target, and used bows and arrows! One of the players, Michael Rose, said: "It went well until some of us tried firing the bows. One of my arrows disappeared into the passage-way and got embedded into the windowsill!"[7] In 1967 the team was the outright winner of the Battle of Britain Darts Cup organised by the Hastings RAF Association. Denny Gower, later a world darts champion and landlord of the Warrior's Gate in the 1970s, was team captain.[8]

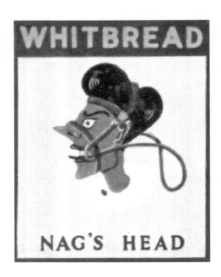

Norman Arms
Norman Road

The original 'Norman Hotel and Tavern' opened after 1845, 20 years before the completion of Warrior Square. The pub was designed by 'the builder Voysey in 1845', and is listed in the Hastings Directory for 1855.

In that year the Norman club room was the headquarters of the St Leonards Town Improvement Association, and was also the venue for Vestry meetings of the St Mary Magdalene church which set the local Poor Rate and elected the St Leonards Overseers.

Two valuations of the Norman carried out in the 1850s inform us of the number of rooms and bars in the building and the value of its fixtures, fittings and stock. The first valuation in February 1854 states that the 'Norman Hotel and Tavern' was a public house consisting of a parlour, bar and tap room with a kitchen, scullery and 'chicken house by the back door', plus a club room, 3 bedrooms and 3 'small chambers' upstairs.

The contents of these rooms included stoves, cast iron fenders, hearth rugs, cocoa matting, roller blinds, arm chairs and five cast iron spittoons. The bar had 11 feet of fixed bench seating, a spittoon, a 5 pull beer engine, cribbage, cards, pewter spirit measures, rummers [glasses], ale glasses and a painted water can to water your whisky. The tap room contained an incredible 25 spittoons and '7 old Windsor chairs of no value'.

The stock included barrels of Porter, barrels of 'XXXX' ale at 48/- a barrel; barrels of 'XXX' ale at 36/- a barrel; plus all the usual spirits and cordials. The total value of fixtures, fittings and stock was £350. But all was not well and landlord 'Alfred Holland secretly left the house in December' 1858. The Norman and its freehold was then auctioned off at the Swan.[1]

When new landlord William Mumford Palmer, a builder, took over in 1858 a second valuation increased the value to £425. The parlour and the tap room had been replaced by a smoking room and coffee room; the six bedrooms were accompanied by a sitting room, and a wine cellar had been installed. The total number of rooms had increased from 12 to 14.

The contents had also changed. New mahogany furniture was enhanced with Kidderminster carpets, dimity curtains and valances [tasselled drapery] hung from the beds and pelmets. The decor was supplemented with stuffed birds in cages, pictures in gilded frames, pier glasses and gas pendants with globes. Bagatelle was available

PUNCH DRUNK.

An affecting incident occurred on Saturday afternoon. Police constable Sharp after driving Punch, known as William Barnet, to his special friends, from Western-road, found him drunk and noisy in Roddas yard. Several persons assembled. Prisoner went to the door of the Norman Hotel, and the boys now called out "Punch is drunk". Witness took the prisoner into custody. Punch now handed in a letter in which he asked £10 for performing four nights to some parties in Warrior-square. – Fined 10s. and costs. Prisoner asked for time. Mr. Scrivens – With such a lucrative business as yours, you can pay at once.

1868 [2]

in the smoking room, and artificial flowers, 'an eight day time piece'
and 'an oil painting by Blake' decorated the bar. Unsurprisingly
there was not a spittoon in sight![4] Thus William and Eliza Palmer
took over the Norman at a time of change, from an average licensed
premises to one catering for the upper middle class residents and
'fashionable visitors' to St Leonards. The cost of these changes
possibly bankrupted Alfred Holland. Six years later in 1864 William
Palmer was also bankrupt. However, he died in December of that
year.

ST. LEONARDS.

ESTABLISHMENT OF A ROWING CLUB.—On Tuesday evening
a meeting was held at the Norman Hotel to consider the expediency of
forming a rowing club for the young men resident at the west part of
the borough. The Chairman disclaimed any hostility to the Hastings
Club, and called attention to the long distance most of them would
have to go before they could reach the Hastings shed to enjoy what
was one of the best possible means of recreation after a day's
confinement—a good pull afloat. Mr John Bray said there was plenty
of room for two clubs in such a length of foreshore. He moved the
general resolution—"That it is desirable to establish a Rowing Club at
St. Leonards," which was carried without comment. The hon.sec. of
the Hastings Rowing Club shortly addressed those present in tones of
encouragement of the movement. He thought the heartiness with
which the west end regattas had been carried on was an augury of the
success of the Club—a point upon which he saw no reason to doubt.
On the part of the Hastings Club he would welcome that at St.
Leonards, and before long he hoped to see them join in friendly rivalry.

1874 (Edited) [5]

On becoming a widow Eliza Mumford Palmer took over the licence. Her descendant Sonja Eveleigh said: "Eliza's four brothers Newton, Albert, Henry and Charles Parkes were successful local businessmen involved in cattle breeding, milk production and butchery as well as property. Newton had a share in the collier 'The London', and lived in one of the grand houses on the front. The coal, unloaded on the beach, was stored at the rear of his property before distribution. He also had shares in the Hastings Gas Company, Hastings Pier and the Royal Victoria Hotel."[6]

The Norman always had competition. From the 1850s to the 1870s a second pub, the Mason's Arms, was located nearby and at a later date a beer house, the Warriors Arms, was to be found next door.

As Warrior Square developed, the Norman's public bar became a rendezvous for the grooms, valets, coachmen and servants employed by the Victorian families of the square.

In 1905 the licensing magistrates considered closing the Warriors Arms. They noted that the Norman was doing a good trade but that the customers of the Warriors Arms were 'undesirables', 'loose and idle people who generally stand at street corners'. The Warriors Arms was consequently closed in 1905[7] and is now a coin and stamp collectors' shop.

c1911

During the First World War Warrior Square became an overseas drafting depot. The Women's Auxiliary Army Corps, founded in 1917, was billeted in the square and took over some of the properties, including number 64, which it used as an orderly room. Female volunteers for military duty were issued with uniforms, vaccinated, and drilled in front of the statue of Queen Victoria, before marching up the square to their mess hall. Off duty hours were quietly spent in the Norman and for many this was their last experience of England before being sent to France, from which many never returned.[8] The first draft of WAACs left for France in August 1917, 15 months before the war ended.

After the First World War, the Norman became the headquarters of the St Leonards Bowls and Quoits Club, which had at least two active teams in the 1920s.[9] From 1925 until 1953 the landlord was Leonard Collinson ('Colly'). As vice president of Hastings & St Leonards Snooker League he provided a first-rate billiards saloon, used by many successful pub teams who entered the annual *Hastings Observer* Snooker Championships.

The old pub stood for about 90 years until it was demolished and rebuilt by Wilfred Shippham of Kent in 1938.[10] During its rebuilding, the Norman stayed open and provided a minimal service. A popular feature of the new pub was the teak panelled dining room locally renowned for its selection of cheeses. In 1939 it was reported that a practical joker took a pony upstairs and tied it to Colly's bed! His response to this prank is not recorded!

The Demolition of the old "Norman," and Erection of the New, were carried out by

WILFRID SHIPPAM

(Who has undertaken many important Building Works in his native county of Sussex)

The whole of the Joinery, including teak panelling and counters, being manufactured in his workshops at

ASHFORD, KENT

1938

In the Second World War the Norman, unlike some other local pubs, never closed, although it was bombed by the Luftwaffe,[10] the local population was depleted by evacuation and supplies of beer were at times very poor. The billiards saloon in particular stayed open throughout the war years, when it was much in demand by the military personnel billeted in the nearby Adelphi Hotel. Members of the Home Guard also used the pub for concerts and social evenings.

The Normando Jazz Club ran for a period in the 1990s and in 1995 the Norman closed for a short period after the joint licensee absconded, owing a large sum of money to Watneys.

The pub sign at that time simply said: 'The Norman', underneath Watneys Red Barrel. The most recent sign, stored in the cellar, depicts a Norman soldier. It is made of fibreglass and according to a recent landlord its image was downloaded from the internet.

The Norman closed again in 2013.

Pig in Paradise
Palace Court, White Rock

1970s

The Pig in Paradise, formerly the Palace Bars, is located on the ground floor of one of Hastings' most prominent buildings. The first building on this site was the Seaside Hotel, built in 1835, which in 1872 became the Seaside and Pier Hotel. It was rebuilt in 1886 as the Palace Court Hotel but like other Victorian hotels in the town, for example the Old Golden Cross or the Havelock, the investment required did not produce an adequate return and consequently its prices were higher. In 1889 a glass of wine in the Palace cost 6d [2½p] whereas elsewhere in town it was 4½d although the Palace claimed its wine 'was as good as the Bodega' (now French's Bar).[1] After more investment and alterations in 1894, it reopened 'with electric light in all public rooms' powered by dynamos installed in the caves behind the building.[2]

The wages earned by barmaids came to prominence in 1891. In that year a barmaid was dismissed for misconduct and applied to the courts for a month's pay of 30s [£1.50] in lieu of notice. The manager, when asked the reason for her dismissal, said she had been kissing the customers. The question is, asked the magistrate, "Did she kiss a customer or did a customer kiss her? Did she kiss or was she kissed?" It was established that two male customers had kissed the barmaid, which was technically an assault and therefore she could not be accused of misconduct. She received a month's wages in lieu but lost her job anyway.[3]

In the early 1900s the Palace Bars was one of the meeting places used by the Hastings and St Leonards Debating Society, which met to discuss issues of national and local importance. Alf Cobb, local socialist firebrand, was a regular member of the club, which functioned up until the First World War. In 1909 members debated tax, the budget and Sunday opening hours for public houses. This was a popular topic with the temperance campaigners who were opposed to Sunday opening.[4] In 1917 the Palace Court Company went into liquidation and the building closed, although it had been commandeered by the army during the war. Struggling financially it was described as 'a 30 year failure' and as 'Hastings's white elephant'.[5]

Nevertheless, Captain Vincent Moss, landlord of the Imperial, Queen's Road, took over the bars and restaurant in 1926, after the rest of the building had been transformed into high class apartments. The Palace Bars gained a new lounge designed as 'a bowl of flowers' with giant spikes of gladioli and columns of asters. There were thick pile carpets, a silver service, a Piccadilly chef and wallpaper with a silver tissue pattern over scenes of gondolas. It had a Persian tearoom for 'intimate tête à tête over the tea table'. In the 'swinging 20s' the Palace lounge and the ground floor bars were the place to be seen.[6]

Palace Court 2009

Bar mural 2013

It reopened to acclaim from holiday makers and locals in 1927 and the licensee applied to open up the caves behind the building as a meeting place for the Ancient Order of Druids, which claimed 400 members. Although the caves were fitted out with lighting and ventilation in expectation of being granted permission, the application was refused and the caves were possibly never used.[7]

Pat Dunn remembers the Palace Bars as a smart venue in the 1940s under a head waiter called Lou.[8] Another drinker, Alan Crouch, recalls: "Sometimes we started off an evening drinking Biddenden cider in the King's Head. Because of its strength you were only allowed two pints. Then we made our way to Hastings pier, which had an extension until 11pm, stopping at the Palace Bars on the way."[9]

Cyril Pelluet also has good memories of the Palace Bars. "In the late 1950s", he says, "it was run by Fuller and Swatland. The head barman was Matthew Hart, a sort of big brother or uncle, always immaculately turned out in a white jacket and slicked back hair. It had a very long bar and the right hand corner was known as Matt's corner. His equally affable sidekick Ted was known as 'the stomach in a white coat'. The Palace Bars was quite a smart place. At that time

National Service was still on and a lot of us servicemen and ex-servicemen, used to meet up there—a happy atmosphere and a lot of camaraderie.'[10]

September 2013

Twenty-five years later the Palace Bars, now known as the Pig in Paradise, had become an 'alternative' venue describing itself as an 'Ad Hoc Arts and Performance Centre'. In 1984 Roger Carey celebrated his 1,000[th] gig here, with a collection for Ethiopian Famine Relief.

In the mid-1980s, several events were staged from 'quiet music on the Hammond organ and the Bechstein concert grand', to poetry readings, magic, and rhythm and blues. The Pig also hosted the Hastings Free Festival with a 'broad minded selection of culture for the town's alternative masses'. In 1986 the Pig staged two weeks of daily entertainment ranging from radical poetry, blues, country, string quartets, disco synth, craft, free form music, cabaret, comedy and film. It also included psycho sonic music by local band Turn Blue.[11] Numerous other bands performed here including Pass the Cat and Moire Music.

More recently the large bar has become an occasional cocktail lounge featuring a 'Flair barman' who entertains the customers by the manipulation of bottles, glasses and cocktail shakers. Flair barmen use skills more commonly associated with jugglers.

Bar mural 2013

Pilot and Privateer
Queens Road and Elford Street

Early 1900s

The Pilot was opened in 1834 by a sail maker and former letter carrier called William Nabbs. He was first employed by the post office in the High Street at the age of 12 or 13, and later apprenticed as a sail maker to Messrs. Winter and Thwaites who built fast sailing cutters in their shipyard on Hastings beach.

In 1824 he married Sarah Gallop and took up residence in Rope Walk, America Ground, which was the centre of rope making and sail making in Hastings. He later set up as a sail maker in John Street.

The Nabbs were an historic Hastings family. William Nabbs' father, also called William and also a sail maker, owned and captained a privateer licensed by the government to raid French boats in the 18th century. His in-laws were licensees of the Bo Peep in 1794.

The Pilot was one of a number of public houses built when the exodus from America Ground took place in 1835. Others included the Wheatsheaf in Bohemia, and the Angel and the Plough on West Hill.

The Pilot was also one of at least four Hastings' pubs associated with early Liberal politics. Charles Bolingbroke, a political associate of Nabbs, undertook a similar role at the Red Lion up the road in Stone Street. Henry Morley, another radical politician, took the Angel on West Hill, and John Bean became landlord of the Kings Head.

The large Nabbs family of 18 ran the Pilot until the 1840s, after which period they transferred to the Swan Shades in Swan Terrace.

The 1872 Licensing Act created some confusion for the Pilot.

THE Landlord of the Pilot Inn, seeing a man with clayey boots which looked as if they had traversed many a weary mile that morning, could not find it in his heart to refuse the man a glass of beer within closing hours on Sunday last. He therefore bade him drink and be gone; but while there two other men came in, equally as thirsty, but the landlord, not feeling they had the same claim upon his tap as the first arrival, declined to serve them with the much-thirsted-for refreshment. But so unkind are the gods – whether the constable acted on "information" received from a kindly neighbour, or whether that lynx-eyed constable could see round the corner we know not – Sergeant H. Wood, stepped in upon the scene. The landlord, not a bit dismayed, told him the circumstances of the case as he subsequently deposed to in the witness-box on Thursday; and with a courtesy and honesty that might have softened the heart of even a policeman, bade him do his duty. The magistrates held the offence to be proved, and fined defendant in the lowest penalty they could inflict—£1 and costs, the Mayor adding that the Bench were of opinion that Mr. Love broke the law in ignorance. This is the only salve that Mr. Love can apply to his wounded soul. In whatever light you view law it is a costly commodity. Here is Mr. Love, who has practised at the bar for eight years. Believing he has a right to assuage the thirst of a weary traveller, he draws him "a half-pint." Thereupon he is called upon to pay smartly for his consideration. Mr. Love will know in future that "ignorance is no excuse in law." He had better lay out now a sovereign or two more upon copies of and comments on the Licensing Act, and stick them up in his bar. Whenever he is in doubt he can refer to them. He has paid once for his ignorance of the Act; see how many times he may then be called upon to pay for his acquaintance with it. If he can reconcile the conflicting decisions of the powers that be, and, say, after six months, hard study, honestly declare that he understands the law, he will have accomplished more than I should give mortal man credit of being able to do.

1874 [1]

Between 1906 and 1928 the Pilot had 14 different landlords. However, it was doing a better trade than most other pubs in the area (e.g. Bedford, Imperial, Fountain, Palmerston, Red Lion and the Tiger). It was a free house before being taken over by the Kemptown Brewery of Brighton. It was granted a music, singing and dancing licence for wireless only, in 1927. But in 1934 the licensee, William Davey, died suddenly and his widow was affected by a clause in the brewery tenancy agreement which gave her only 14 days notice to quit the pub. The Magistrates Court declared that this was wrong and deleted the 'unfair clause'.

Minnie Howlett and her husband were customers of the Pilot after the Second World War, when Stan and Dolly Barton ran it from 1948 to 1956. 'The Pilot was a very popular public house', she said. It had two bars 'one up and one down because it was built on the slope of a hill'. (It was on the corner of Queens Road and Stone Street.) 'It had stairs between the bars and sometimes when it was crowded we sat on the stairs at the back. It was always full of customers and my brother-in-law Chick Howlett played the piano there'.[2]

In its final years the Pilot was well known for its cider, and in 1970 it was selling 700 pints of cider a week. It was possibly the only Hastings 'cider house' at that time. It closed in 1971 and is now an electrical appliance shop.

Another public house with a nautical name, the Privateer, was located in a nearby street. In the mid 19th century this popular pub had bonfire boys, 'girls on the town' and railway employees among its customers, and was noted for its involvement with the traditional Hastings Rock Fair then held annually on the White Rock.

In 1859, and again in 1861, landlord William Brett was cautioned for selling alcohol in a booth at the fair. He had been wrongly informed by the Excise that the fair was legal and that he could sell liquor, but was told by the police that this was an offence as the fair was 'illegal'.

In June 1869 the pub changed hands and an inventory of furniture and effects was taken. The Privateer had a bar, a 'Little Parlor', (French spelling), and a smoking room. These later became the bar, saloon and lounge respectively. The inventory listed the following:

Smoking Room, 1 deal table, 7 Windsor chairs, 8 rush bottom chairs, 1 roller blind, 1 iron fender, 6 spittoons, 1 gas globe, 3 pictures, 1 puff tube and darts, a bagatelle board with cue, balls and a marking board.
Bar, 9 ale glasses, 14 large ale tumblers, 14 small ale tumblers, 7 common tumblers etc. 3 large beer cans, 2 stone jugs, 2 stone 1 gallon bottles etc. 12 quart pewter pots, pewter spirit measures, 4 cordial bottles etc. dominoes, cribbage board.
Little Parlor, A tea table, pictures, floor cloths, teapot, meat dishes, vegetable dishes, 10 large plates, 5 small plates, cutlery, candlesticks.
Washhouse, main water tub and tap. Total value: £28 – 5 – 0.'[3]

The most interesting item on the list is the 'puff tube and darts', an early form of modern darts almost certainly an attraction at the Hastings 'Rock Fair'. A description of puff and dart is found in the book: *Played at the Pub,* by Arthur Taylor.

'Puff and dart', he says 'was depicted in the 1870 edition of *The Boys' Own Book*, subtitled *A Complete Encyclopaedia of All the Diversions, Athletic, Scientific & Recreative of Boyhood & Youth*. This reference describes puff and dart as an 'old fashioned tavern game', which has 'lately found its way into private houses, where it enjoys a certain kind of popularity under the name "Drawing-room Archery".'

The game was played with a brass tube and 'needle-pointed' darts, using a target consisting of concentric rings.

However, in her *Glossary of Northamptonshire Words and Phrases,* of 1854, Anne Elizabeth Baker described a target that appears to have been closer in design to the modern dartboard. Puff and dart, wrote Baker, was 'a game played by puffing or blowing a dart through a long narrow tube, aiming to strike the numbers painted on a circular board hung against a wall: the various figures are arranged like those on the face of a clock.'

'In 1868', she said, (only one year before the game was listed at the Privateer), 'the catalogue of a games supplier called WH Cremer of New Bond Street, London, described puff and dart as, "An Old English game".'

Sussex Puff and Dart board

Arthur Taylor introduces some local, Sussex evidence: 'A persuasive ... piece of evidence that puff and dart provided a model for modern darts is this photograph of a tiny board (of perhaps seven inches in diameter), which appeared in *The Countryman* magazine in ... 1947. Described as a board used for puff and dart in Sussex pubs ... in the 1880s, it is ... immediately recognisable as an early version of the modern dart board.'[4]

The Hastings Rock Fair came to an end in about 1860, although there were attempts to revive it outside the town boundary. (See Tivoli Tavern.)

The Privateer continued until the First World War when, in 1917, it was closed temporarily by the Liquor Control Board presumably because it had allowed soldiers to get drunk.

It never reopened and the building became a private house, now also gone. All that remains is a sad and derelict open space in a Hastings back street. The Privateer, the Rock Fair and puff and dart have disappeared from local history.

Pissarro's
South Terrace

1913–1916

Pissarro's, formerly known as the Princes, was first licensed in 1864.[1] Among its first customers were visiting cricketers and fans, who came into Hastings for matches on the former Central Cricket Ground, now the Priory Meadow Shopping Centre opposite. The first landlord was Alfred Vidler followed by international cricketer John Wells, who very quickly became bankrupt and the pub had to be sold in 1865.

In 1950 the pub sign was featured in Whitbread's series of miniature inn signs.[2] It showed the two nephews of Richard III, who were declared illegitimate by parliament and executed in the Tower of London in 1483. Sometime after 1960, Whitbread repainted the sign to show the princes no longer holding hands.

From 1977 to 1981 the licensees were Alan and Marie Garaty, who remember the pub with fondness. "It was quite a small pub", they said, "it only had the two bars, public and saloon. Next door, where the restaurant is now, was a furniture depository whose employees were regular customers."

Sponsored cycle ride to Eastbourne
Marie and Alan Garaty are in the centre of the picture

Marie with customers c1980

They continued, "We organised wheelbarrow races and a cycle race to Eastbourne, to replace money stolen in a burglary. We had a swear box in the public bar that took a lot of money. All the proceeds went to the children's department of a local hospital. We also ran a successful Princes gun club for clay pigeon shooting on Sundays."

Marie recalled: "We never had any really bad incidents, only some minor ones. I used to deal with most of it, but then I was trained by Whitbread to deal with incidents in the bar. The brewery's idea was that a man wouldn't hit a woman whereas he might well attack another man. So they relied on their landladies. But most customers were supportive.

"The building on the other side was a private house. So you see with only two bars we couldn't develop it much further. There wasn't any space for a children's room, something then coming into demand, nor was there any outside space for a beer garden."[3]

Sometime after 1981 the pub expanded into both the former furniture depository and into the private house next door. In 1992 it was sold and became a freehold premises and hotel. Two years later it was renamed Pissarro's, after Lucien Pissarro (1863–1944) who lived in Hastings briefly in 1918. He painted eight local landscapes, including one of All Saints' Church.

Pissarro's website suggests that it is 'neither pub, wine bar, bistro or restaurant but the best of all of these. A meeting point, a subtle fusion of tastes—visual, audio and gastronomic'. Pissarro's has been voted the south-east's premiere jazz, blues and soul venue. But regardless of its new image it still retains the atmosphere of a traditional pub.

On its reopening, the pub rock and jazz scene welcomed its addition to the reduced number of live music venues in the town. At the time the Carlisle was under threat of closure (but was later reprieved), Mr Cherry's had already closed and Blades Club at the Yorkshire Grey was about to close.

Pissarro's was the location of the first Hastings 'Beatles Day' in December 2000. This was designed as a one-off event but was so successful that another date was set for the following April, it being obvious to everyone that a larger venue was needed.

In April 2001, 2002 and 2003 Beatles Day was held at the Marina Pavilion, St Leonards, and Pissarro's became one of the first sponsors. In 2004 Beatles Day moved to Hastings Pier—an excellent venue and home to much of the town's music history. Since 2006 Beatles Day has been held in the White Rock Theatre and this marathon 10 hour event has become one of the most important annual gigs in the Hastings music calendar. 2011 saw the 12th

anniversary with 300 local performers, and Pissarro's is still a major sponsor.

Local groups who play Pissarro's regularly are Engine, Clutch and Gearbox, Pass the Cat, the Liane Carroll Trio (Ronnie Scott's Award & double BBC Jazz Award winner) and singer Chris Hutchinson (aka the Mellow D Man) whose father Leslie Hutchinson was an outstanding and famous cabaret singer of the inter-war years.

A regular is 80-year-old Dennis Neeves, who plays piano sometimes on Sundays, when the main group takes its interval break. He has been playing piano for several years and also occasionally plays the intervals at Porter's Wine Bar in the High Street and elsewhere.

Picture window 2013

Pissarro's 2013

Prince Albert
Rock-a-Nore

Fisherman outside the Prince Albert

The Prince Albert, Rock-a-Nore Road, was formerly a fishermen's lodging house, built in 1789, and tucked away among the net huts. It became the Foresters Arms in 1847 and the Prince Albert in 1852, when it was one of at least 14 fishing pubs around the Stade. Before the First World War, along with the Nelson, Royal Standard and Dolphin, it was a popular fishermen's pub.[1] The famous Winkle Club, a fishermen's charity for poor children, was founded here in late 1899 and held its first charity supper on New Year's Eve 1899/1900.[2] The pub is now defunct but its immortality is guaranteed by this fact.

A group of local fishermen who used the pub discussed the idea of raising money for children of poverty-stricken families in the town. In those days there was no welfare state and many working class families, especially throughout the winter, existed in dire poverty and deprivation.

The fishing community decided to organise a self-help charity but were stuck for a name until somebody suggested the Hastings Winkle Club. And so it was. No time was lost in getting the club under way and the history of the club's early days is one of inevitable development. It was decided that every member would have to carry a winkle. The mortal remains of the original occupants of the shells were removed and their places filled with sealing-wax. On being asked to 'winkle up', the luckless person caught without his badge of membership, the winkle, had to pay a fine—a penny in the early days—and the challenger likewise had to report him or pay a fine too. An elaborate system of such penalties developed.[3]

Over the years the club also organised events at the fish market, including festive sports days and banana races, where competitors had to race with a ten-bushel basket full of bananas on their head. There was also a Winkle Band that marched around Old Town collecting money.

The main event was the children's Christmas party. Ironical then, that the landlord was summonsed and fined £1 in 1920, for allowing children into the room where the Winkle Club was in session, although they used a side entrance.

This type of charity was not unique to Hastings. Mass Observation's, *The Pub and the People* mentions similar charities called Dolly Clubs operating from pubs in the north of England, where every member had to carry a small dolly or pay a fine. Equally another Hastings pub, the Royal Oak, had an Acorn Club, where members were required to carry an acorn at all times.

In the 1930s a second Winkle Club was formed, at the Tivoli Tavern in Silverhill.[4] Both clubs operated on the same principle but with one major difference; the Tivoli Winkle Club had several female members whereas the Hastings club was exclusively male and banned women from its ranks. Cyril Fletcher wrote a poem poking fun at the men only rule. Here is a verse from it:

Bessie from an Old Town pub
Had joined the famous Winkle Club
When Winkles Up was cried with zest
She raised hers higher than the rest.
She wore her winkle night and day
She wouldn't put the thing away
Even when swimming in her vest
The winkle glistened on her chest.[5]

With 150 members, the club closed during the Second World War, except for two concerts organised for evacuee children billeted in the town. In 1948 the Winkle Club held its first dinner for nearly 10 years because of wartime food shortages. The Prince Albert closed in 1954 and its licence was transferred to the Duke of Wellington in the High Street. The Winkle Club moved to the Jolly Fisherman until 1959 and moved again to the Lord Nelson until 1964, when it finally found a new home at the Fishermen's Institute where it remains to this day.

The Winkle Clubs of Hastings were thereafter remembered by an unusual pictorial link between Hastings and Basingstoke in Hampshire. In 1967 a pub sign was commissioned and designed for a new public house in Basingstoke called the Winkle. This pub is located on Winklebury Way near the Iron Age camp on Winklebury Hill. Its sign shows a winkle shell, the Hastings town arms and a silhouette of Winston Churchill gazing out across the English Channel.

The Hastings Arms represents Hastings as the chief Cinque Port. The winkle represents the historic Winkle Clubs, while Winston Churchill is included as he was an honorary member of the Winkle Club and Lord Warden of the Cinque Ports.[6] The Prince Albert is now the Mermaid Restaurant adjacent to Winkle Island, and a monument of a winkle shell.

The building in 2009

Prince of Wales
Western Road, St Leonards

2011

The history of the Prince of Wales in Western Road follows a pattern common to many St Leonards pubs. Originally a bakery, it started selling beer in the 1850s and in 1855 was listed in the directory as a simple beer house, when George Sutton was the landlord.[1]

By 1858 it was known as the Prince of Wales.[2] The next landlord was John Snelling, who applied for a full licence which was refused

A collier delivering coal to St Leonards in 1854

in 1862.[3] He had other businesses in Western Road and was the proprietor of a livery and private stables servicing the residents of the emerging Warrior Square.

Other trades in Western Road at the time included blacksmiths, undertakers, coach builders, washerwomen, saddlers, corn and forage contractors and a bath chair man, all of whom would have used the pub.

Other customers included the men who unloaded the colliers hauled up onto the beach opposite London Road and the carters who delivered the coal locally. As 'bona fide travellers' the men crewing the boats could legally be served out of hours whereas the carters couldn't. This aspect of the law led to much trouble in the local pubs.

One Sunday morning in 1864 a police constable saw some men standing outside, drinking out of hours. On seeing the constable they went inside. He followed and they exited into the yard at the back. He continued to follow and found them in the kitchen of the house next door with pots of beer. The next door neighbour explained to the policeman: "They have only come to look at my cage birds and the beer was delivered from the Old England yesterday!"[4] On other occasions the same policeman was met with 'several expressions of a violent and vulgar character' from some customers.[5]

As the years went by, the Prince of Wales beer house occasionally came up in the local news. In 1878 the *Hastings and St Leonards Chronicle* reported on a secret campaign carried out by a private detective into the town's beer houses. The object was to spy on beer houses that were thought to be selling spirits illegally. The Prince of Wales was caught out when it served rum to the detective. He had been hired by the Hastings Licensed Victuallers' Association, whose members all held full licences. However, when the case went to court it was dropped over a technicality.[6] On another occasion the pot boy had his trousers stolen from the kitchen by an old man called John Love, who was a fern hawker. The police caught Love later in the day in Hastings and the potboy got his trousers back.

After the Second World War the pub was allowed to sell wine as well as beer but was still prohibited from selling spirits. The pub applied for a full licence in 1949, but was refused on the grounds of poor interior decoration.

The brewers replied that: "Some landlords prefer a bare floor and some customers prefer benches and forms, to plush seats". But it did apparently need some decoration and new interior fittings, which were near impossible to purchase after the war.[7] At that time it had two small bars.

Pat Dunn recalls that in the 1950s they did bed and breakfast. "They had a small sign up: 'B&B 7/6d' [37½p] and the landlady played piano." More than 40 years later Pat was barmaid there herself. "There were characters, of course. One I remember was 'Nobby No Toes' who somehow had lost his toes."[8]

The Prince of Wales is a common pub name but the pub sign in this case refers to Edward the Black Prince (1330–1376). The three plumes of ostrich feathers are from his coat of arms. There were three other pubs with the same name in Hastings but their signs referred to Queen Victoria's eldest son. One in Pelham Street closed after the First World War and another in Bohemia Road closed in 1971. There was also a Prince of Wales Beer House in Waterloo Passage from 1849 to at least 1869.

Prince of Wales from Cross Street 2014

Railway and Royal Hotel
St John's Road

The Railway

The Railway Inn opened in 1854 as a beer house and got a full licence in 1862. Its first landlord, Frederick Campbell, was supported by two certificates of character including one from 'an influential inhabitant of Maidstone', the location of his previous pub. This was just as well as the chief constable had heard that the Railway Inn had been 'rebuked by a gentleman of high position in St Leonards', following the wedding of a local brickmaker whose workmates 'behaved in an indecent manner causing a complaint'.[1] The Railway got its licence but Frederick Campbell was warned that it could be withdrawn at any time.

Scoring was a 19th century custom of credit in public houses.

Charged with Assault
The result of running up a score

On Thursday Frederick Campbell, landlord of the Railway Inn, was charged with assaulting George Rummers, brickmaker. Complainant, it seems, had run up a rather long score at defendant's house and on Saturday hearing he was at the Bo Peep hotel and fearing he would not return he went after him. They had some words, and complainant was very abusive, whereupon defendant struck him drawing blood. Fined 1s and costs 12s.

1863

In 1876 his wife Mary Campbell, now a widow, took over the new hotel, which had been built on the adjacent corner. At first she called it the Railway Hotel.[2] Having a Railway Inn and a Railway Hotel within a few yards of each other was obviously not a good idea and it was soon renamed again, this time to become Mrs Campbell's Hotel, 'two minutes from the sea'.

In the late 1870s Hastings was once again visited by the military in the build up to the Anglo-Zulu wars in South Africa. The 'billeting question' was a contentious issue with publicans, who were legally required to provide cheap accommodation for soldiers, at their request. In a court case of 1877, Starr vs. the army, a claim was made for a soldier billeted upon Mrs Campbell's Hotel. She claimed she could not accommodate him and a servant was sent with the man to find him a bed at the soldier's allowance of 4d a night [1½p]. The soldier was found a bed at Mrs Starr's guest house down the road, but Mrs Starr thought that 1s [5p] was a more reasonable rate, took the case to court and won.[3]

In 1884 the hotel changed hands and was renamed again as the Royal Hotel,[4] after the nearby Royal Concert Hall (originally the Warrior Square Opera House) and now the site of Royal Terrace flats.

The Railway, meanwhile, shot to fame when one of its customers was summonsed to a coroner's inquest in 1891. Early one morning, the body of a young girl was found deep in Bo Peep railway tunnel. She was carried to the station and identified as a girl named Polly from Alexander Road, who worked as a domestic servant in Warrior Square.

At the inquest, witnesses contradicted each other, and suspicious circumstances created a great deal of interest and a large attendance of the general public. The town held its breath while the inquest was adjourned three times.

A doctor stated: "She died in the night from a large wound on the head. Her handkerchief was saturated in blood but it was dry and stale, about a week old. Had I seen the body in another place I would not have the opinion that she had been struck by a train. There were no marks of a struggle, only blood."

Station employees suggested that she could easily have walked into the tunnel at night, but couldn't explain why anyone run over by a train would have an injury to such a small area of the body. She was found lying between the rails, but her fingers were stained as though she might have crawled some distance before dying. No

ROYAL
FAMILY & COMMERCIAL HOTEL
OPPOSITE
WARRIOR SQUARE STATION.
BASS'S ALE & STOUT
ON DRAUGHT
CIGARS OF THE CHOICEST BRANDS
St Leonards-on-Sea
CHARLES BESSELL,
PROPRIETOR
TELEPHONE, HASTINGS 581.
WINES & SPIRITS OF THE FINEST QUALITY.

The Royal Hotel 2011

train doors were open so she could not have jumped, and all the engines were clean. Her hat was lying beside her.

The inquest was told that she had claimed her employer had ill-treated her. Her employer claimed that she had secretly left his house in Warrior Square at 10.20pm on the night she died, after which time he was drinking in the Railway. The inquest found the evidence wholly unsatisfactory and concluded that she was 'found dead with no evidence to show the cause of death'. Was she killed by her employer and dumped in the tunnel before he went drinking in the Railway? Did someone else kill her, or did she commit suicide? The mystery remains unsolved to this day.[5]

The Royal Hotel suffered a severe blow during the First World War, when the landlady was charged under the 'treating' regulations of the Defence of the Realm Act. The barmaid served a soldier and his girlfriend in the private bar, through a service window that didn't always allow sight of the customers. The police claimed the barmaid had served the soldier with more than one drink, one for himself and one for his girlfriend. This was 'treating', an illegal act in the First World War, for which they were charged. Although there had been no complaint against the Royal in living memory, the landlady was fined a massive £30 (£10 for each of three offences). According to the historic retail price index, £30 in 1915 would be about £1,600 today.[6]

Then, in 1919, it was the Railway's turn. Food and drink inspectors visited several pubs incognito asking 'for a drop of whisky', which they then examined for quantity, strength and price. The Railway was fined £5 for overcharging, after barmaid Elizabeth Shoesmith made the unfortunate comment: "We have to make big profits because of the rates."[7]

Spittoon

In 1927 a window cleaner threw a spittoon at the landlord of the Royal. Spittoons went out of use after the First World War, so this one must have been part of the décor. The spittoon pictured here is typical of a century ago and came from the Dorset Arms in Silverhill and is now the property of Dot Mitchell.

Pat Dunn, who was born in 1931, recalled: "I was bought up in St Leonards and the Royal Hotel was one of the pubs used by my family. They drank in the saloon bar from about 1926 and I used to go there as a child. I was allowed to sit in the corner with a lemonade, if I kept quiet. I started drinking there myself in about 1947, when I drank ginger wine. At that time it had three bars—a large public bar, a small private bar and the more upmarket saloon.

"My parents also used the Railway during the war years and after. I think it was just one bar and a jug and bottle. My mother told me that when the sirens went off during the air raids they would all go down into the cellar. That's when she started drinking pints so she didn't run out. I remember one local character Bill Elf and his friends drinking at 11am one Sunday morning, a good hour before opening time. When the police came in he joked with them: We are a committee meeting of the underwater sky diving club', he claimed and got away with it."

The Railway was used by the performers from the Regal Theatre (now Ocean House office block), which towers above Warrior Square station on London Road. Stars who performed in the variety shows there included Leslie Hutchinson (Hutch), the famous cabaret singer of the interwar and post-war period. His son Chris Hutchinson sings in Pissarro's today.

In the 1960s the Railway was run by Carl and Judy Burton and in the 1980s Jim and Di Davidson came from the Cambridge to run it. They ran it well and Di was a 'no nonsense' landlady.[8]

Cyril Pelluet, remembering the 1960s, remarks: "As teenage jazz fans, one of the clubs we went to was the Railway Workers Social Club [British Rail Staff Association] opposite the Royal and just a few yards up from the Railway. I'm sure they served 'Grotney's' Red Barrel. I think they also featured other bands from time to time, such as pop/rock bands from the emerging 60s pop and rock revolution."[9]

Of course jazz fans and others who didn't want to drink 'Grotney's' went across the road to the Royal or the Railway.

From 1931 until 1953 the Royal was tied to Edlin's Brewery, Brighton, and following this it was tied to Tamplin's and then to Charrington's. It is now a free house with all the original bars now one. The Railway still has brown glazed tiles indicating it was once tied to Fremlin's.

Red House
Emmanuel Road

The Red House was built in the mid-1870s as a small hotel, in the new development of the West Hill estate. It has an attractive corner turret—a common feature of local domestic architecture—and is now a private house.

The Red House was first fully licensed in 1876 and quickly became renowned for its comfortable, middle class hotel accommodation and facilities.

By the mid-1880s however, the Red House was beginning to suffer from the effects of the economic depression and trade started to fall off. Like many other pubs it ran a savings club. This one was known as the West Hill Benefit Society and had over 100 members. It paid out a lot of sickness and unemployment benefit in the hard times towards the end of that decade.

During the late 1880s and 1890s it developed a reputation as a musical house where customers sang and played musical instruments at 'harmonic evenings'. It was advertised as 'three minutes from St Clement's Caves and the lift to George Street, with a lyric club every Tuesday and accommodation for bean feasts'.

The Red House Harmonic Society carried on for a number of years until it finally amalgamated with the Harmonic Society of the King's Head, Old Town, Hastings' oldest pub. The amalgamated society alternated between the two pubs for 'harmonic Saturday evenings' during the final years of the 19th century.[1]

One evening in 1894 the society hosted a beef pudding supper and musical programme for its members. Herr Jeckel, a native of Coblenz, sang Monte Carlo, with a piano accompaniment. It was reported that 'his broken English added charm to the song'.[2]

By the time of the Edwardian era, the Red House was drawing custom from members of both the Liberal and Conservative parties, who held political meetings here, and from the local bowls club. But by 1903 it seems to have become a radical house, with a Liberal landlord who chaired meetings to discuss, among other things, 'the coming of the trams to Hastings'.

At the turn of the last century it was competing with several other pubs within a few hundred yards. These included the Plough (which is still extant) and the Little Brown Jug, Whitefriars, Angel, Edinburgh Castle and Manor, which have all closed. However, the nearest public house of the same class was the Langham, a mile away.

Just before the First World War the chief constable opposed the renewal of the Red House licence on the grounds of redundancy, when the magistrates queried a fall off in trade. It was pointed out that 'the interior accommodation was extremely good', that it had some 'jug trade' and organised a popular bowls club. A customer with a sense of humour, who appeared as a witness, said the fall off in trade was because, 'the landlord had changed his politics. He got a little controversial.' [Laughter in court.][3]

In 1917 the landlord, James Brown, was called up by the Hastings Military Tribunal, although he 'could not do much walking'. The Tribunal exempted him for one month only, to allow the transfer of the licence to his wife.[4] However, he survived and continued as landlord until 1922.

In 1921 the Red House was offered a handsome compensation of £3,000 if it would close down, but the brewers successfully appealed. Smith & Co., family brewers of Lamberhurst, sold the pub for the same amount to Kemp Town Brewery of Brighton in the same year.

In the Second World War the Red House was lucky. The Emmanuel church across the road was a prominent landmark for German bombers but neither the church nor the pub suffered any damage.

Percy Gardener was the landlord for its last 28 years until 1953, when it was finally declared redundant. He was ill in his final years and had to be brought into court on a stretcher. During 1951 the police visited every pub within a quarter of a mile to establish the custom. All of the pubs had an average of between seven and 16 customers except the Red House, which had only two.[5]

Red House in 2009 now a private residence

Robert de Mortain
The Ridge

2009

This pub is located some three miles from the town centre. The building was originally a lodge house; a large property adjacent to Netherwood House, occupied between the wars by a 'socialist commune', and then during the Second World War partly occupied by an Army Records Office.

As a pub its history revolves around two men from the past whose time in Hastings was nearly 900 years apart. The first is Robert De Mortain, half-brother of William the Conqueror, from whom the pub takes its name. Robert de Mortain is thought to have been responsible for the building of Hastings Castle.

Netherwood House

In the section of the Bayeux Tapestry below, Robert Count of Mortain (right) sits on the left hand side of his half brother, William Duke of Normandy, (William the Conqueror). Robert's full brother Odo sits to William's right, implying his seniority. This scene is thought to be somewhere local, immediately before William ordered the castle to be built on the cliff top, before the Battle of Hastings.

A section of the Bayeux Tapestry

Aleister Crowley

The second person in the pub's history is Aleister Crowley, occultist, satanist, magician and mystic. Crowley lived at Netherwood House from 1945 until his death in December 1947, allegedly practising 'sex magic' and black magic. By this period in his life he had gained a notorious reputation. He has been referred to as 'the beast' and 'the wickedest man in the world'. His detractors believe that he is the secret grandfather of George W. Bush and moreover, that he was responsible for 'putting the curse on Hastings'.

Crowley's ghost haunts the pavement outside the pub and is said to be inspired by some former mischievous activity of his. The pub itself is not thought to be haunted but an energy line or ley line runs through it. Two houses in Netherwood Close, adjacent to the pub, have experienced 'severe weird happenings' in recent years and the High Priest and Priestess of White Witches who live in Hastings have been called in twice to perform exorcism ceremonies there.[1]

In an odd twist in local belief, it is thought that at one time Crowley also lived in an old house against the cliffs beneath Hastings Castle, thereby linking him with Robert De Mortain.

In September 1946 Leney's Brewery of Wateringbury, Kent purchased the freehold of the lodge house, then known as Ripon Lodge Hotel. Following refurbishment, this modern and substantial building was converted into a public house and opened in December 1946, exactly a year before Crowley's death.

Its licence was transferred from the Bedford Hotel in the town centre, which was bombed during the Battle of Britain in 1940. The Bedford licence was held 'in suspense' by Leney's Brewery from 1941 until 1947. The first landlord was Geoffrey Taylor and a successful application[2] was made to change the name from Ripon Lodge Hotel to the Robert de Mortain in April 1948.

The first pub sign, a double-sided sign, was included in Whitbreads miniature inn sign series in about 1950. It was designed by Violet Rutter, who also designed other Hastings Whitbread miniatures.[3] The current sign is a bland Green King multiple.

In the hurricane of 1987 the Robert De Mortain suffered extensive damage and had to have its roof replaced. This unfortunate incident has also been attributed to Aleister Crowley's sinister connection with the pub and with the area!

Roebuck
High Street

Roebuck with Breeds brewery office on the right

The Roebuck public house was an old property situated next to Bourne Passage (now Roebuck Street). Formerly the Star, it originated from a brew house occupied by Thomas Hovenden from around 1778 and was first licensed in about 1800.

In 1839 the Star was the location of a Chartist meeting facetiously reported in the conservative *Sussex Express*:

> **THE CHARTISTS.**— On Wednesday evening, that which the Chartists will doubtless call "a demonstration," took place in a room at a small public-house, called the Star, in High-street. On the morning of that day a few bills, stuck about the town, announced that a meeting of the Chartists would take place as above, at half-past seven o'clock; when Mr. Osborne, from Brighton, would attend. At the appointed hour five persons had strayed into the room, lighted by three candles. At eight o'clock some 30 persons, mostly from curiosity, were present when the

renowned Mr. Osborne asked if someone would take the chair, to which no response was made, and the parties were at a standstill. After a considerable pause a young fellow named Yates, as we understood, said "I will take the chair," and immediately jumped into it, without either vote or other approbation being passed. Mr. Osborne then proceeded to address the meeting at great length, denouncing as vagabonds, thieves, scoundrels and cowards, every sober-minded person who presumed to differ from him and his party. His speech, however, produced but little effect, for, except the now and then a solitary "hear, hear," of the landlord, small indeed was the applause that greeted the vituperative harangue of this agitator from Brighton. At the finish of the orator's observations, he was suddenly seized with a fit of modesty, and could not bring his impudence to move a resolution, but hoped there was some *honest man* like himself, who would do so' but none could be found for a long time who could "screw their courage to the sticking place," to place themselves on a level with so much *honesty*. The chairman, however, having written one, declaratory of their approval of the principles of the Charter, requested some *honest* man to move it. Another pause ensued, when Mr. Perry said he would move it, if any one would second it, but for a long time no one would even do that. At length one appeared in a person from the crowd. Mr. Morley then put some questions to Mr. Osborne, which the other refused to answer, because he considered them personal; and the meeting becoming impatient, the question was put and carried by a large majority—so the Chairman said. The people were then requested to sign the petition, and the meeting ended, without a subscription being proposed!!! Such are the demonstrations so much boasted of in the "National Convention."

1839 [1]

On becoming a coaching inn in 1842, it changed its name to the Roebuck after a privateer, a ship of the same name. 'The privateer was commissioned as a "man of war" under "letters of marque", to cruise against French, Spanish or "rebellious colonial" ships (i.e. American ships) and to take any goods, wares or merchandise from them.' In other words they had government permission to engage in piracy on the high seas. The crew of the Roebuck were recruited at the George Inn, George Street.[2]

The pub's 19ᵗʰ century customers, apart from the stagecoach drivers and their passengers, included the ostlers and stable boys who worked in the stables in Roebuck yard at the rear of the building. In 1854 a carter arrived at the stables to collect a load of dung. It was disagreeable and hot work and the landlord gave him the usual pots of beer and several measures of 'bull'.

'Bull' was a drink concocted by the landlord, by swilling boiling water in gin hogsheads, rum barrels and brandy casks and mixing it together 'for fishermen when they returned from a voyage'. The landlord didn't know the strength of 'bull' but it was literally a killer. The carter died within a few hours of drinking it, but oddly enough at the coroner's inquest which followed, the landlord was only cautioned.

In 1860 the Victoria Tavern, a beer house opposite, was granted a full licence, and the Roebuck, then a century old, complained that it would lose custom. With the Mason's Arms described as 'a tramps' lodging house next door, there were now three pubs within a few yards of each other.[3] In the 1870s yet another beer house, the Duke of Wellington, opened on the south corner of Roebuck Yard, previously Breeds Brewery office, and is still open today.

Drawing of Roebuck yard 1875

243

Roebuck yard c1875

In the 1880s the Roebuck became the headquarters of the St Clement's Bonfire Boys, who organised for bonfire night and held socials and dinners there. Another group, the St Clement's Harmonic and Tradesmen Society, met weekly 'for social intercourse, vocal and instrumental harmony'.[4]

During this period the Roebuck introduced early 'magic lantern' shows, and at least two films were shown to the paying public.

The pub was a privately owned free house until 1894 when it was sold to A.F Styles, the Kent brewers, who owned it for four years. In 1895 the old house was about to be pulled down and new plans were submitted, but for some unknown reason nothing happened.[5]

In 1915 the landlord was called up into the army and sent to war. In 1917 the new licensee fell foul of the Defence of the Realm Act which stipulated that all pubs had to close at 9pm, and at 12.30 one night, a policeman saw a light on and three people in the bar. The three people were the potman, his wife and his brother—a soldier on leave from France. The landlord, Frederick Peppin, was charged and fined £10 for 'allowing people in licensed premises during prohibited hours'. The soldier was fined 1s [5p] 'as he might not have known about the law'.

Tenants of other Hastings' pubs similarly convicted (the Fountain in St Leonards and the Jenny Lind, for example), lost their licences and were replaced by the brewery. In the case of the Roebuck, the brewers were at first lenient because Peppin's wife was dying of cancer.

Two months after this incident, a priest from a Jesuit college on the Ridge, Ore, was seen buying two bottles of beer before the official opening time. In court, Peppin produced a letter from a doctor stating that an invalid priest at the Jesuit college had been ordered to drink beer twice a day with his meals. This was common practice although the court didn't accept it, and he was fined again. This time he was fined a massive £50 and the priest £5. For these offences the landlord was described as 'a traitor to the nation' and lost his licence.[6]

The chief constable described the pub as an 'ill conducted premises', and closed it down in 1918 'as a warning and example' to the other licensees of Hastings and St Leonards.[7] Frederick Peppin, who had lost his wife from cancer, his licence and his pub, disappeared from the town and the life of the Roebuck came to a very sad end.

Site of the Roebuck Inn 2013

Royal Albion and Albion Shades,
Marine Parade and George Street

Early 1900s

The Royal Albion stands on the site of Whitby House, built in 1689 and licensed in 1730. The house was rebuilt in 1831 and reopened in 1832 as the Albion Hotel,[1] a coaching inn on the then fashionable Marine Parade. Excellent stabling and lock-up coach houses were available at the rear of the hotel in George Street.

At that time, the Albion often suffered from bad weather and high tides from across the road, and in 1836 tempestuous weather and a hurricane blew the windows in. Again in 1855 during a great gale and storm, the sea reached George Street and was so fierce it dislodged the York paving slabs on Marine Parade and threw them against the Albion 'like bits of wood'.[2]

From about 1850 to 1880 the Albion's success fluctuated with the rest of the Old Town which meant James Emary, landlord from 1852 to 1864, was always seeking other business opportunities. After the arrival of the railway in 1851, he procured an agreement with the South Eastern Railway Company allowing his flymen the right to ply for hire at Hastings railway station to the exclusion of some other horse-drawn cabs. He also undercut other cabs by charging lower fares, a move which caused local resentment.[3]

In 1863 he added two adjoining houses to the premises creating new smoking rooms and a billiard room. The annual subscription for the Albion Billiards Room, which was promoted as a sort of gentleman's club, was 10s 6d [52½p] a year.[4]

One landlord in the 1860s was John Ellis who gained a bad reputation for 'furious driving' of his horse and carriage along the seafront whilst drunk, and for drunkenness in the bar. "It's all a pack of lies", he exclaimed, when it was proved that he had thrown dangerous missiles at his wife and when it was further proved that he had kicked and struck a policeman 'in two particular parts'. "The first in the chest and the other in the execution of his duty", quipped a local reporter. In court he was reminded that he had 13 convictions for various offences and was bound over with £20 of sureties to behave. His licence was removed and by 1870 he was working as an under-waiter in Lewes.

In 1877 the hotel had four joint licensees. One of them represented the Glasshouse Colliery of Stoke on Trent and sold and delivered coal on their behalf.[5] The coal arrived by sea and was unloaded on the beach.

ALBION HOTEL

Centre of Marine Parade, Hastings.

Completely sheltered from cold Winds by adjacent Hills.

Susan Emary (formerly of the Castle Street Hotel) respectfully solicits from the Nobility and Gentry visiting Hastings, a continuance of that kind patronage and support so liberally experienced from them, for above 14 years, at the Castle.

N.B. - - - Excellent Livery stabling and Lock-up Coach-Houses, contiguous to the Hotel.

Hastings & St Leonards Guide 1843

HORSES, CARRIAGES, &c.

JAMES EMARY, ALBION MEWS, George Street, and
CASTLE MEWS, Wellington Square, Hastings.

Horses Let by the Day, Month, or Year.
Saddle Horses 1s. 6d. Per Hour, with experienced Riding
Masters.
Carriages suitable for Weddings, Picnics, Visiting, etc.
The description of Carriages kept are as under:—
Diorophas, Broughams, Drotchkas, Sociables, Landaus
Barouches, Mail Phaetons, Cab ditto, Basket Carriages, Pony
Phaetons, Dog Carts, &c.
Funeral Equipages of every description.

1859

In common with several other hotels in the south-east the Albion maintained a 'taproom' known as the Albion Shades, on the other side of George Street. The term 'shades' originated in 19th century Brighton as a synonym for wine vaults, but was also a term used elsewhere as 'oyster shades', signifying the availability of prostitutes.

The Albion Shades came into existence as a beer house in the 1830s and was used by prostitutes and their 'gentlemen' customers from the hotel. It is thought that the original cellars and wine vaults, constructed in 1831 by Francis Emary, provided access between the hotel and the Shades, for their benefit. The Albion Shades consisted of a large bar in George Street and a small private bar in Albion Mews (now the West Hill Arcade). In 1879 it became separately owned and licensed[6] and changed its name to the Albion Tavern, although it was still referred to as the Shades for many years. It continued as an independent beer house until 1916 when it was declared redundant and closed.

None of the initiatives taken by various landlords were enough to compensate for the poor economy and all of the licensees between 1850 and 1890 had difficulties making the hotel business pay.

In 1894 the life of the Royal Albion as an hotel came to an end following a pattern in the town.[7] Palace Court was having difficulties at this time and the Havelock Hotel had closed a few years earlier.

The Swan, the York and the Warriors Gate all provided hotel accommodation at one time, but in the 1880s were rebuilt or remodelled as public houses.

A section of the back of the building in George Street was converted into an off-licence and shops, and the hotel became flats. The magistrates expressed regret at the inevitable change from hotel to public house with three bars, but renewed the licence 'on condition that no bar be connected with any of the flats in the building'. Four years later there were just two bars, the usual saloon and a public bar with swinging doors to attract the 'excursionists'.

Excursionists, or day trippers, were also attracted to the nearby Empire Theatre of Varieties, a music hall designed by architect Ernest Runst and opened in 1899 starring Marie Lloyd and Tiller's Eight Fairy Dancers.

'Marie Lloyd' otherwise known as Matilda Wood, and Ernest Runst were both members of the East End Wood family which had financial interests in a number of theatres including the Empire Theatre of Varieties. In 1899 Marie Lloyd acquired the tenancy of the Royal Albion for her father John 'Brush' Wood who became landlord for two years.

All the visiting music hall stars were of course among his customers including Kate Carney, the Coster Queen who ran competitions on stage with her famous song: 'Tanner mouth organs,

---

PARTY AT THE ALBION.–Quite a family party assembled at the Royal Albion Hotel, at the invitation of Miss Dolly Morell, to celebrate her initial visit to Hastings. Host Pa Wood, father of the one and only Marie Lloyd, provided a capital luncheon, Master Johnnie doing the honours. After the usual toasts, Little Alice McNaughton, May Wood, granddaughters of mine host and Theresa Bathurst, Miss Morell's little niece, kept the company entertained with their really clever attempts at statue dancing. Miss Morell delighted her guests with a new song, entitled "Never Interfere." Miss Edie Rivers and Miss Alice Mosedale helped to keep the ball rolling until it was time to adjourn to the Empire, where all these ladies are performing.

1900 [8]

they sound alright'. Anyone who could play was welcome. The music hall became a cinema in 1913 and is now the De Luxe Leisure Centre.

Another attraction was the West Hill Lift (funicular railway) also situated in Albion Mews. In 1890 a celebratory dinner was held in the hotel to commemorate the laying of the 'keystone' in the tunnel arch. The finished structure containing a million bricks, opened in 1892.

The Royal Albion was closed and unoccupied in 1910 after the building was sold and re-licensed. In 1914 at the start of the First World War it closed again and was very nearly declared redundant. Then at the end of the war it closed yet again from November 1918 to January 1919.

In the inter-war period it had at least 15 landlords and in 1941 it closed for the duration of the Second World War, until 1945.

In 1963 the building had to be evacuated, when a leaking gas main caused a series of explosions followed by a blast, sheets of flame and smoke. Thirty-three people were injured and 22 properties were damaged on Marine Parade and George Street. The scene was described as 'an experience worse than the war and like a miniature battlefield'.[9]

The Albion was a venue on the 'Old Town Rock Circuit' in the 1970s and was also the home of some 'Free Form music'. One evening a local journalist observed 'three musicians huddled in the corner like 19th century impressionists sitting in a street café in Paris. As they attempted to create some new, improvised, experimental music, sometimes they lost their way. But gradually a return to the original theme was perceptible and was greeted almost like a long lost friend.' The three musicians were drummer Dave Saunders, guitarist Adrian Underhill and bassist Roger Carey.

Alan Crouch recalls the Albion in the 1980s: "Nearly all the customers were visitors or holiday makers, particularly in the summer", he says. "There was a very good pianist in the bar who played in the boogie style of Winifred Attwell, which pulled the customers in. The pub was tied to Younger's brewery of Edinburgh and was their most southerly pub. This link with Scotland explains the bagpipes behind the bar and the tartan designs set into the wall panels."[10]

Royal Standard
East Beach Street

The Royal Standard is a fishing pub opposite the Stade. The deeds of this quaint building date from 1707 when a shoemaker lived there. It became a beer house in 1822 and in 1856 John Webb was granted a full licence. The magistrate was facetious: "You would rather sell spirits with a licence than without I suppose?" "Yes Sir", he replied.

John Webb was a keen landlord and by 1858 he had acquired a lease to a part of the Stade, opposite the Royal Standard, where he owned a rope and net shop. These facilities were for the use of customers loyal to the Royal Standard. This was a common practice among the fishing pubs. From the 1840s to the 1880s at least, beach leases were held by the Cutter, London Trader, Jolly Fisherman, Eagle and the Dolphin, among others.[1]

In the 1880s when pubs were feeling the effects of competition from grocers with beer licences, the Royal Standard started selling tea and groceries. It became the distribution agent for all tea sold in Hastings' pubs which at one time amounted to 15 hundredweight [762kg] a week.[2] This was helped, no doubt, by the system of allowances for fishing families (see below).

In 1913 this part of Hastings was described as very 'crowded when the fish come in'. The Royal Standard was one of the early morning pubs opening at 5am for boat crews, boys ashore and fish buyers, who sheltered in the pub waiting for fishermen to call out 'sole buyers' or 'cod buyers'.[3] Other customers included boat skippers, mates and the sub coxswain of the lifeboat.

Three boat crews and their boys ashore (a crew member who worked ashore) had allowances in this pub. The allowance enabled them to drink on credit, until the skipper paid the bill on a 'day of settlement'. Fishermen's wives also had allowances, but with the butcher and the baker, who were paid in the same way.[4] The Royal Standard, the Dolphin, the Lord Nelson and the Prince Albert were considered to be the authentic fishermen's pubs according to witnesses at an appeal. Although there were of course several other pubs in the area used by fishermen.

At this appeal in 1900, the fishing pubs lost their early morning licences on the basis that the fishing industry was in decline due to traditional sailing trawlers being out-classed by new steam trawlers. This meant less fishing and less employment for fishermen. An early licence was again refused in 1915, when wartime restrictions on pub opening hours were imposed.[5]

As a fishermen's pub it had a tough reputation, demonstrated by a particular landlady. In 1920 a customer refused to pay up and threw a two gallon [4½ litre] jar of lemonade at the landlord. He was physically thrown out by the landlady, who held him down by the scruff of his neck until he was taken away by the police. He was sentenced to one month's hard labour.

Nowadays the Royal Standard acts as the base for the marble championships on Good Friday and is popular with visitors to the Jack in the Green Festival on May Day. The festival is based on a tradition which started in the 1830s but died out at the start of the 20th century. Revived in 1983, it is now an annual event that takes place during the May Bank Holiday weekend and has become a tourist attraction.

Jack is a 'green man', who represents the spirit of the forest. He is covered in branches and leaves, wears a crown and a green face. He leads a procession and is escorted by dancers dressed up as trees. These people are called bogies or spirits and live in dark places. There are several different groups, including the Hastings Bogies and the Gay Bogies. Behind Jack there are groups of drummers and people carrying sponges soaked in green paint, which are used to dab the noses of spectators. The festival ends at Hastings Castle, where Jack is slain and the spirit of summer is released.

The Royal Standard is tied to the Shepherd Neame Brewery of Faversham. The brewery produces a beer exclusively for the festival. The 4.1% Jack in the Green Special is described as pale and golden with a clean, fruity taste. It is brewed with Maris Otter pale ale malt, sun-dried golden oats, gently kilned caramalt and pure local honey. Shepherd Neame brews only a dozen or so barrels for the festival, which are sold in the Royal Standard, Hastings Arms, Anchor, Ye Olde Pump House and the Stag.

The Royal Standard and its sister pub, the London Trader, have a history of flooding by high tides. Flood marks are recorded on the front of the bar with dates of when the sea has come through the door. In 1967 a deluge of rain at high tide brought floodwater three feet [91cm] high. Thirty-five stranded customers had to stand on the chairs and tables.[6] More recently, in 2007, there was a flash flood about a foot deep [30cm]. With rising sea levels, watch this space.

The Royal Standard usually means the flag of Queen Victoria. This first pub sign shows the flag of King Harold, used in the Battle of Hastings in 1066 when he was defeated by William the Conqueror. Therefore it was unique to Hastings. It was recently replaced by the second sign on page 256.

Smugglers
White Rock

A drawing of the White Rock area in 1844 shows an open space where the site of the Smugglers is today, although it is listed as the Wellington in *Kelly's Directory* for 1845.[1] On 24th June 1850, Anthony Harvey laid a foundation stone on Robertson Street and after the ceremony, the party, accompanied by a band and the builder Richard Cramp, went to the Wellington for a celebratory lunch.[2] In 1852 two employees of Rock's Coach Works, two doors away, went swimming at midnight after an evening in the pub. Only one returned. The verdict: 'Drowned whilst drunk'.[3]

HASTINGS & ST. LEONARDS.—

BUYING A BABY.—At the Borough Bench, on Tuesday last, EDWARD WALTER WELLERD, (60), carpenter, of Vine's-passage, appeared (on bail) in answer to a charge of being drunk and using abusive language.—P.C. Weeks stated on the previous afternoon he was in Robertson-street, and saw prisoner striking a woman with his fist at Claremont.—Prisoner denied that he was drunk, and said he bought a baby, and paid for it like a man, and that was the cause of the disturbance.—Sergeant Dennis stated that prisoner was drunk when brought to the station-house by P.C. Weeks.—Prisoner, in defence, said—I was at work in Stratford-place, and went in to have have my 'lowance, and whilst I was there three women came in and offered a baby for sale. I said, "I'll give you a pot of porter for it." I bought the "youngster" and took it to the Standard to buy it a cake, and when I went back they all fell at me, and I was not going to have my skylight and brains knocked in. I never suffer a man to hit me, much more a woman. I am too good a man for it.—The Mayor—You could not suppose the women were going to let you have have the baby.—Prisoner—She might have had it back, but there was no occasion to drop it on me like that. Women hit pretty hard, you know.—The Mayor—You should not go buying babies.—Prisoner—I will buy anything in the world, if it's old tin.—The Mayor told prisoner it was proved that he was drunk and using abusive language in the street, and they had decided to fine him 5s. and costs. He would advise him not to get drunk and go buying babies again.

1867 [4]

In 1868 landlady Sarah Barton was summonsed for 'allowing bad characters to assemble in her house'. A police constable looking through a side door saw nine women and seven men. He asked the landlady if she 'knew what class of females she had got there'? "No", she retorted, "but I know they are pert and lively".[5] Ten years later the pub had become more respectable, with a billiards room serviced by a billiard marker and the usual barmaids and potboy.

In 1891 a shoe black (a 'shoey'), who lodged at the Bee Hive in the Old Town, was drinking whisky in the front bar with two others when he collapsed. The head barman, Edmund Clarke, and the under barman carried him along the passage to the pot room where he lay covered in blankets. When they returned at 11.30pm he was dead. An inquest decided that he had died from natural causes, but they couldn't discover his name and he was buried anonymously.[6]

In 1894 the pub was taken over by Mrs Frances Harvey, the widow of a well-known Hastings bookmaker. The police suspected the pub 'might become a resort of bookmakers and betting men' and she was warned.[7] They need not have worried as four years later she married the proprietor of Café Monaco next door and the Wellington was taken over by Albert Todd, who was to remain for some 30 years.

Before the First World War, Todd was busy challenging the competition on this part of the front line. In 1914 he protested that the Wellington was losing its middle class customers to the bar of the newly opened Grand Restaurant, opposite Hastings Pier (now the White Rock Hotel). He claimed his pub was their equal and could 'serve all social classes with liquor', indicating perhaps a social change in his customer base.

Late 1950s

But then came war and restrictions. No one was allowed to 'treat' another person or buy alcohol for soldiers and in 1916 when two recuperating Canadian soldiers wanted a drink, someone went into the Wellington and bought them a bottle of whisky, which they drank in the Palace Bars (Pig in Paradise). This person was fined a steep £20.[8]

After the war, Todd opposed the licence for a restaurant at 38 White Rock, as its customers had, up until then, bought alcohol from him. In 1924 he supported changes in pub opening hours for Hastings and was criticised for it by the local churches and the Temperance Association. In 1926 he opposed the reopening of the Palace Bars, before he retired in 1927.

In 1946 the landlord, James Beaven, was summonsed for serving after hours. In court he claimed: "We were having a session on spiritualism and forgot the time".[9] In the same year there was an outbreak of smuggling along the south coast. A Hollington man was fined £300 for smuggling whisky from France and admitted supplying the Wellington with nine cases. This incident accurately indicated the pub's future name; however, for these two convictions James Beaven lost his licence.[10]

The next landlord was Arthur Barber, a saxophonist and leader of the Harmony Aces Dance Band, which included his brother Bill, who played drums. The band started playing at the White Rock Pavilion in 1929 and provided entertainment for the troops during the war. In the 1930s they played on a floodlit raft in the sea between the pub and the pier and also at the West St Leonards Holiday Camp. He retired in 1968.[11]

In 1995 an accident occurred when draymen were making a delivery. After opening the delivery flaps in front of the pub, an elderly woman with poor sight fell into the cellar and sustained bad injuries. Courage, the brewer, was fined £3,000 plus costs.

The original sign showed the Duke of Wellington. After the Second World War it was replaced by a sign of a Wellington bomber, whose pilots were stationed at a local training camp.[12] According to one source, this changed again in the 1970s to the Wellesley Arms, the arms of the Wellington family.[13] Another drinker pointed out that it probably changed because of a post war feeling that reminders of the war should be forgotten. The sign changed again in 1995, to the Smugglers. The Smugglers closed in 2010.

c2008

Smugglers' banner

Engine, Clutch & Gearbox at the Smugglers

Stag
All Saints Street, Old Town

The Stag is a listed building dating back to the 16th century. It is on record as a beer house after the 1830 Beer Act and opened the Stag Benefit Society in 1835. In 1838 the Stag applied for a full licence[1] which indicates that it was not a fully licensed public house at that time. It may have been licensed in a previous century but there is, as yet, no evidence to support a claim that it has been a public house since 1547.[2] The earliest deed held by the brewery is dated 1876.[3]

A report the following year in 1877 described the Stag as: 'An old fashioned Victorian house where plate glass, guilding and brilliant lights are unknown.' 'The bar is still a small compartment for serving liquor.'

An annual event was:

BEATING THE BOUNDS.—All Saint's parish observed the time-honoured custom of perambulating the parish boundary, on Ascension Day. The bound-beating party consisted of the rector, the Rev. G.A. Foyster; the vestry clerk, F. Langham, Esq.; The churchwardens, Messrs. D. Wood and J.B. Ayers the overseers, Messrs. Veness and Kent; Mr. Piper, assistant-overseer; a few parishioners, and seventeen boys from the parochial and Saunders's endowed schools. Starting from the Stag Inn, All Saints-street. The party traced the line indicated on the parish maps and by the bound-stones, up the Old London road to the Hare and Hounds Inn. Thence to the Down Barn, Fairlight road; across to the Pindles, and to Barley lane, down the valley to Ecclesbourne coastguard station. Following the edge of the cliff and high-water mark, the party came to the south-west corner, at Mercer's Bank; thence through Messrs. Burfield's brewery, up the course of the bourne, until the starting point, the Wilderness, was reached. The trip occupied a considerable time, during which the usual process of "impressing" the boundary points on the boys was performed; and there was a scramble for nuts, halfpence, and oranges. The day's proceedings were finished up by the demolition of a supply of creature comforts, provided at the Stag Inn.

1869 [4]

The Stag is best known as the former residence of a witch and her two cats. A notice in the bar explains:

According to legend the French raids upon the towns of the Cinque Ports during the middle ages led to new methods of defence being devised, although only Hastings had a form of aerial surveillance. At Hastings a witch named Hannah Clark was employed for the purpose. Riding on her broomstick, together with her two cats, she became a familiar sight and gave advance warning of many assaults. Her cats kept the Old Town free of rats. The iniquitous Hearth Tax of 1622 brought these events to a close. The tax was collected by ruthless men who took all they could find, in lieu of cash. At the Stag, then, as now, enduring hard times, the tax collectors took everything including the gruel bubbling on the hearth. They even took Hannah's broomstick from a ledge in the chimney where she used to sleep above the embers. In despair Hannah left Hastings in search of a new broomstick, but never returned. Her cats remained but from that day they caught no more rats. During the Great Plague of 1665 Hastings suffered like the rest of the country and it was commonly believed that cats and dogs were to blame, and so it came about that Hannah Clark's cats were bricked into the fireplace, on the ledge where they used to sleep.

Mummified cats and rats

Treasure Trove at The Stag

The discovery years ago of a hoard of gold coins at the Stag Inn, All Saints'-street, was mentioned in an article in a recent issue of the "Observer," and more information about the find has since been given by Mr. Edward Hook, of 33, Sedlescombe-road South. At the time of the discovery, about 45 years ago, he was employed by a local builder, Mr. J.H. Towner, who was carrying out a good deal of work on public houses for Breeds Brewery.

Mr. Hook was apprenticed to Mr. Towner, and he recalls that he was at work in his employer's workshops in Emmanuel-road one day in the year 1905 or 1906 when news came about the discovery of the gold coins at the Stag Inn.

Mr. Hook went to the inn next day and learned that, during alterations in the public bar, another employee of Mr. Towner, Mr. William McConnell, was taking down a headline in the ceiling near the front entrance to the inn, when out rolled a quantity of spade guineas and Spanish doubloons.

The coins, which were covered in dust, were taken to the police as treasure trove and, after several months, rewards were paid out in varying amounts to various employees of the firm. Mr. Hook's share was £2.

HIDDEN BY SMUGGLERS?

To the best of his recollection, Mr. Hook thinks there were between 20 and 30 of each type of coin, and it was the opinion at the time of the discovery that someone in the room above the bar, perhaps smugglers, must have hidden the gold coins in the space between the ceiling and the floor of the upper room, probably taking up a floor board to do so.

Exactly how the coins came to be there, however, will probably always remain a mystery.

Mr. Hook thinks that the mummified cats, now hanging from a beam in the bar, must have been found at a later date.

1951 [5]

The Stag was also home to an unusual pub game. In the 1980s customer Mark Pennington found an historical reference to a game called 'loggats'. In 1603 the landlord of an alehouse nearby was 'not permitted to allow cards, dices, tables, quoits, loggats, scailes, bowles or other unlawful games'. Mark decided to revive it.

The original game was played out of doors and was a variation of bowls. According to Arthur Taylor, the jack was a wheel of hardwood, nine inches in diameter and three or four inches thick. The loggats, long wooden cones about two feet long, were thrown at the jack holding the thin end. The object was to get as close to the jack as possible. In Shakespeare's time loggats was played with bones. In *Hamlet* as an irreverent grave digger buries the corpse, the Prince asks Horatio, "Did these bones cost no more the breeding, but to play loggats with them?"

These two door panels were being used as cloches in the Stag garden and were rescued by Tommy Read in the 1950s [6]

The medieval atmosphere of the Stag has also lent itself to the occult. On Halloween night 1982, 60 people attended a four-hour prayer meeting at All Saints' Church, to combat 'the occult forces of evil' in the neighbourhood. Meanwhile, six people in fancy dress, one dressed as a werewolf, held an 'occult convention' at the Stag, which is just 100 yards from the church. The landlord said: 'They weren't going to do anything. It was a joke.'[7] But the prayer meeting may have influenced the fact that by the 1990s the landlord was taking no chances. He became a member of the Parochial Church Council in 1995.[8]

The Stag 2009

St Leonard
London Road, St Leonards

c1950

One of St Leonards' earliest pubs, designed by architect Walter Inskip, the St Leonard, formerly the Warrior's Gate, opened in 1833[1] when it was occupied by George Hyland. The original building included hotel accommodation and was much larger than the current pub.

In 1839 the Adelaide Lodge of the Oddfellows was established here, with 450 members and average annual receipts of £700. In the Lodge Room, each member paid a joining fee of between 5s and 20s [25p–£1] according to age and drew sickness benefit of 12s [60p] a week for up to a year, with a free local doctor. The lodge also paid death benefits of £12 and £6 on the death of a wife. It was described as 'one of the most secure investments among the Friendly Societies in the country'. In a typical initiation ceremony, a new member was blindfolded and taken to the lodge room. His proposer and seconder knocked three times and gave a password to a doorkeeper. A member then shook his hand and asked if he had joined of his own free will. A declaration of principles was read aloud, a litany was chanted and a long clay pipe, a symbol of purity, friendship and peace, was handed to him. With his right hand he pressed the clay pipe to his heart and snapped it with both hands. An oath of secrecy was read out which he repeated. The blindfold was then removed to reveal the chairman in regalia standing on a dais before an altar. All present formed a chain and danced around him singing Auld Lang Syne, which was followed by a welcome speech and drinks all round.

Every Whitsun hundreds of members celebrated with a grand parade. This started at the pub and complete with banners and bands marched to White Rock, where they joined other branches from pubs such as the Anchor, the Crown and the Swan.[2] The day ended with eating and dancing, usually to the music of the St Leonards Quadrille Band, which included Thomas Brett playing guitar and Tom Reed, a 'hard handed violinist and untiring fiddler'. A typical

Thomas Brandon Brett

'soiree' held in 1860 was attended by 120 Oddfellows who had an 'excellent tea' at 4pm followed by dancing 'with other amusements until the following morning'.[3]

For several years in the 19th century the Oddfellows Lodge secretary was Thomas Brandon Brett (1816–1906). Brett was a renowned figure in the St Leonards community. Apart from his role as lodge secretary he was also the proprietor, printer and journalist of the St Leonards (& Hastings) Gazette and a noted local historian.

As a dancing master he also taught the Oddfellows to dance and there are accounts of him giving lessons, in particular, on how to dance the

1913–1914

quadrille, to which he supplied the music with the St Leonards Quadrille Band.

In 1917 the building was reduced in size and partly converted into shops and flats. The pub was then located at the junction of Norman Road and London Road. The Warriors Gate was one of five pubs bombed in 1943. The pub burst into flames, trapping and killing a number of people including the landlord, his wife and a customer, who were rescued from the basement.[4] The pub was totally destroyed by the bombing and the brewers applied to erect wooden huts as a temporary measure. They were opposed by the council on the basis that this might hold up postwar town planning. "If we allow this", a spokesman said, "we would soon have a town of wooden shacks".[5] The pub was rebuilt in 1950 on the corner of Shepherd Street, and the post office now stands on the original site.

In the 1970s, darts champion Denny Gower became landlord. He captained the Warrior's Gate darts team into the finals of the Vernon's Treble Top in 1976, and in the following year he achieved two world records. One was for playing three games of 301 in the amazing time of 2 minutes 9 seconds, which required each game to be played in 40 seconds—the average time most players take to decide what to aim for(!) and the second record was for an 'arm's

Denny Gower 1979

length round-the-board-on-doubles' feat, which he did in 9.2 seconds. Gower was also Sussex champion from 1968 and overall won 200 silver cups.[6] Pat Dunn recalls that he also played bass guitar with a band. She heard him play in the Angling Club in the Old Town at about this time, and according to Pat, he was a much better darts player than a musician.[7]

At the time Denny Gower considered changing the pub's name to the Darts Inn, but this never happened.[8] The pub's first name was Warhouse Gate, after a lime kiln that originally stood on the site. It kept this name for seven years until 1840, when it was changed to Warrior's Gate, the name of a planned Regency housing estate designed by architect Lewis Vulliamy in 1843, on the site of what is now Warrior Square. However, Vulliamy's plan never came to fruition.[9]

Before the First World War it was known as the Warrior's Gate and London Distillery. Its last two pub signs referred to the Norman invasion, as portrayed on a section of the Bayeux Tapestry. In 1950 the sign was included in Whitbread's collection of miniature inn signs.[10]

The Warrior's Gate closed in 2006 and reopened as St Leonard in 2012.

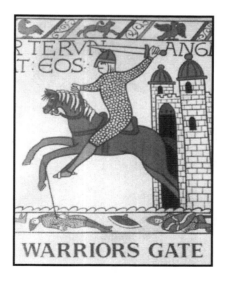

St Leonard 2013

Tivoli Tavern
Silverhill

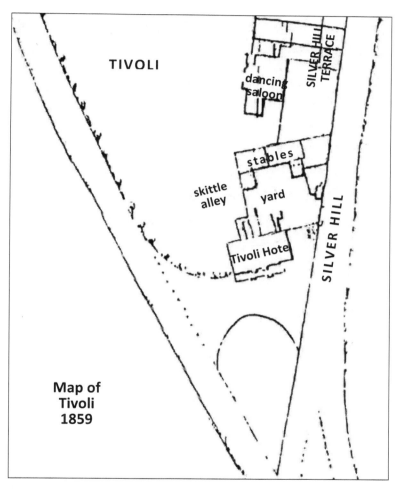

TIVOLI

dancing saloon

SILVER HILL TERRACE

stables

skittle alley

yard

SILVER HILL

Tivoli Hotel

Map of
Tivoli
1859

There is no known photograph of the original Tivoli Tavern

The Tivoli Tavern first opened in about 1836 on a site at the junction of the Silverhill crossroads. It was then owned by William Mantell Eldridge of the Crown Brewery St Leonards and the first landlord was William Edlin.

Its brief history of 24 years can be gleaned almost entirely from newspaper reports.

The rural character of the area was revealed in a court case over a fatal 'Prize Fight' which took place in a field next to the Tivoli Tap Room in 1838. The fight was reported in the county press:

FATAL PRIZE FIGHT

On Monday last a fight took place in a field nearly opposite the Tivoli Tavern, between a man of the name of John Bean and Charles Lee, one of the gypsy tribe. They fought for about one hour and a half, and in the last round, Bean fell down senseless, and expired the following day at the Tivoli Tavern. An inquest was held on the body before N.P. Kell, Esq., on Tuesday, and the following evidence was adduced:- 'Wm. Edlin, landlord of the Tivoli, sworn: The deceased was brought to my house a little after twelve on Monday; some of the party who brought him in, I believe, had been engaged in the fight. When he was brought in he was laid on the table on his back, in the tap-room; he was not sensible, he appeared to be stunned. I did not observe that he was much bruised; I washed his face with some brandy and water; he laid on the table about one hour. A surgeon was sent for; and Mr. Whitworth arrived immediately; he bled the deceased, and ordered him to be put to bed. I had the deceased put to bed; he had all the attention that could be given to him since he has been in my house, by myself and Mr. Whitworth, the surgeon. He died about 10 o'clock this morning; I have not seen him since he was carried up stairs until the present moment.

Frederick Handley sworn: I live in the parish of St. Mary in the Castle, Hastings; I am a printer; I was present at the fight, and saw a person of the name of Charles Lee, who is a labourer, and lives in Hastings, fighting with deceased. Charles Lee, sen., seconded his son; he is a sweep. The deceased was seconded by W. Henbrey; he lives in Castle-terrace; he is a labourer. I do not know how long they fought before I got there. I think they fought about three-quarters of an hour after I arrived. I suppose there were between 30 and 40 persons witnessed the fight. The deceased did not appear exhausted, he laughed and sung. He fell with a broken neck. Lee fell upon him. He stood before his man a second or two sparring then staggered and fell. Verdict: Manslaughter against the principle Seconds.

1838 [1]

Brett informs us that another landlord, Thomas Phillips, had an agreement with William Eldridge whereby he need only pay rent when monthly beer sales achieved a certain level. He tells the story that "so salaciously did Phillips attempt to keep just under the stipulated quantity that on one occasion when a party of huntsmen appeared (who were) likely to threaten sales Phillips moralised on moderation and set a limit on their beer."[2]

The Tivoli Tavern was adjacent to the Tivoli Pottery, also owned by Eldridge who unsuccessfully put both businesses on the market 'for sale or let' in 1839.

TO BREWERS, TAVERN KEEPERS, & OTHERS.
Most eligible opportunity for Business or Investment.

TO BE LET OR SOLD, with immediate possession, the TIVOLI TAVERN, and extensive gardens and pleasure grounds, and gardener's cottage, covering about 5-acres of land with excellent stables and yard, well supplied with water, now occupied by William Edlin, situate about a mile distant from Hastings and St. Leonards, at the junction of and fronting the two London Roads, forming a triangle with, and so placed as to catch the whole ingress and egress (either on business or pleasure) to and from those celebrated places. The gardens are calculated for nursery and horticultural purposes, and the pleasure grounds consist of nearly 3 acres of wood covered with timber and underwood, intersected with walks, arbours, and fish ponds, and opening to beautiful views of the country and sea. Adjoining land might be had admirably adapted, and partly formed, for cricket ground and bowling green, etc. No place could be better calculated in the hands of a spirited occupier to give amusement and recreation to all classes, and ultimately to become a most attractive and profitable concern. It must be seen to judge of its advantages.

The owner being anxious to realise, is prepared to make liberal terms with an eligible tenant or with a purchaser.

N.B. The owner has also a brewhouse and beer-shop adjoining it, now let to John Evenden, situate near the Saxon Hotel, at the entrance between Hastings and St. Leonards, and he will treat for the sale of these if a purchaser should wish to connect the two properties, so that one might assist the other, and give together a most eligible business.

To view the premises, apply to the tenants, and for further particulars to Mr. WALTER INSKIPP, London Road, Saint Leonards or to Mr. BEECHAM, Solicitor, Hawkhurst, postage to be paid.

1839 [3]

The hey-day of the Tivoli was undoubtedly the 1840s and 1850s when the attractions of the Tivoli Gardens were regularly advertised. In 1845 Richard Harman formerly of the Hastings Arms, became landlord and attempted to continue the 'Hastings Rock Fair' then in the process of being banned from the town. Silverhill being outside the Hastings boundary doubtless led Harman to believe he would be free to hold it there. However, the Excise soon reminded him that the fair was illegal putting a stop to the plan.

TIVOLI TAVERN AND GARDENS, HASTINGS

R. HARMAN (late of the Hastings Arms Inn, Hastings), having taken the above splendid establishment, respectfully informs the public that as

ROCK FAIR

Has been forbidden by the authorities, to be held within the Borough of Hastings, in future that

ANCIENT FESTIVAL

Will be held at the Tivoli, on the 26th and 27th of July as from time inmemoria. R.H. In thus making known his intentions, hopes to give universal satisfaction.

The splendid grounds open to the public daily for lunch, dinner or tea parties accommodated on the shortest notice. Choice wines and spirits, prime East India and other ales, Dublin and London stouts in draught or bottle. Excellent beds and stabling.

Coaches to and from the Staplehurst Station daily.

Any communication in reference to Rock Fair is requested to be sent, addressed to Mr. RICHARD HARMAN, Tivoli, Hastings. Standings for booths, exhibitions, and stalls free. Tivoli is one mile from Hastings and St. Leonards, and without the limits of the Borough.

1846 [4]

Nine years later, in 1855, Tivoli advertised its gardens again:

TIVOLI NEW ORNAMENTAL GARDENS,
HASTINGS AND ST. LEONARDS.

FIRST GRAND FETE AND GALA will take place on MONDAY next, 13th August. Magnificent display of Fireworks, Rockets, Shells, Mines, Golden Rain and Coloured Fires, concluding with a spectacle, a scene in Macbeth.— witches with boiling caldron of liquid fire.

The gardens brilliantly illuminated with many hundred variegated lamps. An additional Band in attendance.

A Montgolfier Balloon will ascend at Six o'clock. Fireworks at half-past Eight.

The Mechanical Exhibition will be lighted up on this occasion.

Admission 6d. Each till Four o'clock; after Four. 1s. Children half-price.

1855 [5]

And also in 1856:

TIVOLI GARDENS. -the principal point of attraction among our resident and visiting gentry, seems at present to be these magnificent grounds. Considering the short time they have been re-laid out and enlarged by the present proprietor, the beauty and luxuriance they exhibit on all sides, is really surprising. Annuals, perennials, and choice flowers of every description are showing forth in their richest varieties,. In the course of another week, upwards of 150 standard roses will be spreading around their splendour of colour and perfume. Variegated parterres, intersected with well-arranged walks, collections of statuary grouped in different parts of the gardens, clean cut lawns, and shady bowers with their full foliage, are objects well worth an hour's enjoyment during the present season of the year. Some of our principal boarding schools, as also of the families of the gentry who have paid a visit to the Tivoli gardens on the select and private days, have found that these by no means exhaust the attractions of the place. Mr. Hutchinson has taken care to place at different spots about the grounds pretty little amusements for pretty little folks, which, with the curious clock-work performer on the organ, the mechanical exhibition with its grotesque assemblage of moving drolleries, &c., are the delight of the juveniles. Shortly there is to be a grand display of fireworks upon a scale similar in extent to those of last year. This, however, will be an evening attraction, and will in no way interfere with the more private visits and select picnics of day visitors.

1856 [6]

By 1857–8 James Barnett, formerly of the British Queen, St Leonards was in charge. But his time here was cut short when in 1858 the estate was sold to a property speculator and in 1860 the Tivoli Tavern was demolished.

SILVERHILL, NEAR ST. LEONARDS

The Tivoli Hotel, with its beautiful and extensive pleasure Grounds, several Dwelling Houses and Cottages, an old-established Pottery, and sundry plots of Building Ground, in a healthy and picturesque situation, commanding fine sea and inland views.

Mr. V. J. Collier

Has received peremptory instructions TO SELL BY AUCTION, at the Swan Hotel, Hastings, on Thursday, 23rd September, at Two for

Three o'clock precisely, in lots, a valuable and highly improvable FREEHOLD PROPERTY, distant but little more than a mile from Hastings and St. Leonards, comprising a spacious and substantially built house, known as the Tivoli Hotel, with the cottage, stabling, and premises attached, a small residence contiguous; and extensive well-planted pleasure grounds in the rear, laid out with considerable taste, and occupying altogether a large and valuable surface in a beautiful spot, bounded on two sides by the turnpike roads, leading to Battle, Sedlescomb, and Hawkhurst. There is an ornamental shrubbery in front, forming a valuable addition to the property, which, it is suggested, might be advantageously converted into a private residence, in which case the license might be removed to another part of the estate. Also a neat double Cottage residence, three single Cottages, and a large Building, formerly used as a distillery, in Silver Hill Terrace. An old-established pottery and six labourers tenements, together with several plots of building ground, affording admirable sites for the erection of villa residences.

1858 [7]

James Barnett then took over another house further along the Battle Road also named Tivoli Tavern which has only recently closed. The *Sussex Express* noted that "Mr Barnett has obtained a transfer from his old house to his new one at Tivoli" and also that the bones of a mammoth type animal were found during the demolition:

A DISCOVERY OF FOSSILIZED REMAINS

was made on Tuesday last. Some workmen were engaged in excavating a drain for the new house erecting by Messrs. Carey and Aveling for Mr Newton Esq., of St Leonards, on the site of the old Tivoli Tavern, when they discovered a number of petrified bones of immense size. There is reason to believe that the skeleton of an animal of the mammoth or antediluvian epoch is embedded on the spot. The largest bone exhumed is the shank of a leg which measures 2ft. 8in. in length, with a proportionate circumference. The soil is marl, and the remains were found about six feet from the surface.

1860 [8]

Tower
London Road

1910–1914

This pub is named after a former toll gate and tower on London Road. It opened in 1866 with 12 rooms, two parlours and a bar. In the final years of the 19th century, there were reports of customers drinking 'pots of gin hot and eating Welsh rarebit'. The custom of 'hustling the hat', a means of deciding who paid for the drinks, was practised here. Each participant put a (marked) coin into a hat which was shaken and tipped out, and all coins showing heads were withdrawn. The tails were put back into the hat, the process repeated and the final or 'true tail' had to pay for 'pots all round'. This was a custom that

THEODORE LODGE, RAOB
LADIES NIGHT

A grand concert was held on Wednesday evening last at the Tower Hotel, the room in which the above took place being artistically decorated with plants and bunting by the host and hostess (Mr and Mrs Squires), each lady and gentleman receiving a button-hole.

An excellent programme was carried out by the following artistes: Mr Collins (vice-chairman) opened the ball with "My Daddy's a gentleman", being loudly applauded. Following on came a duet by Mr. W. Beverley (banjo) and Mr. E. Martin (violin), which appealed strongly to all lovers of music. Next came that sweet pathetic song "Good-bye", which was faultlessly rendered by Mrs. Holdstock. After this was a comic song by Mr Whyborn, who convulsed the company with "Dottv-otty". Mr L Guttridge's rendering of "Jack's the boy", from the "Geisha", was acknowledged the hit of the evening. Mr Bernard Theodore, "The Entertaining Comedian", was responsible for the funniest song of the evening, entitled "Look at me looking at you", which caused roars of laughter. The next on the programme was Mrs. Hughes, who delighted her hearers with an old-fashioned song, "Ring-dum-dah", after which the Chairman (Mr. F Hunt) sang that most popular of songs, "Sail away", which filled those present with delight, the swinging chorus being taken up unanimously. Following came a trio by Miss Buchanan (mandoline), Mr. W Beverley (banjo), and Mr. E. Martin (violin). Mr. Whyborn again delighted the audience with "Running up and down our stairs", after which Mr. Freeman gave that touching song from "Humanity". "Only a Jew", being greatly appreciated. And now comes the grandest turn of all the items in the programme, "Merlin—Magician". This gentleman simply held the company spellbound by his marvellous manipulation of cards, balls, etc., etc. The committee of this entertainment should congratulate itself on being so fortunate as to secure so wonderful a magician. Mr. J. Fuller, "The Local Comedian", met with his usual success, singing "Let her drown", which convulsed the company, especially the ladies. Perhaps the cleverest and most talented entertainer of the evening was Mr. C. Harris, whose imitation of birds (with his throat alone) was simply marvellous, his imitation of the skylark and nightingale wonderfully true to nature, and little short of miraculous. Mr and Mrs Squires and the concert committee are to be congratulated on the manner in which they conducted the above.

1903 [1]

The Tower House and Toll Gate, from an Oil Painting by JR Mitchell, 1865

sometimes led to trouble and was frowned upon by the police.

In 1943 the pub was bombed by the Luftwaffe and a thousand pound bomb landed in the cellar, but miraculously failed to explode. It was defused and lifted out through the cellar flaps. In 1991 the pub was threatened again. This time with demolition to make way for the proposed Hastings bypass. An interesting wooden sign in the bar states that: 'Members of the Hastings Temperance Society are banned from this pub'.

Bomb in the cellar

PATRICK KAVANAGH is a former bomb disposal officer who now lives in Coventry. Here he recounts the day that he and his colleagues were called to St Leonards in 1943.

SUNDAY 23rd May, 1943, was the date on which an unexploded bomb landed in the cellar of a public house in St Leonards.

The area was evacuated and the Bomb Disposal Squad, of which I was a member, was called in to deal with it. We diffused the bomb, rendering it harmless, and on the following Monday morning removed it through the cellar.

A photographer from the Hastings Observer was called and recorded the event. All of us in the company purchased the paper that week and the following week, but no photograph ever appeared it it, or in any subsequent following weeks. On checking we discovered that had the photograph been published the editor could have been sentenced to life imprisonment in the Tower of London, as this was classified information and no photographs allowed.

My daughter is now living in Springfield Road, St Leonards, and whilst there recently on holiday, deciding to have a drink one evening, I strolled down to what seemed to be the nearest public house. Talking to a customer who was recalling a wartime incident of an unexploded bomb, I told him about my wartime experience, but could not recall the name of the pub to which we had been called. He suggested I should see a photograph of a bomb being removed through a cellar. "The Tower" in which I was drinking was the self same pub of those many years ago.

I must say I was delighted to see the photograph bringing many memories back of brave men who did not survive the war, through the dangerous and perilous work they carried out.

Bombing became part of the daily life of the people of the area as older residents will remember, after the bombs, the "Doodle Bugs" and rockets had been inflicted on them, with their menacing wailing.

It was nostalgic to have those times brought back to me, happily now buried under half a century of time. Those of us still alive who served in that company will be old men now, sometimes reliving those days of uncertainty and hazards.

1990 [6]

Union Bar and Dripping Well
Cambridge Road

The Union Bar, formerly the Carpenter's Arms, is listed in the directory for 1845[1] and was a beer house for some years before that date. In 1884 it was renamed the Cambridge Hotel.[2] A lot of its history is centred on the upstairs club room, which must be one of the most widely used pub rooms in Hastings. For many years it was the meeting place of printers' and compositors' trade union branches, known as chapels. The printers themselves worked next door in the *Observer* building and at Parsons print works on Claremont.

In the 19th century, printers also used the room for smoking concerts. A typical printer's 'smoker' had singers and soloists playing the cornet, mandolin and violin and 'comic recitations', among other acts.

In 1900 it was the room where 43 local army volunteers received an honorary breakfast, accompanied by speeches from the mayor, before leaving for South Africa and the Boer War.[3] From 1937 the same room was home to the semi-finals and finals of the Annual *Observer* Darts Tournaments, although the Cambridge darts team itself was unlucky.[4]

From 1907 until 1934 the landlord, James Bargent, was a well-known Hastings' personality, and before the First World War he was the secretary of the London Cab Company. He was a member of the Buffaloes and received every Buffalo honour, including Provincial Grand Primo for Sussex. He ran the refreshment bars at the Central Cricket Ground and at the bowls tournaments at White Rock.[5]

During the Second World War, the clubroom was used to promote campaigns in support of the war effort. In his book *Hastings at War,* Nathan Goodwin says that 1940 was the year that 'Alderman Blackman launched the Hastings Spitfire fund in an attempt to raise £5,000 for a new Hastings Spitfire'. Donations came from all over town including its many pubs. The Cambridge darts team was contributor to the fund and all scores under 10 required a halfpenny in the Spitfire tin. Hastings eventually got its Spitfire, known as the 'Hastings', which went to war with a Polish crew about a year later.[6]

Jim and Di Davidson took over in 1961 and for the next 20 years the Cambridge was Hastings' most popular pub. Jim remembers: "At one time the brewery lorries from Maidstone carried enough beer for four Hastings' pubs. At the height of our popularity we had a lorry load of beer to ourselves. Many different people used the pub; all of the Hastings trade union branches met in the upstairs room. These included ASLEF (the train drivers' union), railwaymen, taxi drivers and others. The printers' chapels had always met there." It was the meeting place for Hastings Trades Council from at least the 1950s to the 1970s.

Jim continued: "Numerous clubs and societies also met upstairs, including the Cage Birds Society and the Hastings Hill Walkers. In the 1960s when traditional Latin mass in the Catholic Church was banned by Rome, the local congregation hired the big room and held mass there. At first we didn't know what they were doing,

The Fantastic BEER ENGINE

57 CAMBRIDGE ROAD • 420074

Every Wednesday Night

Forfeit, Prize & Quiz Nite!

Try a totally fun night out - including the 1 minute Bar Dash

Saturday 1st October 1994 at 8pm

The British Armwrestling Association

Presents

OVER THE TOP

PRIZES & TROPHIES

Mystery Beer Competition!

WIN A MOUNTAIN BIKE

THE ONLY PUB WITH THE

88p-a-pint Recession Session Bitter

If you're looking for something fun & different
Try The Beer Engine!

ONE NIGHT COULD CHANGE YOUR IDEA OF A GOOD NIGHT OUT!

1994

but they met there for about two years and had a drink afterwards.

"Ed Burra, painter and printmaker, and John Banting, surrealist painter, both with work in the Tate, drank there regularly, as did George Melly. Another customer in the 1970s was *Observer* editor, Gary Chapman. The Cambridge was one of his favourite pubs. We were having problems with the high rent charged by the brewery at the time and Gary wrote some criticism about the brewers in the paper. The brewers didn't want negative publicity and 'encouraged' us to move, which we did in 1982."[7]

In the 1960s Peter Skinner was a reporter on the *Observer*. "One of the regulars", he reminisces, "was a guy called Frank Rhoden, who ran the Hastings International Chess Congress—one of the biggest in the world. Because of Frank, all the Soviet Grand Masters and people who were legends in the chess world came into the Cambridge during the congress. They dressed up as English parsons in grey flannel trousers, tweed jackets and pipes. They did this because they had a notion of what the middle classes in England were like and they aped it. All these Grand Masters sitting there, looking like country parsons. They wandered down because Frank was the organiser, they came to an English pub and they would play chess with the customers. I played with a number of them.

"Probably because of Frank, there was a thriving chess community. I played chess at lunchtimes with printers or other journalists. Jim kept the boards. He was a very easy going and likeable guy. The other thing, it was only 250 yards from the Hastings Chess Club, the only club in Britain which had its own building and which opened from 1pm to 11pm, every day of the week.

"Hastings has a great chess tradition and the players would walk down to the Cambridge. I played with Smyslov and a Dutch player, whose name I can't remember. All the great players of the 60s would come in and play. Some of them would play everybody in the pub at the same time, without even thinking about it. But they loved the notion of the pub—an English pub.

"It was an eclectic mix of printers, journalists, artists, chess players and darts players. It really was a socially mixed pub—there was no notion of class, and everybody went into the public bar."[8]

In the early 1980s the *Observer* moved and in 1982 longstanding landlord Jim and his wife Di moved to the Railway in St Leonards. The incoming landlord changed the name to Tavern in the Town and created a nostalgic Victorian atmosphere, supposedly reminiscent of the seaside at the turn of the previous century. The downstairs bars became one and various artefacts including a bathing machine; sign boards and a collage of Victorian seaside postcards were installed.[9] In the mid-1990s the name changed to the Beer Engine and then became a teenage, gothic pub called the Tubman, before becoming the Union Bar in 2013.

Meanwhile, the Dripping Well next door started life about 1850 as a beer house run by Elizabeth Collins, who advertised herself as a 'Baker, Grocer and Beer Retailer'. About 20 years later it was licensed to her son, Joseph Montegue Collins, and had acquired the name the Dripping Well after a popular Victorian era natural attraction located in Hastings Country Park.

From 1894 until 1937 the premises were run by Dennis Coppard and were shared with Charles Lane, a wholesale confectioner. Dennis Coppard was one of the longest serving landlords in the town with over 43 years' service.

Although it was policy to close one pub where two were adjacent, both pubs have escaped this fate. Both are situated on the slope of Cambridge Road, and the Dripping Well is built on two levels with one bar overlooking the other.

DRIPPING WELL

"Dripping Well" is a small stream, in a beautiful and romantic glen, about three miles from Hastings:—

Away, away to the Dripping Well!
In the wild and far ravine,
Where towering cliff and shady dell
And spangling moss are seen!
It seems as though I felt the thrall
Of a deep and solemn spell.
As I list the tinkling waters fall,
Of the lonely Dripping Well!

Away, away, from the city's din,
To that sweet secluded spot,
Where the pang of care, and the lure of sin,
May be alike forgot!
Ah many a bright and happy time
I have roved in that fair dell;
While my heart was sooth'd by the gurgling chime
Of the lonely Dripping Well!

J.P. Douglas 1853

Dripping Well c1960

The Volunteer
Middle Street

Elizabeth Beale 1920

This small beer house in Middle Street was run by at least three generations of the Beale family. Margaret Beale (known as Minnie), who was born 1920 in a cottage behind the Hole in the Wall, Hill Street, grew up in the Volunteer.

The photograph on page 291, of Elizabeth Beale, Minnie's aunt, was taken outside the pub in about 1920. Minnie's father, grandfather and great-grandfather were all licensees of the Volunteer one after the other from 1910–1947. All three landlords had the same name: Frederick Edwin Beale, as did Minnie's brother. Minnie's mother was Emily Beale, Minnie's grandmother was Mildred Beale although her great-grandmother's name is unknown.

Watney's Pimlico Ale, advertised at the top of the building, has an interesting history. Pimlico Ale was originally brewed on a farm (Pimlico Farm) in Derbyshire and sold in London pubs. It was eventually brewed at the Stag Brewery in what later became the Pimlico district of London. Thus an area of the capital is named after an old ale. It had a reputation as a strong ale and those who drank it were considered serious drinkers. Although the reputation of this beer had changed by the time of the photograph the name still

Minnie Howlett

carried overtones from the past and in Hastings it was popular with fishermen.

"We had a lot of customers from the fish market", began Minnie, "and from the fishing community generally. Mother's home-made cheesecakes–a cheese pastry–had a local reputation; they were much talked about and in demand. The fishermen queued up for them on Sundays when mother gave them out for free.

"The Volunteer had two separate small bars and a big room at the back used for darts, cribbage and shovepenny. On Saturday evenings we had a pianist who played and sang in there and people danced. Women came into the pub but were always accompanied by their husbands. They never came on their own. Thursday night", added Minnie, "was volunteer drill night in the 'shed' and so Thursday nights were very busy and packed with volunteers.

"The Priory stream ran underground through the area and sometimes flooded the cellar. I remember the bottles clanking about in the cellar as they floated in the flood water. I was there in the Second World War when the area was bombed. I can remember the bombing of Middle Street and the reverberations which shook the pub, but the Volunteer itself wasn't hit. The pub closed during the Blitz in 1940, reopened, then closed again in 1947 when father died."[1]

A new landlord, Edward Booth, took over in 1948 and at 20 became the youngest landlord in Hastings at that time. The late Ron Fellows remembered that: "Teddy Booth was brought up in the Clarence two doors away where he was fostered by my uncle Fred and aunt Edith (Frederick and Edith Standen 1943–1949). I think they had some influence in getting him the licence of the Volunteer."[2]

Teddy Booth was granted a wine licence in 1949, ending the Volunteer's 82 years as a beer house. It stayed open for another seven years until it was finally declared redundant by the magistrates and closed in 1956.[3] The pub sign is now in Hastings Museum.

Double-sided pub sign

Wheatsheaf and Bricklayers Arms
Bohemia Road

Wheatsheaf

Bohemia's early history is peppered with the surname of Jinks and many members of the Jinks (extended) family once resided in the district. In the second half of the 19th century, at least 25 people with this surname, in six family branches, lived along Bohemia Road. Their adult occupations ranged from the building trades, shop keeping (one was a greengrocer), taking in laundry and running pubs.[1]

Bohemia's first pub, the Wheatsheaf, was built by John Jinks, a bricklayer who had previously been a squatter on the America Ground, where he had a ready-made clothes shop. This was approximately where 40 Robertson Street is today (Hoagies Reloaded Café).

When the 'Americans' were given notice to quit in 1835, John Jinks moved to Spittleman's Down, later called Bohemia Place and now a part of Bohemia Road. He built the sandstone wall on the eastern side of Bohemia Road (probably the walled garden), houses in White Rock and Prospect Place, and ornamental brickwork in Warrior Square. He was also an early landlord of the Wheatsheaf.[2] From 1848 to 1911 the Wheatsheaf was run by the Pratt family. In 1856 when the pub was advertised for sale, its stables (now the Pizza Hut takeaway) and skittle alley were especially mentioned.

During the time of the Pratt family, the Wheatsheaf was popular with skilled artisans and respectable tradesmen, who regarded themselves as superior to the unskilled labouring classes. These men, dubbed the 'Aristocracy of Labour', usually wore bowler hats and ties and in the 1870s they set up a number of branches of the Conservative Working Men's Association in Hastings. The Bohemia and Silverhill branch met at the Wheatsheaf and had at least 100 members. Their secretary, George Upton, was also one time landlord of the Prince of Wales.[3]

From 1913 until 1922 the pub was known as Ye Olde Wheatsheaf. In the latter year it was sold by the brewery for £4,000 and reverted back to its original name. In 1917 the landlord was fined a steep £5 for serving a soldier with a bottle of beer[4] and in 1919 he was fined again, this time for overcharging.[5]

A short distance from the Wheatsheaf, a beer house known as the Bricklayer's Arms was located at 21 Bohemia Place from at least 1853 (when it was licensed to a Miss Young) to 1868. In 1865 it was licensed to another member of the Jinks family, Fanny, probably John's niece, a young widow aged 32. She fell foul of the law when she was summonsed for 'failing to admit the police' at 12.15am.

When the police eventually got into the house 'they found two men drinking beer in an upstairs room'. The summons was dismissed after a caution with the comment: "We want to teach beer house keepers that the police must be admitted immediately".[6] However, she was summonsed again in 1866 for 'keeping bad time'. Her brother appeared in court on her behalf.

'P.C. Marchant stated that about half-past eleven on Sunday night he was at Bohemia and heard a noise at defendant's house. He went there and on looking in one of the windows, saw several men sitting in the room smoking. He saw one of the men take up a quart pot and drink from it. The door was unlocked and he went into the house. He saw defendant's brother who said their clock was fast enough and that no beer had been drawn after 11 o'clock.' Fanny Jinks was fined £1 with costs.[7]

James Standen is listed as the next licensee in 1867/8 but 21 Bohemia Place is not listed as a beer house after that date. It was most likely a free house as there is no reference to it being tied to a local brewery.

It was probably the case that after two offences the Excise refused to renew Fanny's licence or that she couldn't cope with further scrutiny by the police. Equally, James Standen probably didn't wish to be associated with the name of the Bricklayer's Arms. In any case after 1868 it reverted to an ordinary residential house which later became number 132 Bohemia Road after the road was renumbered.

The 1871 census lists John Jinks (bricklayer) and family now living at 31 Bohemia Place and Fanny Jinks (widow) and family living at 26a Jinks Passage, possibly a twitten off Cornfield Terrace. She was then working as a laundress.

Some time between 1868 and 1871, James Standen became the licensee of another beer house at 29 Bohemia Place. This beer house later became known as the Barleycorn and later still as the Hearts of Oak.

The Pelluet family moved into number 132 in the 1930s and Cyril Pelluet was born there in 1940. He says: "As a child I always believed the house to be haunted and my father insisted it had been a pub sometime in the past and that there might be a connection between the pub and a ghost."[8]

Although 132 Bohemia Road is the site of the Bricklayer's Arms, the original house seems to have been rebuilt. The more modern pair of semi-detached houses that stand today do not resemble the small mid-19th century terraced cottages that flank them either side. After 174 years the Wheatsheaf finally closed in 2010 and is now a Chinese restaurant.

Site of the Bricklayers Arms 2014

Wishing Tree and Hollington Oak
Wishing Tree Road, Hollington

Wishing Tree 2009

The Wishing Tree public house took its name from Wishing Tree Road, which for many years was thought to be the location of an actual 'wishing tree' connected in mythology to a pagan custom that took place on 12th night.

The Hollington Wishing Tree however, has also been known as the Scrag oak or Smugglers oak, at one time a rendezvous for the tubmen carrying brandy inland from the coast. Hastings Museum claims it was given the name Wishing Tree in the 1850s after a children's game. Henry Bullock, author of *A History of the Church in the Wood, Hollington*, thought that changing traditional names for new ones was contemptuous and criticised the practice.[1] However, as late as the 1920s it was still remembered as the 'Smugglers Oak'.

The tree was removed from its location in Wishing Tree Road at the beginning of the Second World War, and replaced in 1948 with a sapling oak. At the planting ceremony groups of children danced around the tree singing: *To English folk the mighty Oak is England's noblest tree.*

Alternative locations for the Wishing Tree or Smuggler's Oak are Robsack Wood and Ironlatch roundabout, although the trees that stand on the roundabout today are not oaks. To confuse the issue further some think that the tree in question was the original Hollington Oak—the name of another pub further down Wishing Tree Road.

The Hollington Oak opened in 1950 when the licence of the Royal Oak, Castle Street, was transferred to the Southlands Court Country Club. Originally Stone House Farm, it was built in 1740.

Southlands Court Country Club

The Wishing Tree, a relatively recent pub, opened in 1946.[2] Its licence was transferred from the Swan, Old Town which was bombed in 1943.[3] The Swan was believed to have many ghosts and it is said that some accompanied the licence on its journey to Hollington.

Since 1946 a lot has been reported about the paranormal activities of the Wishing Tree. Several landlords are on record as having

2009

experienced contact with the supernatural. There have been so many 'sightings' and experiences that the BBC made a film about the pub in 1972, and at least three authors have since written about it.

John Northwood, landlord in 1968 said: "I am convinced there's a ghost here and it's one of the old ladies. First it was the dog, she started howling for days on end for no apparent reason. Then, one night I was talking to a customer and heard, bump, bump, bump over my head. I thought that's Mike, our son, out of bed and went upstairs. Yet he and his sister were fast asleep." More puzzling was his young son's side-splitting chuckles at all hours of the night. Usually he was a sound sleeper. "It was obvious something was making him laugh, something which he called 'Funny face'. There were many times we sat in the kitchen and felt an unseen something brush past."[4]

In May 2010 Gerry Foster, then managing the bar during the day but landlord from 2003–2004, revealed: "The two Victorian ladies are still quite active. One evening just before closing time I went upstairs leaving my wife Sylvia behind the bar with the last customer. Sylvia suddenly felt a push from behind and thought that

I had come back downstairs. But I hadn't! The last customer, who couldn't believe his eyes, sobered up very quickly and exclaimed, 'I saw that woman push you but there's no one there!' That was in 2004.

"On other occasions the wall lights in the bar have lit up or gone off without being switched and on several occasions the cistern in the ladies toilet flushes itself leaving women customers to believe the toilet is occupied."[5]

One of the ghost sisters was reputed to be a practical joker responsible for pulling the funny faces that make children laugh, an unusual occupation for a ghost. She was also in the habit of pushing a pram into the path of oncoming cars in the road outside. The greatly perplexed driver screeched to a halt only to find no one around. It took a particular sense of humour to appreciate this kind of practical joke! The other sister who was more of a poltergeist was the one who made all the noise.

When Leney's Brewery applied to have the licence transferred in 1946, their representative, Harold Miskin, unveiled the first pub sign to the magistrates. It showed a young woman under a moonlit tree dreaming of marriage. The famous advice of Mr Punch 'Don't' was printed underneath. The second pub sign of a similar theme was included in the first series of Whitbread's miniature inn signs published in the early 1950s. The sign showed two young girls who, I am told, were there to remind us of the legend of the two sisters who haunted the building.[6]

The Wishing Tree Social Club was an independent organization associated with the pub. During the 1950s the club was at its peak, providing leisure activities, including sports, carnivals, torchlight processions and bonfires on Guy Fawkes night. This extract from the report on the 5th November 1959 in the *Hastings & St Leonards Observer* gives a good example of the activities of the club:

The Wishing Tree Social Club has arranged a big celebration at Hollington tonight. A 13ft. 'Guy' has been constructed and an additional feature this year is that, as well as lights there is a microphone concealed in its head. An interesting point about the head of this guy, which is replaced by a similar one without the electrical fittings just before it is hoisted onto the fire, is that it is now about 40 years old. Originally the property of the Bohemia Bonfire Boys, it was handed onto the Wishing Tree Club, and has been in use for many years, by them.

Guy Fawkes night outside Wishing Tree — late 1950s

The Wishing Tree was demolished in 2013.

HOLLINGTON OAK

THE WISHING TREE

INN BUSINESS

WHITBREAD

WISHING TREE

Ye Olde Pumphouse
George Street

2009

Ye Olde Pumphouse in George Street, at first glance, appears to be one of the oldest pubs in Hastings. However, as a pub it is a mere 58 years old, having opened in 1956. Before the Second World War it was three separate dwellings centred on a well-known boot and shoe shop owned by two brothers, Sidney and William Carey.

As with many Old Town premises after the war, this complex of buildings lay empty and derelict. Fire broke out in 1953 destroying practically the whole of the building, which over the next three years was reconstructed by a Canadian builder called Anthony Newman. Some old timbers from badly war damaged houses in All Saints' Street were incorporated into the front of the building. A written statement by a researcher some years ago notes that the original building was extensively rebuilt 'but this did not quite extend to a new building'. However, details were not given.

Turning modern buildings into 'olde' ones was not so unusual at the time. After the war, damaged buildings were bought up cheaply, 'tudorised' in the style of Mock Tudor and sold at a good profit.[1] Another example of this is the old cottage next door to the Cinque Ports Arms, in All Saints Street.

Regardless of its origins, Ye Olde Pumphouse has maintained its value as a building and in 1982 it was included in 'a million pound deal' by Whitbread, when it purchased a number of pubs in the south-east. Soon after it became a grade II listed building.

The first landlord from 1955 to 1959 was Sydney Cole who had previously been the licensee of the St Leonards Pier Pavilion and Lounge from 1952. The pier was immobilised during the war and never reopened but Sydney Cole held the Pavilion licence 'in suspension' until 1955 when it was transferred to the newly opened 'Pump Room' in George Street.[2]

Cyril Pelluet frequented the Pumphouse as a teenager in the late 50s. "There was only the downstairs bar at that time which was decorated with sailors' hatbands. We liked it because it was frequented by the 'Teds' or teddy boys and was a local centre of fashion with drape jackets, drain-pipe trousers and DA [duck's arse] hairstyles. This was about 1957/8. Later John Kilroy took over as landlord. An Irishman, John had a magnificent handlebar moustache and with his wife, Noreen, transformed the upstairs bar into the place to be seen on a Saturday night and it's where we met up with our girlfriends later in the evening. John Kilroy was the epitome of a gentleman and we all had the utmost respect for him. Another landlord, Arthur Wilkinson Bell, introduced curry evenings in the early 1960s, which was quite revolutionary at the time."[3]

Michael Rose recalls: "Prior to 1957 when I was on leave from the navy, I used to drink in the Horse and Groom at lunchtime and in the Pumphouse in the evenings before moving on to the pier, which had an extension licence. In these two pubs I would meet up with mates on leave. The Pumphouse had a lot of naval customers then and a collection of naval memorabilia, hats and so on."[4]

Peter Skinner drank there in the late 1960s, by which time it seems the image had changed. "The Pumphouse", he believed, "was more middle class, more conventional, [and served] salesmen and people on the make. The Pumphouse was the pub to meet women. I met my first long term girlfriend there when she was a student from Norway. I spilled some lager over her because I was drunk and that led to one thing and another. We lived together for 10 years.

"I never saw the Pumphouse as a very old pub, even though it had mock beams and so on. The Anchor seemed much older with its warren of little rooms. The Pumphouse was a harbinger of things to come, a little artificial, a little more knowing and commercial than the other pubs in that area. It was a nice pub, always a little different, not rough, and it was more friendly. Women found it more friendly."[5]

A customer from the 1970s known only as Steve remarked: "To the surprise of many, including me, this beautiful pub is not Elizabethan but was crafted from old timbers after the Second World War. It matters not. I don't know whose idea it was to create this exquisite feature of George Street, but I'd like to shake their hand. It is quite extraordinarily well done for the period.

"I was a regular as a teenager in the little snug bar at the back during the years 1978 to 1980. Beer, vodka … darts, conversation and Space Invaders. The cosy glow in the bar and the snow blowing outside. Companionship inside. Thin Lizzy and the Boomtown Rats on the jukebox. I love that pub."[6]

The pub's name is derived from the site of a freshwater pump which provided this part of Hastings with some good quality water, filtered by the local sandstone. The pump, which never ran dry, is now attached to the front of the half-timbered building and is thought to be 400 years old. Thomas Daniels, landlord of the Anchor opposite from 1805, owned the pump in the early 19th century and for many years it was known as Daniel's pump. The ground floor of the Pumphouse was used by the Anchor as a store for wine and spirits.

Up until the Second World War, a tax of one penny was paid on the pump every year.[7] In the past, the pump was a valuable property, producing a substantial income from water sales for the owners. Most other pubs in the Old Town used its pure water and would use no other for the 'breaking down of spirits'. Before the First World War, spirits were supplied to pubs at a high strength and publicans were required to break them down with water. The legal maximum dilution of spirits was 25 degrees under proof for whisky, brandy and rum and 35 degrees under proof for gin. So as a supplier of pure water, this site has had a relationship with the pubs of the Old Town for more years than it has been a pub itself.

The original building before the fire in 1953

Two views of the Pumphouse interior c1960

York Hotel
Wellington Place

York Hotel, Albert Memorial and Hastings Castle, 1891

York Buildings, now a shopping centre, was originally a cluster of private lodging houses. These buildings once looked out over the Priory Bridge and the shanties of America Ground before the construction of Robertson Street from 1850. In 1852 Susannah Osborne was granted a licence for a York Tavern[1] and in 1853 Thomas Coussens appeared to have been granted a licence for a second York Tavern opposite.[2] Not surprisingly, the first York Tavern changed its name to the Freemasons in 1854.

The Albert Memorial, erected in 1862 in front of the York, quickly became the most important landmark of Hastings town centre. By 1866 James Hayter was the licensee and the buildings had become commonly known as Hayter's York Tavern.

The York Tavern was the pub of the boxing community.[3] One of its more famous customers was Tom Sayers (1826–1865), the Brighton-born, 19th century champion bare-knuckle fighter, who stayed at the York when in Hastings. In 1857 Sayers became heavyweight champion of England (unofficial, since boxing was then illegal) and was the last holder of the title before the introduction of the Queensberry rules in 1867. But it seems he didn't always pay his bills.

> THE CHAMPION OF ENGLAND NOT UP TO THE "SCRATCH" —
> Same v. Thomas Sayers—Board and lodgings, £18.
> The defendant, who is the champion fighter of England, while training to meet one of his recent pugilistic engagements, "held forth" at the York Tavern, and managed, as his fraternity are very liable to do, to leave his name on the landlord's books. He failed to put in his appearance to-day and immediate order was made upon him.

1858 [4]

In the 1870s the police became concerned about the numerous fish hawkers causing obstruction outside. Several hawkers were summonsed more than once for allowing the public to gather around their whelk carts at closing time. When a constable asked one to move on he was 'answered in three or four warm sentences, pungent with bad language'.[5]

A fraudulent business scheme referred to as 'the Liberal Association and York Hotel case' in 1878 provoked a local outburst. Controversially, the York was auctioned off on the cheap, to purchasers who knew that Hastings Corporation would have to purchase the property to carry out road improvements. The owners made a large profit at the ratepayers expense. Hayter, a Liberal councillor, probably tipped them off and in 1879 a new York Hotel was erected.[6]

THE YORK HOTEL.

A week or two ago we announced that the York Hotel had been sold to Messrs. Ellis and Co., and on reference to our advertising columns, our readers will see that, in consequence of extensive structural alterations to premises, the trade fittings, fixtures, &c., will be sold by auction on Wednesday next. by Mr. Joshua Godwin. Licensed victuallers, furniture dealers, and others will do well to avail themselves of this rare opportunity to secure the effects, which include massive mahogany-top counters with hard metal mouldings, mahogany shelves and brackets, a very handsome bar cabinet, painted and grained partitioning, two nearly new beer engines with ebony and plated handles by Warne, mahogany frame seats with velvet cushions, the whole of the partitions to bars, mahogany screening with engraved glass sashes, all the hard metal fittings comprising drainers, basins, &c., the bar furniture, and the whole of the plate glass windows and sashes to bar, four globular-shaped lamps with supports, and innumerable other articles, which will be on view the day previous and morning of sale.

1888 [7]

In the 1890s it became known as the York Hotel and London Distillery. The ground floor bars were designed on the lines of a gin palace with fast service from the beer engines and decorated with ornate mirrors and etched glass. In short, a Victorian Wetherspoon's with cheap and plentiful supplies. On the other hand, the lavishly furnished upstairs lounge was described as looking like a high-

The upstairs lounge of the York Hotel and London Distillery 1899

class club. 'A thick Turkey carpet covers the floor and on the walls a rich Japanese paper has been used, surmounted by a hand painted tulip garden frieze....' The stained glass windows were curtained in gold silk, the bar was walnut and the whole lounge was approached by 'a flight of marble steps'.[8] The York applied several times to have its off-licence at the rear of the building in York Gardens changed. As an off-licence it could only sell liquors and wines in bottles. The landlord claimed that customers often wanted to taste the wine before buying and had to go round to the bar. The applications were always refused.[9]

During the First World War, the licensee was charged with allowing soldiers to get drunk. The police claimed that he was not a fit and proper person to run a public house and opposed his licence. They also claimed the York was used 'by low class women and persons of bad character' and 'by some of the worst persons in the town who were in and out all day long'.[10] A renewed licence was at first refused but then allowed, although the magistrates noted a complaint by the local commanding officer that large numbers of the Royal Field Artillery were being arrested for drunkenness in the town centre. The evening street scene outside the York was described as a drunken 'khaki crowd'. Soon after, a new manager was appointed.[11]

The York was also popular with the military in the Second World War. Retired Police Inspector, the late Charles Banks recalled that "Hastings police were once called to the York Hotel. There, a G.I. got into a quarrel with two English soldiers and the American had suddenly drawn an automatic pistol from his tunic and fired two rounds into the pub ceiling. The two English privates quickly disarmed the G.I. ... and he was detained in a police cell. The G.I. was charged with 'carrying a concealed weapon'; recklessly firing two rounds into the York Bar and disorderly conduct. After a full hearing he was sentenced to 12 months imprisonment."[12]

The upstairs lounge of the York was still popular in the 1950s and early 1960s, especially with courting couples.[13]

In 1964 the lease on the York Tavern came to an end and the licence was transferred to Falaise Hall in White Rock Gardens. The two upper floors were removed and the lower floors became Hastings Information Centre. It is now Costa Coffee.[14]

The Albert Memorial clock tower synonymous with the York Hotel as the centre of Hastings since 1862, was demolished after a fire in 1973.

The building in 2011

Reference Notes

The following abbreviations have been used in the references:

ESRO	East Sussex Records Office
HG	Hastings Local History Group
HSLC	*Hastings and St Leonards Chronicle*
HSLG	*Hastings and St Leonards Gazette*
HSLN	*Hastings and St Leonards News*
HSLO	*Hastings and St Leonards Observer*
HSLT	*Hastings and St Leonards Times*
OD	*Osbournes Directory*
SE	*Sussex Express*
SWA	*Sussex Weekly Advertiser*

Admiral Benbow
1 Hastings Directory 1884
2 HSLO 13-8-1898
3 HSLO 23-3-1905
4 HSLO 4-6-1993
5 Trefor Holloway interview

Anchor Inn and Coach & Horses,
1 Brett v1 p97
2 HSLC 31-8-1881
3 SE 23-8-1845, 29-8-1846, 5-12-1846
4 Michael Rose interview
5 HSLO 11-3-1950

Anchor Inn, George Street
1 Manwaring-Baines 1986 p361
2 SE 4-8-1838
3 SE 15-6-1839
4 Prince p70
5 SE 30-11-1852
6 HSLC 28-6-1871
7 HSLC 25-10-1876
8 HSLC 6-3-1882

Angel and Plough
1 Manwaring-Baines 1986 p361
2 Census Return 1841
3 HSLC 15-2-1860
4 HSLC 30-8-1871
5 HSLO 12-2-1921
6 HSLO 26-2-1977

Barrattinis's Sports Bar
1 HSLO 7-6-1975
2 HSLO 2-12-1975
3 HSLO 9-1-1981
4 HSLO 21-1-1984
5 HSLO 21-4-1988
6 HSLO 5-7-1990

Bo Peep
1 Brett HB v1 p98
2 ESRO SAS/DD248
3 SWA 14-1-1788
4 SWA 14-2-1803
5 Barry's Guide 1797 p72
6 Prothero v3 p261, v4 p349

7 Brett v3 p265
8 Brett v3 p294
9 HSLC 22-8-1877

Brass Monkey
1 Julian Deeprose interview
2 John Hodges interview

Bulverhythe
1 Sussex Directory 1855
2 SE 23-8-1845
3 HSLO 31-3-1900
4 HSLO 7-5-1910

Carlisle
1 Brett v2 p173
2 HSLC 27-8-1892
3 HSLO 18-8-1894
4 HSLO 28-10-1899
5 HSLO 9-12-1933
6 HSLO 16-4-1938
7 HSLO 14-5-1945
8 Terry Huggins interview
9 Julian Deeprose interview
10 HSLO 10-7-1992

Cinque Ports Arms
1 Manwaring-Baines 1986 p362
2 Brett v.2 p155
3 HSLC 15-5-1878
4 HSLO 3-8-1989

Clarence
1 HSLC 2-9-1868
2 HSLC 17-4-1889
3 HSLO 15-5-1872
4 HSLO 3-2-1894
5 HSLO 28-4-1894
6 HSLO 15-12-1906
7 HSLO 10-11-1906
8 Late Charles Banks interview

Clive Vale Hotel
1 HSLC 27-8-1879, 28-8-1883,

23-9-1885, 22-9-1886
2 HG Newsletter 7. 2008
3 HSLO 15-5-1909
4 HSLO 7-2-1920
5 HG Hastings Voices p40
6 HSLO 3-12-1987
7 HSLO 8-12-1988

Clown
1 HSLO 11-2-1905
2 HSLO 10-3-1928
3 HSLO 22-3-1930
4 HSLO 6-2-1954
5 Roger Povey interview

Cricketers
1 HSLC 31-8-1864
2 Ball 1973 p97
3 Tressell 1955 p179

Crown Inn
1 Brett Historico Biographies v3 p178
2 ESRO dhbe/DH/B/136/137
3 HSLC 21-6, 26-7, 30-8, 18-10-1854
4 ESRO dhbc/DH/B/98/1–12
5 HSLC 4-1-1893
6 HSLO 24-3-1900
7 HSLO 19-3-1921
8 Philip Littlejohn interview

Cutter
1 Quoted in HSLO 11-9-1971
2 HSLC 1-1-1862
3 HSLC 15-4-1868
4 HSLC 7-2-1872
5 HSLC 19-3-1892
6 HSLO 27-1-1995

Dripping Spring
1 Sussex Directory 1866
2 HSLC 28-8-1893
3 HSLO 3-6-1916
4 HSLO 5-2-1938
5 Whitbread inn signs. Series 1 No. 8

6 Cyril Pelluet interview

Duke of Cornwall
1 SE 25-10-1862
2 HSLO 14-6-1924
3 ESRO SPA 5/1311

Electric Stag
1 OD 2-11-1861
2 HSLC 9-11-1861
3 HSLC 2-9-1868
4 HSLC 27-8-1893
5 HSLO 29-9-1894
6 HSLO 26-2-1944
7 Peter Skinner interview
8 HSLO 6-2-1971

First In Last Out and Prince of Wales
1 ESRO dhbc/DH/B/136/392
2 HSLN 26-8-1853
3 HSLO 28-8-1869
4 HSLC 28-8-1901
5 HSLO 9-1-1910
6 HSLO 9-3, 20-7, 27-7-1929
7 HSLO 1-11-1930
8 HSLO 18-3-1933
9 HSLO 6-2-1954
10 HSLO 20-11-1982

Flairz
1 HSLN 24-8-1857
2 HSLC 28-8-1867
3 HSLC 27-8-1890
4 HSLO 23-12-1899
5 Whitbread inn signs. Series 1 No. 5

Foresters Arms
1 Brett v2 p148
2 HSLC 20-8-1856
3 HSLN 3-1-1851
4 HSLC 9-3-1864
5 HSLC 21-10-1874
6 Hastings Directories 1886-90
7 HSLO 4-3-1905

8 HSLO 18-3-1933
9 HSLO 16-2-1952
10 HSLO 20-9-1969

Fortune of War
1 Manwaring-Baines 1986 p362
2 Brett v2 p205
3 HSLN 27-8-1850
4 SE 29-5-1866
5 HSLC 20-5-1885
6 HSLO 14-2-1903
7 HSLO 11-4-1903
8 Michael Errey interview
9 HSLO 5-10-1968

Fountain
1 HSLN 28-8-1853
2 Coleman 1929 p5
3 HSLC 26-3-1879
4 HSLO 1-7-1916
5 HSLO 13-2-1937
6 Whitbread inn signs. Series 1 No. 4

Fox
1 Sussex Directory 1855
2 Russell 3/2011 p43
3 HSLO 21-10-1933
4 HSLO 11-3-1939
5 Alan Crouch interview
6 HSLO 18-5-1940
7 HSLO 11-4-1942
8 Michael Monk interview
9 Pat Dunn interview
10 Whitbread inn signs. Series 1 No. 7

Frank's Front Room
1 HSLC 31-8-1864
2 HSLC 24-5-1865
3 HSLC 17-6-1891
4 HSLO 26-8-1899
5 HSLO 26-8-1916
6 Roger Povey interview

French's Bar and Priory Tavern
1 HSLN 30-8-1851
2 HSLN 27-08-1850
3 HSLC 1/3/1865
4 ESRO BUR2/1/160
5 HSLN 2/11/1866, HSLC 26/10/1866
6 Betty Austin interview
7 HSLO 13/7/1994
8 Sayer p501-4

General Havelock
1 Russell 3-2011 p52
2 SE 27-6-1868
3 HSLC 25-3-1874
4 HSLC 28-11-1883
5 Goodwin 2005 p84
6 Cyril Pelluet interview

Hare and Hounds
1 HSLO 30-6-1962
2 HSLO 7-7-1962
3 Cooper 1891 p52
4 HSLO 6-2-1909
5 HSLO 22-12-1933, 5-1-1934

Hastings Arms
1 Manwaring-Baines 1986 p363
2 Brett v2 p157
3 Brett v3 p262, p323
4 SE 1-2-1840
5 SE 4-11-1843
6 HSLN 7-2-1851
7 HSLN 25-7-1851
8 HSLO 27-1-1917
9 HSLO 29-4-1961
10 HSLO 9-8-1980

Hole in the Wall and Kicking Donkey
1 Manwaring-Baines p363
2 HSLO 13-3-1926
3 HSLO 9-1-1937
4 HSLO 12-3-1938
5 Aspect Southern no.16 1992
6 HSLO 16-2-1952

7 HSLO 14-8-1971
8 Sussex Directory 1855
9 HSLO 15-2-1936
10 HSLO 15-3-1947

Horse and Groom
1 Brett v1 p5
2 Brett op cit p38
3 Brett v2 p125, v3 p262
4 Brett v1 p100
5 Brett v1 p107
6 SE 21-5-1853
7 HSLO 24-2, 14-7, 21-7-1917
8 HSLO 17-10-1985
9 HSLO 25-6-1999

Jenny Lind
1 HSLO 19-1-1918
2 HSLO 9-9-1933
3 HSLO 15-2-1941
4 HSLO 17-2-1951
5 HSLO 24-1-1959
6 HSLO 21-8-1982
7 HSLO 7-9-1990

Jolly Fisherman
1 HSLC 16-1-1856
2 HSLN 26-1-1855
3 HSLC 3-10-1883
4 HSLO 16-1-1915
5 HSLO 28-3-1925
6 HSLO 14-2-1959

Lord Nelson
1 Manwaring-Baines 1986 p364
2 HSLN 27-10-1882
3 HSLO 11-2-1905
4 HSLO 18-2, 4-3, 27-5-1911
5 HSLO 19-3-1938
6 HSLO 11-3-1967
7 Peter Skinner interview
8 Terry Huggins interview
9 HSLO 3-8-1989

Marina Fountain
1 Prothero v6 p567
2 1851 Census
3 HSLG 28-1-1860
4 HSLC 5-10-1864
5 HSLO 14-7-1917
6 HSLO 20-4-1968
7 Trefor Holloway interview

Merry Christmas
1 ESRO dhbc/DH/B/98/1-12
2 ESRO dhbg/DH/B/99/1
3 SE 24-11-1849

Moda
1 Sussex Directory 1866
2 HSLC 14-9-1870
3 HSLC 12-5-1875
4 HSLC 12-10-1887
5 Late Charles Banks interview
6 Tommy Read interview
7 HSLO 1-12-1945
8 Longmate 1975 p216
9 Whitbread inn signs. Series 1 No.1

Nag's Head
1 HSLN 26-8-1853
2 HSLN 24-8-1855
3 HSLC 10-9-1862, SE 25-10-1862
4 HSLC 25-11-1885, 7-11-1888
5 Ball 1973 p97
6 Whitbread inn signs. Series 5 No. 28
7 Michael Rose interview
8 HSLO 3-2-1968

Norman Arms
1 ESRO BUR2/1/27
2 SE 8-4-1868
3 SE 27-3-1869
4 ESRO BUR2/1/75
5 SWA 5-5-1874
6 Sonja Eveleigh interview
7 HSLO 4-3-1905
8 HSLO 3-8-1957

9 HSLO 15-3-1920
10 ESRO DH/C/6/1/13872

Pig in Paradise
1 HSLC 2-1-1889
2 HSLO 28-4-1894
3 HSLC 30-9-1891
4 HSLO 19-6-1909
5 HSLO 10-3-1917
6 HSLO 31-7-1926, 21-8-1926
7 HSLO 14-4-1928
8 Pat Dunn interview
9 Alan Crouch interview
10 Cyril Pelluet interview
11 HSLO 13-3-1986

Pilot and Privateer
1 HSLO 12-12-1874
2 Late Minnie Howlett interview
3 ESRO VID2/2/66
4 Taylor p23-25

Pissarro's
1 HSLC 31-8-1864
2 Whitbread inn signs. Series 1 No. 3
3 Alan & Marie Garaty interview

Prince Albert
1 HSLO 15-3-1913
2 Dyer & Vint 1972 p12
3 Dyer & Vint 1972 p10
4 HSLO 9-1-1937, 15-1-1938
5 Dyer & Vint 1972 p44
6 HSLO 17-6-1967

Prince of Wales
1 Sussex Directory 1855
2 HSLC 21-4-1858
3 HSLC 27-8-1862
4 HSLC 13-7-1864
5 HSLC 11-12-1867
6 HSLC 12-6-1878
7 HSLO 12-2-1949
8 Pat Dunn interview

Railway and Royal
1 HSLC 27-8-1862
2 HSLC 30-8-1876, 20-9-1876
3 HSLC 10-10-1877
4 Hastings Directory 1884
5 HSLC 16-9-1891
6 HSLO 10-2-1917
7 HSLO 8-11-1919
8 Pat Dunn interview
9 Cyril Pelluet interview

Red House
1 HSLC 18-10-1893
2 HSLO 6-1-1894
3 HSLO 15-3-1913
4 HSLO 27-1-1917
5 HSLO 17-3-1951

Robert de Mortain
1 HSLO 26-2-2010
2 Russell 3-2011
3 Whitbread inn signs. Series 2 No.47,48

Roebuck
1 SE 27-4-1839
2 HSLO 16-9-1961
3 HSLC 29-8-1860
4 HSLC 25-11-1885, 28-11-1888
5 HSLC 28-8-1895
6 HSLC 28-8-1917
7 HSLC 13-4-1918

Royal Albion and Albion Shades
1 ESRO dhbj/DH/B/182/115, dhbj/DH/B/182/29
2 Brett v4 p194
3 HSLC 27-6-1855, HSLC 22-11-1865
4 HSLC 11-12-1867
5 HSLC 10-1-1877
6 HSLC 27-8-1879
7 HSLO 29-9-1894
8 HSLO 15-2-1900
9 HSLO 13-7-1963
10 Alan Crouch interview

Royal Standard
1 ESRO dhbf/DH/B/147/83
2 HSLC 12-10-1887, 4-4-1888
3 HSLO 15-3-1913
4 HSLO Ibid.
5 HSLO 16-1-1915
6 HSLO 1-7-1967

Smugglers
1 Sussex Directory 1845
2 Brett v4 p50
3 Brett v4 p224
4 SE 13-4-1867
5 HSLC 23-9-1868
6 HSLC 11-11-1891
7 HSLC 27-10-1894
8 HSLO 3-5-1916
9 HSLO 2-2-1946
10 HSLO 9-11-1946
11 HSLO 8-3-1947
12 Dunkling & Wright 1987 p287
13 Prothero v7 p761

Stag
1 SE 25-8-1838
2 www.shepherdneame.co.uk
3 email to author from Shepherd Neame
4 SE 14-5-1869
5 HSLO 1951
6 Tommy Read interview
7 HSLO 6-11-1982
8 HSLO 1-9-1995

St Leonard
1 Brett. v1. p86
2 Russell 9-2011 p48-9
3 HSLG 11-2-1860
4 Goodwin 2005 p80
5 HSLO 28-5-1943, 3-7-1943
6 HSLO 26-02-1977
7 Pat Dunn interview
8 HSLO 27-3-1976
9 Prothero v4 p393
10 Whitbread inn signs. Series 1 No. 6

Tivoli Tavern
1 SE 17-11-1838
2 Brett v2 p147
3 SE 17-8-1839
4 SE 20-6-1846
5 HSLN 10-8-1855
6 SE 21-6-1856
7 HSLC 1-9-1858
8 SE 30-6-1860

Tower
1 HSLC 27-5-1903
2 HSLO 29-9-1990

Union Bar and Dripping Well
1 Sussex Directory 1845
2 Hastings Directory 1884
3 HSLO 24-2-1900
4 HSLO 13-2-1937
5 HSLO 17-2-1934
6 Goodwin 2005 p34
7 Jim Davidson interview
8 Peter Skinner interview
9 HSLO 5-2-1983

Volunteer
1 Late Minnie Howlett interview
2 Late Ron Fellows interview

Wheatsheaf and Bricklayer's Arms
1 Research into the Jinks family.
  Cyril Pelluet, 2009 (unpublished).
2 Brett v1 p107
3 HSLO 18-1-1873
4 HSLO 10-2-1917
5 HSLO 23-8-1919
6 HSLN 17-11-1865

7 HSLC 30-5-1866
8 Cyril Pelluet interview

Wishing Tree and Hollington Oak
1 Bullock p291
2 HSLO 29-6-1946
3 Russell 9-2011
4 HSLO 1-7-1972
5 Gerry Foster interview
6 Whitbread inn signs. Series 1 No, 2

Ye Olde Pumphouse
1 Prothero v1 p256
2 Russell 2011
3 Cyril Pelluet interview
4 Michael Rose interview
5 Peter Skinner interview
6 Steve M on twitter
7 HSLO 6-3-1926

York Hotel
1 HSLN 27-8-1852
2 HSLN 26-8-1853
3 HSLG 12-5-1860
4 HSLC 1-9-1858
5 HSLC 9-2-1876
6 HSLC 27-8-1879
7 HSLT 7-1-1888
8 HSLO 22-8-1896
9 HSLO 28-8-1897
10 HSLO 3-7-1915
11 HSLO 10-3-1917, 7-4-1917
12 Late Charles Banks interview
13 Alan Crouch interview
14 HSLO 8-2-1964

Bibliography

Hastings Directories: 1852–1974 Hastings Reference Library

Sussex Directories: 1828–1866 Brighton History Centre & ESRO

Census Returns: 1841–1891

Parliamentary Papers: Select Committee on Public Houses 1852–1853.

Books:
Anon (2000) *Tales from around the Wishing Tree.* University of Sussex: Centre for Continuing Education.
Ball, F.C., (1973) *One of the Damned.* London: Lawrence & Wishart.
Bullock, F.W.B., (1949) *A History of the "Church in the Wood" Hollington, Sussex.* St. Leonards-on-Sea: Budd & Gillatt.
Coleman, G.D., (1929) *Queen's Road in 1929.* Hastings Reference Library.
Cooper, T., Sidney (1891) *My Life.* London: Richard Bentley.
Cousins, H., (1920) *Hastings of Bygone Days and the Present.* Hastings: F.J. Parsons
Cresy, E., (1850) *Report to the General Board of Health ....*
Dunkling, L. and Wright, G., (1987) *A Dictionary of Pub Names.* London: Routledge & Kegan Paul.
Dyer, W.H. and Vint, A.K., (1972) *Winkle Up! The Story of the Hastings Winkle Club.* Hastings Winkle Club.
Funnell, B., (1999) *The America Ground.* Hastings Area Archaeological Research Group.
Goodwin, N.D., (2005) *Hastings at War.* Chichester: Phillimore.
Harrison, B., (1971) *Drink and the Victorians: Temperance Question in England, 1815–1872.* Keel University Press.
Hyde, A., (2004) *The Breeds of Hastings: Merchants and Brewers. 1762–1931.* Brewery History Society.
Jennings, P., (2007) *The Local: A History of the English Pub.* Stroud: Tempus.
Longmate, N., (1975) *The GIs: The Americans in Britain 1942–1945.* London: Hutchinson.
Manwaring-Baines, J., (1986) *Historic Hastings.* St. Leonards-on-Sea: Cinque Port Press Ltd.
Mass Observation (1945) *The Pub and the People.* London: Ebury Press.
Prince, N., (1996) *'That's All Folks' The Cinemas of Hastings and St Leonards.* Wakefield: Mercia Cinema Society.
Russell, D., (2013) *Register of Licensees for Hastings & St Leonards 1500–*

2000. St. Leonards-on-Sea: Lynda Russell.

Russell, D., (2013) *The Swan, Hastings 1523–1943*. St. Leonards-on-Sea: Lynda Russell.

Sayer, C., (Ed) (1907) *Correspondence of John Collier and his family 1716–1780*. Two Volumes.

Taylor, A.R., (2009) *Played at the Pub: The Pub Games of Britain*. English Heritage.

Tressell, R., (1965) *The Ragged Trousered Philanthropists.* London: Grafton Books.

Volumes: -

Brett, T.B., *Manuscript History*. Volumes 1–7. Hastings Reference Library.

Brett, T.B., *Hastings Historico Biographies.* Hastings Reference Library.

Prothero, J., Scrapbooks*, Volumes 1–9*. Hastings Reference Library.

Newspapers and Periodicals: -

Aspect Southern No.16. (1992) Hastings Reference Library file World War II.

Cinque Ports Chronicle: 1838–1841

Hastings and St Leonards Chronicle: 1846–1905

Hastings and St Leonards Gazette: 1856–1896

Hastings and St Leonards News: 1848–1876

Hastings and St Leonards Observer: 1866–2000

Hastings Pictorial Advertiser: 1901–1918

Sussex Express: 1837–1870

Sussex Weekly Advertiser: 1749–1847

Oral history: -

Betty Austin, the late Charles Banks, Vic Chalcroft, Alan Crouch, Jim Davidson, Julian Deeprose, Pat Dunn, Sonja Eveleigh, Michael Errey, the late Ron Fellows, Gerry Foster, Alan Garaty, Marie Garaty, John Hodges, Trefor Holloway, the late Minnie Howlett, Tony Howlett, Terry Huggins, Philip Littlejohn, Steve M, Dot Mitchell, Michael Monk, Cyril Pelluet, Roger Povey, Tommy Read, Michael Rose, Peter Skinner.

Genealogical research: -

Jinks family (2008–9) Cyril Pelluet (unpublished).

APPENDIX

Pub–Population Ratio
Hastings 1824–1941

year	public houses	beer houses	total	population	pub–population ratio
1824	15	5	20	6000	1/300
1836	34	____	34	7550	1/ 222
1850	43	33	76	9,500	1/125
1860	70	55	125	14,000	1/112
1864	79	60	139	20,000	1/144
1870	99	*52	151	26,000	1/172
1897	128	52	180	*58,000	1/322
1906	137	37	174	*59,000	1/339
1928				63,000	1/330 Eastbourne 1/574 Blackpool 1/711
1937				65,000	1/331
1941	121	17	138	66,000	1/478

* estimated

sources: brewster sessions, directories, www.visionofbritain.org.uk

Index

E

early morning licence: 130,173
earthenware: 112,125
economic depression: 142,234
Egan, Pierce, author: 51
Elliston, Robert, actor: 146,148

F

false history: 70,137,264
first post office: 135
flooding: 78,255,293
fire: 40,82,148,158,306
fishermen's allowance: 254
flair barman: 206
Free House: 72,176,177
French, John, smuggler: 137,138
Friendly & Benefit Societies
    Adelaide Lodge of Oddfellows: 269,
    270
    Ancient Order of Druids: 108,204
    Buffaloes: 81,108,282,286
    Cinque Ports Foresters: 66
    Clarence Oddfellows: 66
    Dripping Spring Slate Club: 89
    Equitable: 68
    FILO Slate Club: 103
    Hastings Cabmen's B S: 65
    Hastings Equitable: 66,148
    Stag Benefit Society: 264
    Hare and Hounds tontine: 149,150
    Victoria Oddfellows: 25,27
    West Hill BS: 234

G

gambling: 13,14,27,53,102,126,259
games
    archery: 193,194
    Bagatelle: 134,160,196
    battle shoot: 98
    billiards: 55,108,134,135,160,199,
    200,248,258
    bowls: 68,199,235,267,286
    bull: 126
    chess: 45,288

Cribbage: 150,196,293
darts: 28,31,55,73,89,123,126,150,
158,177,181,193,194,286,293,307
football: 131
Four Corners: 112,113
Loggats: 267
marbles: 255
puff dart: 210-212
quoits: 68,69,199,267
ring board: 77,78
shovepenny: 21,126,150,181,293
snooker: 55,56,199
gay pub: 61
ghosts: 28,300-302
girls on the town: 80,209
gold miner: 98
Gower, Denny, darts champion: 271, 272
groceries: 158,254
Guinness Book of Records: 189

H

harmonic evenings: 65,234,244
Hastings
    Bank: 153,154
    Town Crier: 153,154,190
    town gaol: 153,154
hawkers: 65,85,155,184,312
Hells Angels: 56,178
hop pickers: 180
horse dealers: 122,181
Hovenden, Thomas, landlord: 38,241
hustling the hat: 135,136,281,283

J

Jack in the Green: 35,255
jazz: 99,200,217
Jesuit College: 245
Jinks family: 295,296,297
Jones, Isabella: 39

K

Kean, Edmund, actor: 146
Keats, John, poet: 39,180